RACE, CLASS AND POWER

RACE, CLASS AND POWER

Ideology and Revolutionary Change in Plural Societies

LEO KUPER

DUCKWORTH

First published in 1974 by
Gerald Duckworth & Company Limited
The Old Piano Factory, 43 Gloucester Crescent, London N.W.1

ISBN 0 7156 0757 X

Typesetting by Specialised Offset Services Ltd., Liverpool
Printed by Unwin Brothers Ltd., Old Woking.

CONTENTS

TO HILDA

PREFACE

The chapters of this book were written mostly over the last five years. They deal with situations of extreme racial and ethnic conflict, and seek to develop appropriate theoretical perspectives. My own deep commitment is to interracial co-operation in achieving radical change by nonviolent means. I am aware that there is a tension throughout between this commitment and the attempt to confront some of the intractable realities of racial conflict, and that this tension is not resolved.

Inevitably over the years there has been some change of perspective, on such problems, for example, as the relations between race and class. I have, however, not attempted to eliminate inconsistencies in chapters already published, which thus offer slightly different perspectives on some of the issues, and I present them as originally published, with only very minor alterations. Translations have been added throughout for most French quotations. Some references have been harmonized and there is a single bibliography and index.

The research reported in this book has been supported largely by a grant from the National Science Foundation, and I would like to express my gratitude for this assistance, and also for help from the University of California, Los Angeles, and its African Studies Center. I would like to thank the research assistants who have helped me over the years: Sondra Hale, Arnold Green, Bob Edgar, Terence Freiberg and Anne Bailey. I am also grateful to colleagues who have contributed criticism of one or other of these chapters, or stimulated my thinking: Edna Bonacich, Howard Elinson, John Horton, Adam Kuper, Hilda Kuper, Neville Layne, Hans Rogger, M.G. Smith, Sam Surace, Andre Tiano and Ralph Turner.

'Three of the chapters – 'Ideologies of Cultural Difference in Race Relations', 'On the Theme "Black is Beautiful" ' and 'A Personal Statement on Revolutionary Change in Race Relations' – are hitherto unpublished. The last two were delivered as Special Lectures in Anthropology at the University of London. I would like to thank the University of London for the facilities accorded me, and the editors of the following publications for permission to include reprinted articles.

Civilisations, 'Race Structure in the Social Consciousness', vol. 20, no. 1 (1970), 88-103.

International Sociological Association, 'Ideologies of Violence among Subordinate Groups', paper presented to the Sixth World Congress of Sociology in September 1966 and published in the Transactions.

Cahiers d'études africaines, 'Continuities and Discontinuities in Race Relations: Evolutionary or Revolutionary Change', vol. 10, no. 3 (1970), 361-83.

University of California Press, 'Political Change in White Settler Societies: The Possibility of Peaceful Democratization', in Leo Kuper and M.G. Smith, *Pluralism in Africa*, 1969, 169-93.

Comparative Studies in Society and History, 'Theories of Revolution and Race Relations', vol. 13, no. 1 (1971), 87-107, and 'Race, Class and Power: Some Comments on Revolutionary Change', vol. 14, no. 4 (1972), 400-21.

International Social Science Journal, 'Political Change in Plural Societies: Problems in Racial Pluralism', vol. 23, no. 4 (1971), 594-607.

Race, Review of *Class and Colour in South Africa – 1850-1950*, by H.J. and R.E. Simons, April 1971, 495-500.

I would also like to thank UNESCO for permission to quote from the paper 'Le Rôle de la culture dans la lutte pour l'indépendance' prepared by the late Amilcar Cabral for the conference on Race, Identity and Dignity, and from the paper by Roger Bastide, 'Millenarianism as a Strategy in the Search for a New Identity and Dignity', prepared for the same conference.

London, March 1973   Leo Kuper

PART ONE:

IDEOLOGIES

1

Ideologies of Cultural Difference in Race Relations

Ideologies of cultural difference are an almost invariable phenomenon in race relations. They convey racial character-izations and derive from them principles of race relations. They are linked to the structure of the society, generally either supporting or challenging domination. They are a significant element in structures of race relations and may perhaps serve as an index of the state of these relations. The types of characterization conveyed by them, their functions, and the interaction between ideologies, whether consonant or in dialectical opposition, may be indicative of conservative tendencies, or of processes conducive to peaceful change, or of polarization and impending violence.

1.

Dehumanization is the most common process in the charac-terization of subordinate races by a dominant race. It is expressed, in its extreme form, in conceptions of the subject race as animals or demons or objects, and in a less extreme form, in the conception that the subject race is characterized by a falling-off from the fullness of human quality and human dignity.

Descriptions in terms of animal analogies and animal qualities are related to the culture of the dominant race, its animal world and zoological conceptions, its stereotypes of the subordinate race, and the structure of the society. There

is no doubt some insane logic which governs these characterizations, so that one type of animal conception, say baboon,
is applied to a particular race, but is regarded as quite
inappropriate to another race, for whom the conception,
monkey, may be reserved.[1]

The characterization of a group in animal terms is not
specific to structures of race relations. It is found also in the
relations between ethnic groups, religious communities and
social classes of the same race. Thus the term baboon
(*bobbejaan*), freely applied by Afrikaans-speaking whites in
South Africa to Africans, was a common enough characterization of Afrikaners by English-speaking whites, before
Afrikaners began to assume political power. Jules Roy (1960:
18) refers to the characterization of Arabs by French *colons*
as *bicots* and *ratons*. Religious groups practising circumcision
often react to the uncircumcised as being like animals: within
a religious community, women may be conceived as being
ineradicably creatural. Names of animals may be used to
characterize different levels in a hierarchy (as, for example,
among the Swazi, *Ngwenyama*, i.e Lion, for the King,
Ndlovukazi, i.e. Lady Elephant, for the Queen Mother, and
tinja tetfu, our dogs, in aristocratic parlance, for the
common people, or more prestigious, *tinkomo*, cattle); or the
animal characterization may be reserved for the very lowest
strata, as in this description of class structure in the USA:

Well, while they're fixing supper for us I just want to mention one more
class. Now, this one is really a lulu. These are the families that are just
not worth a goddam. Now, they're not immoral — they're not
unmoral — they're just plain amoral. They just simply don't have any

---

1 D'Hertefelt (1960: 118-19) refers to a very old stereotype, in
Central Rwanda, recited before the declamation of a story, which
summarizes the results of the Tutsi conquest over the Hutu. It runs, in
translation, as follows:

> There existed [once] and there should never [more] exist
> Dead are the dogs and the rats
> Left over are the cows and the drum.

morals. I'll tell you they just have animal urges, and they just respond to them. They're just like a bunch of rats or rabbits (Warner, 1949: 51-2).

The animal world is a rich source of models for systems of stratification, and an especially happy hunting-ground in systems of race relations. Fanon (1963: 42) writes that when the settler seeks to describe the native fully in exact terms, he constantly refers to the bestiary.

The 'demonization' of a subject race is a somewhat rare form of dehumanization. Cohn (1967: 240 ff.)[2] deals with this phenomenon in the context of 'the truly murderous kind of antisemitism . . . where Jews are imagined as a collective embodiment of evil, a conspiracy dedicated to the task of ruining and then dominating the rest of mankind'. He associates demonization with Christian antisemitism, feeding on the collective fantasy of a Jewish world conspiracy, and a conception of Jews as 'demonically super-human'. In this form, demonization is quite specific to Christian antisemitism. In a less threatening form, but carrying connotations of sorcery or magical practices or evil, it is sometimes found in systems of race relations in the characterization of small 'pariah' groups of different culture and religion.

Objectification of the subject race seems to be as ubiquitous as reduction to the animal world. It consists in a denial of the right to self-regulation or the capacity for self-regulation. In its ultimate form, members of the subject race are equated with objects, with things; deprived of autonomy in many spheres, they are regulated by the dominant race. The fullest expression of this state is to be found in chattel slavery. Depestre (1969: 2) refers to the process of zombification, the zombie, according to a Haitian myth, being a person (*le mort vivant*) from whom one has stolen spirit and reason, and to whom is left only the force of work: he describes the history of colonization as a process of

2 De Reuck and Knight (1967: Chapters 17 and 18) contains an interesting discussion of the processes of dehumanization.

the generalized zombification of man. In a milder form, the reduction to the non-status of objects is also to be found, in appreciable measure, in the South African Government's regulation of African labour, as indicated in such conceptions as the 'canalization' of Native labour, or the concept of 'redundant' labour, or in the systematic control of the flow of labour, along the lines of the marketing of commodities, under the Bantu Laws Amendment Act (see Leo Kuper, 1965: 61).

A second form of objectification consists in the subordination to an object, rather than in the reduction to an object. This form is analysed by Simmel (1950: 253), who cites Russian bondage as a situation in which a concrete object governs the domination, the bonded subject being only the appurtenance of the land, and sinking psychologically to the category of a mere thing, since he is subordinate by virtue of belonging to a thing. Again, South Africa provides an example of this extreme form of racial oppression, Africans being subordinate to a document, the pass, which governs their very right to move and be abroad in the greater part of South Africa (Leo Kuper, 1965: 61-6).

Less extreme dehumanization is conveyed by a wide range of characterizations, which do not constitute a reduction of the subject race to animals, demons or things, but express a falling-off in human quality. Conceptions of the subject race as savages or barbarians are somewhat close to the animal analogies. Depersonalization has an element of the reduction to an object. It consists essentially in the relegation of the subordinate race to a category. Memmi (1967: 83-9) describes depersonalization as including characterization in the form of a series of negations, and in the substitution of anonymous collectivity for individuality. Sometimes the rejection or depreciation of the culture of the subordinate race is treated as a process of depersonalization (see, for example, Depestre, 1969: 1); this denigration of the culture of the subordinate appears to be an invariable element in systems of racial domination, and is often institutionalized, as in the French and Portuguese African colonies, where conferment of equality in status (*assimilado* or *évolué*) was dependent on the acquisition of the culture of the dominant race. The expressions of devaluation are almost infinite in their variety, some seemingly benevolent as in paternalist conceptions of the childlike qualities of the subject race, others harshly rejecting as in conceptions of polluting contact, or of evil and depravity (Fanon, 1963: 41-2).

Ideologies of cultural difference are the main channel for conveying the dehumanizing conceptions of the subject race. Some of the ideologies are simply a framework, providing a series of cues for thinking about, and behaving towards, members of a subordinate race, as for example, animal analogies which offer convenient explanations for political and economic discrimination, social exclusion and denigration, overcrowding and other manifestations of poverty. Other ideologies are fully formulated, stating a general theory of society, nature or divine creation, and applying this theory to explain differences in the character, culture and role of the dominant and subordinate races. Obvious examples are theories of evolution, distinguishing dominant and subordinate races as representing higher and lower levels, and relating differences in capacity (say for abstract thought), differences in culture (as between monogamy and polygyny), and differences in role (as between rulers and ruled), to these postulated differences in evolutionary level. Theories of evolution may be biological, distinguishing different species, or social, and providing such ideological categories as primitive, barbarian and civilized societies. Theories of divine ordinance, in the form of punishments for improper behaviour as in the curse of Ham, or of rewards and punishment for performance or neglect of duty as in the Tutsi myth defining the characters and roles of Tutsi, Hutu and Twa in traditional Rwanda society, are often the basis for ideologies of cultural difference.

Ideologies of cultural difference are sometimes viewed as expressions of personality needs, but this does not explain the phenomenon of collective ideologies (see de Reuck and Knight, 1967: 261-2). More generally, they are interpreted as functions of the systems of domination.[3] In much the same way that theories of the culture of poverty may serve the function of blaming the poor for their poverty (Valentine, 1968: 15), so too ideologies of cultural difference may serve to place responsibility for subordination and suffering on the subordinates themselves. They provide legitimation for domination and they justify racial discrimination. At the political level, in colonial and white settler societies, the civilizing mission and other ideologies of cultural difference legitimized the monopoly of political power, exclusion from the vote, or a qualified franchise, and the system van den Berghe describes as 'Herrenvolk Democracy' (1969: 73). At the economic level, these ideologies justified forced labour,[4] migrant labour, low wages, exclusion from skilled labour and discrimination in stipends for ministers (Leo Kuper, 1965: 210-12). In living conditions, the ideologies justified segregation, the provision of rudimentary housing for members of the subject race and extreme racial discrimination in amenities. In terms of human freedom, conceptions of cultural inferiority were used to justify slavery, restraints on freedom of movement, dual standards of justice and harsh physical punishment. Ideologies of religious differences have served to justify genocide, pogroms, slavery, serfdom and innumerable milder forms of hostility, oppression and discrimination.

The consequences of these ideologies of cultural difference for the subordinate race have not been exclusively negative: the positive contributions were considerable in the extension of aspects of Western education, technology, economic skills, health services, and so on. There is hardly a domain which has not been affected by the consequences of ideologies of

3 Memmi (1967: 79-89) in an interesting discussion of the relations between colonizer and colonized, argues that the colonizer's economic and basic needs shape and explain each of the traits assigned to the colonized. See also Memmi (1964: 41-7).

4 James Duffy (1963: 129-34).

cultural difference, as they shaped and rationalized the policies of dominant races towards subordinate races.

The great flexibility of ideologies of cultural difference is no doubt an important factor in their relative ubiquity and pervasiveness. There is flexibility in the relationship between the ideological emphasis on cultural difference and the actual extent of cultural difference. Ideologies may understate cultural difference, when it is considerable, or emphasize cultural difference when it is in fact negligible. The curious phenomenon of the shibboleth, in which some particular item of cultural difference becomes symbolic of alien cultural worlds and antipathetic societies, demonstrates a measure of independence between subjective perceptions and objective differences. Language sometimes serves as a shibboleth so that a member of a dominant race may insist that subordinates address him in their own language or in a debased form of it,[5] even though the subordinates are quite fluent in the language of the dominant race. As cultural differences diminish, the emphasis on cultural difference may increase, or conversely, the shared elements of culture may suddenly become significant, when the power of the dominant race is seriously threatened.

There is flexibility also in the exclusiveness or inclusiveness of ideologies of cultural difference. The ideologies may raise a permanent barrier between the races, as for example, where the cultural differences are linked to biological differences, or to different levels of evolution, or to the laws of science and the ascendancy of the superior, or to divine sanction. Or the barriers may be conceived as temporary and permeable.[6]

5 Basil Davidson (1969: 221) refers to the refusal of the District Commissioner in Northern Rhodesia to converse directly in English with Kaunda (now President of Zambia). The DC spoke English but insisted on his clerk translating what he said into Bemba, though Kaunda himself continued to speak in English.

6 Ideologies of cultural difference need not necessarily imply inferiority. A curious example of this is the ideology of apartheid in South Africa in one of its many deceptive formulations. The ideology,

Where the barriers are permanent and impermeable, the
ideologies establish exclusive categories of being. Where they
are transient, where the culture of the dominant race is
conceived as simply acquired and accessible to all, where
quality of participation is linked to the acquisition of this
culture, then the ideology is inclusive in its implications for
race relations, and may be persuasive to members of the
subordinate races, as for example to educated Africans at a
particular stage in the evolution of colonial societies.

2.

Ideologies of the ruling race are infinitely more effective, as
instruments of domination, if they are accepted by members
of the subordinate race, and a common theme in the
literature of black protest is precisely this acceptance by
subject races of the negation of their culture and of
themselves. Thus Fanon (1967: 38-9), in analysing the
relations between colonizers and colonized, comments that
the colonized were brought to admit that their misfortunes
resulted directly from their racial and cultural characteristics,
and that they tried to escape the guilt and inferiority they
experienced by proclaiming total and unconditional adoption
of the new cultural models and irreversible condemnation of
their own. Depestre (1969: 2-3) describes the policy of
cultural assimilation as one by which the colonized was led in
certain cases, to deny his cultural singularity, the specific
reactions of his sensibility to 'la vie, l'amour, la mort et l'art',
his countenance and his colour, which became to him a
constant source of trauma and frustration; he comments
however, that the colonized peoples, despite everything,

---

while repudiating the ranking of cultures, emphasizes cultural differences, the desirability and indeed obligation to maintain these cultural
differences, and the inappropriateness of democracy where there is
heterogeneity of culture. In the USA, the doctrine of cultural pluralism
does not imply inferiority, but affirms the desirability and enriching
quality of cultural differences, presumably in the private domain.

resisted the total foundering of their social being.

There is abundant documentation for the thesis that in many situations, members of the subject race accepted the devaluation of their culture. I mention by way of examples, a presidential address delivered by the Reverend Zaccheus Richard Mahabane (a former President of the African National Congress in South Africa) to the 1959 Conference of the Inter-denominational African Ministers' Federation, in which he described Africa as having emerged from ignorance, superstition, vice, degradation, barbarism, savagery, psychic unconsciousness, intellectual insensibility, and mental unawareness (Leo Kuper, 1965: 194); or the chant, *Mayibuy' iAfrika* ('Let Africa Return'), a theme song of the African National Congress in a decade of militant campaigning during the 1950s, which had the refrain, *Sisesebumnyameni* ('While We Were Still in Darkness');[7] or the myths reported among many peoples in Africa, which find the origin of the inequality of the races in divine ordinance (Görög, 1968: 290-309).[8]

But the theory that subordinate races came to accept the denigration of their cultures is expressed largely by the Western educated among them, and is almost certainly a

7 We black people,
  We cry for Africa,
  Which was taken by the English,
  While we were still in darkness.
                    (Translation; see Leo Kuper, 1956: 13)

8 Görög comments as follows on the acceptance of white evaluations: 'On peut, en effet, se demander si, en s'attribuant les défauts, les Noirs n'approuvent pas en quelque sorte l'opinion que les Blancs se font d'eux, et si les qualités prêtées à ces derniers ne traduisent pas l'admiration que provoquent leur savoir et leur superiorité technique. Ceci est corroboré, dans de nombreux récits, par un certain sentiment d'impuissance et plus encore par la volonté de parvenir à égaler le Blanc, dont les contes les plus récents font fréquemment état' (300). In certain myths, the black ancestors were said to have committed grave social or ritual faults, and Görög advances the hypothesis that the myths have the conservative function of reaffirming the importance of the ancient rules of conduct (301).

projection of their own cultural ambivalence. Scholars have
not studied extensively the reactions of different strata of the
subject races to ideologies of cultural superiority. Generalizations are based on research, limited in scope, and not
highly sensitive to indications of covert resistance. Our
conceptions are certain to change, as scholars probe beyond
the apparent acceptance and find the indications of resistance
they seek. There can be no doubt that reactions by
subordinates to cultural differences must have been quite
varied, ranging from an intractable revulsion for the culture
of the rulers, or a relatively unreflecting and selective
adaptation or syncretism, to a fervent affirmation of the new
incoming values, and the rejection of the old traditional
values.

In societies experiencing their first contacts with colonizers of a different race, there would arise the need to define
the newcomers; presumably recourse would be had to
existing categories. Hilda Kuper (1970) shows how, in the
case of the Swazis, the existing categories were inadequate
for the classification of whites. They were not conceived of as
'people', since they lacked the quality of 'humanism' or
'humanity', they were not 'witches', though they were
considered to have power equal to that of witches, and they
were neither 'animals' nor 'ancestral spirits'. A special
category had to be created to define them, and clearly the
creation of a special category has ideological implications,
serving to maintain existing categories of thought and values.
With the passage of time, there would be many changes in
perception of cultural difference, and varied modes of perception, related to the course of interaction between dominant
and subordinate races, and to the changing structures of the
society.

Ideologies of cultural difference between races are much
less developed among subordinate races than among dominant races. Fanon (1967: 43) argues that a people under-
taking a struggle for liberation rarely legitimizes race
prejudice, and that it never has recourse to biological

justifications even in acute periods of insurrectional armed struggle; he claims that the struggle of the 'inferiorized' is situated on a markedly more human level, the perspectives being radically new, and the opposition taking the classical one of struggles of conquest and liberation. Though it is not difficult to point to extreme racist ideologies among subordinate races, whether or not this racism is qualified as 'inverse' or 'reverse' racism, there does seem to be substantial truth in Fanon's argument.

Many reasons may be advanced to support the suggestion that subordinate races show less affinity for racist ideologies. It is often suggested that peoples who have suffered under racism naturally find it repugnant, and react by espousing a universal humanism. This is somewhat doubtful as a general proposition. The very suffering and humiliation may add intensity to the hatred, which awaits opportunity for expression. Thus the ethnic and racial prejudices of Afrikaners in South Africa seem to have fed upon the ethnic discrimination they suffered under the British, to attain their extreme form in 'apartheid'. But probably past suffering often does impose some restraint on the espousal of racist ideologies. This is all the more likely since the exclusion from rights and opportunities rests on racial discrimination, and the interests of subordinate races would seem to be served by ideologies which reject racial criteria as irrelevant and immoral. Presumably there is a continuing influence of these ideologies after liberation from racial domination.

More cogent explanations of differences in the commitment to racist ideologies may be derived from the historical context. The rank growth of ideologies of cultural and racial difference is associated with slavery and with colonial and imperial expansion. As members of the white race moved across the world, establishing dominion over many peoples of different race, they found in domination and exploitation the incentives for racist ideologies of interpretation and justification. Moreover the very generality of the phenomenon of colonialism fostered general ideologies. The subordinate races had no special incentive to develop racist ideologies, and for a people belonging to a subordinate race, and isolated in a colonial territory from wider contacts, the situation did not readily encourage the formulation of general ideologies. Instead, ideologies tended to be historically specific to the relationships and events, the past atrocities and the present injustices in a particular territory. When representatives of oppressed peoples came together in movements of resistance to colonial domination, there was already a strong influence of Marxist and Leninist theories stressing the role of economic and political factors in colonialism and imperialism.

Ideologies of racial difference have nevertheless developed among subordinate races, imposed in part by the racism of the rulers. They convey not only characterizations of the dominant race, but also redefinitions of the characteristics of the subordinate race.

Extreme forms of dehumanization of the dominant race as animals, demons or things seem rare. The ideological reduction of people to things is presumably an expression of power over them, and such conceptions are hardly to be anticipated in the ideologies of subordinate races. There is some attribution of demonic quality. In African societies, it seems not to have been uncommon, in the initial stage of contact, for whites to be perceived as having attributes of wizards. The purely ideological demonization of whites is fully developed in the USA in the 'Black Muslim' movement, which characterizes whites as devils created by a black scientist. A.L. Smith (1969: 7) comments, however, that the metaphysics of the Black Muslims have failed to impress many blacks, who must deal with the 'devil' every day.

LeRoi Jones (1969) in a dramatized version of the Black Muslim ideology (*A Black Mass*) presumably finds the demonic quality too appealing and transforms whites into monsters and beasts, creatures of such monstrosity and bestiality that Caliban, by comparison, is the very paragon of beauty, virtue and excellence. In the contemporary black

revolutionary movements in the USA, there is some cultivation of the animal analogy of pigs for whites, though pig
seems also to have rather specific reference to the police.
'Honkie' for whites is presumably also an animal categorization. Sundkler (1961: 207) mentions the description by
African Zionists in South Africa of the type of baptism
practised by white missionaries as bearing the 'Mark of the
Beast' (the beast being the white missionary), but this is
probably inspired as much by religious, as by racial conceptions. Millenarian movements are a major source of ideologies
of extreme dehumanization, in cases where the Manichean
conceptions are linked to race, and the dominant race
becomes the incarnation of evil.[9]

In contemporary political movements by subordinate
races, the dehumanization consists rather in the less extreme
form of the attribution of morally repugnant qualities to
members of the dominant race and their social institutions,
derived from the experience of domination as it is interpreted
within the context of the movement's political ideology.

An essential feature of the ideologies is the rejection of
white 'definitions' of the subordinate race, and their replace-
ment by black definitions. This is a deliberate process among
contemporary ideologists of the 'black revolution' in the
USA. These redefinitions by the subordinate race are closely
related to the way in which it characterizes, and is characterized by, the dominant race. It is common for the ideology of
the subordinate race to define itself as possessing precisely
those human qualities in which the dominant race is so
morally deficient, and some of the very qualities by which
the dominant race defines the subordinate in its milder
characterizations, are affirmed but transformed from denigration to approbation (e.g. 'black is beautiful').

The characterizations are conveyed by ideologies of

9 Y. Talmon (1966) offers an interesting analysis of the varying
characteristics and predisposing conditions of millenarian movements,
including the distinction between particular and universal millenarianism.

cultural difference. In the case of contemporary black ideologies of cultural difference in the USA, there is the initial problem of establishing the very existence of a different culture. Observers of the American scene coming from African societies, in which there are pronounced differences of culture between the races, tend to see black and white in the USA as sharing the same culture, with perhaps minor sub-cultural differences. This was moreover a prevalent view in the USA, encouraged by a national ideology of integration, a commitment to integration among educated middle-class blacks and a widely-held belief that the forms and organization of slavery had been such as to erase the African heritage. Inquiries by Herskovits (1941) into continuities and survivals of African culture in the New World were often felt to be somewhat retrogressive. Now, with the development of movements advocating black separatism, or integration, but only on the basis of the recognition of the distinctive cultural and national identity of blacks, there is a revival of the perspectives developed by Herskovits, and a revaluation of his work. Earlier resentment at the suggestion that blacks in the USA had a distinctive culture is replaced by present resentment at the suggestion that they share a common culture with American whites. Some argue that cultural differences were always present, but suppressed in contact with whites, and that these covert elements of culture are now being brought into the open. There is a search for African survivals and a deliberate cultivation of African culture. Certain items, like a 'natural hairdo' or styles of dress, or a new name, symbolize as shibboleths, a distinctive cultural identity.

This problem of establishing the existence of cultural differences is rare in systems of racial domination. Generally, persistent cultural differences are clearly associated with race, and the ideologies of the subordinates proceed directly to the reassertion of the values of traditional cultures. Particular items of culture may come to symbolize cultural identity and values and resistance to domination, as for example, female circumcision among the Kikuyu in Kenya (Buitenhuijs, 1971: Chapter 3) or the wearing of the veil in Algeria (Fanon, 1965: 35-67).

The process of decolonization greatly stimulated the development of black ideologies of cultural difference. They were an inevitable reaction to the ideologies of cultural difference elaborated and disseminated by whites in the period of their colonial expansion, with particular reference to Africans. To the cultural imperialism of colonialism, the subordinated peoples responded by ideologies directed to the decolonization of social values. Reacting against the declaration of the universality[10] of Western values and the superiority of Western culture, and against the degradation of the values of the conquered societies, the colonized exposed the ethnocentric assumptions of superiority and universality, proclaiming the equal or greater human worth of their own values, and the validity of their own cultures as the basis of distinctive identities..

The black ideologies of cultural difference vary in the degree to which they are inclusive or exclusive, and in the manner in which the differences are defined, whether independently of white ideologies or in opposition to them. *Négritude* in its early formulations by Senghor defined the values of the (Negro) black world in opposition to the European values of discursive reason, instrumental and chrematistic logic: '*Négritude* was intuitive reason, reason-embrace, communional warmth, the image-symbol and cosmic rhythm which, instead of sterilizing through divisiveness, fecundated by unifying.' In its evolution, *négritude*

---

10 The pattern variables developed by Parsons for characterizing social orientations include universalism and particularism, and they are often applied to distinguish 'Western' from 'primitive' societies, so that Western values become identified with universalism. See, on the question of the attribution of universality to Western values, Allen (1962: 321). See also Cohen (1955: 590) who writes of colonialism that 'le maître s'identifie à l'universel et rejette l'esclave dans le particulier'.

came to affirm the values of the 'Negro World' positively and in their own right, as the black contribution, without loss of identity, to the civilization of the universal (Thomas, 1965: 106 ff.).

Africanité expresses the distinctive qualities of what are assumed to be the common elements in African culture. The content of the ideologies may be developed in some independence of the characterizations in the white ideologies, or with a keen awareness of, and a reaction against, these characterizations. The basis of identity for *africanité* is sub-Saharan African societies, and the Arab and Berber societies of the north, as in Senghor's concept of *africanité* in relation to *arabité*.[11] The 'African personality', somewhat similar to *africanité*, is a distillation of the assumed values of African traditional life.[12] To these ideologies must be added the ideological elements developed in the USA over the last decade, expressed in such concepts as 'black is beautiful', 'soul-brother' and 'black experience', which has an ideological basis similar to Pan-Africanism.

These ideologies may be developed in much the same way as the Marxist ideology of revolution, the liberation of the proletariat being the liberation of mankind. So Senghor (Thomas, 1965: 112) conceives the mission of *négritude* as going beyond the dialectic of struggle 'to make the world more human'.

3.

What indications as to the structure of race relations in a society, and of polarization with impending violence, or of

11 See the discussion by the Belgian anthropologist, Maquet (1969) of the sub-Saharan concept of *africanité* and Senghor (1967) for the more continental concept.

12 Ki-Zerbo (1962: 267-82) mentions such values as the authority of the old people and of ancestors, solidarity, personalism.

processes conducive to peaceful change, can be derived from
these ideologies of cultural difference, and from the interaction between them? And what is the rationale for the
assumption that the ideologies can serve as an indication of
the state of race relations?

It is clear that the presence in a society of ideologies of
cultural difference by no means indicates the presence of
racial stratification. Ideologies of cultural difference are
associated with many types of stratification, and are not tied
to systems of racial stratification. Indeed, where the dominant and subordinate strata are of the same race, there may
be an extreme cultivation of cultural difference and an
ideological emphasis on its significance, as if to compensate
for any equalizing tendencies in common racial identity.
Thus, in the black settler society of Liberia, the dominant
stratum of Americo-Liberians cultivated a distinctive style of
life, and discriminated between the 'civilized', that is, its own
stratum, and the 'uncivilized' or 'tribal' local populations.[13]
But although ideologies of cultural difference are not
exclusive to systems of racial stratification, they seem to be
almost invariably associated with them.

Moreover the essential basis for an ideology of cultural
difference in race relations appears to be racial discrimination
and not cultural difference. The objective presence of
cultural difference or cultural pluralism, is seemingly not
crucial. M.G. Smith, in an early formulation of this theory
of pluralism (1965: 63, 89), now substantially revised,[14]
emphasized the primacy of cultural differences, arguing that
racial differences derive social significance from cultural
differences, that hierarchic race relations in a society reflect
conditions of cultural heterogeneity, and that they tend to
lose their hierarchic character as cultural uniformity increases. It seems clear that hierarchic race relations may, on
the contrary, persist as cultural uniformity increases, and

13 See Merran Fraenkel (1964: 14, 196 ff.).
14 See his contributions in Kuper and Smith (1969).

indeed, that there may be greater racial discrimination in reaction to a perceived threat as members of the subordinate race acquire the culture of the dominant group. The really significant factor is the ideological perception. Minor differences may come to symbolize the impermeability of the barriers between the races, and to constitute a mandate for discrimination. Cultural differences between the races may be more greatly emphasized as the cultural differences actually diminish. This is the case under South African apartheid, which places an extreme emphasis on cultural difference in a situation of increasing acculturation and seeks to reverse the trend towards a common culture by policies of education and segregation.

My argument then is that racial discrimination is associated not so much with cultural differences between the races, as with particular perceptions of, or beliefs about, those differences, as they come to be elaborated in ideologies; and that ideologies of cultural difference are almost invariably found in racially stratified societies. If this is accepted, then it should be possible to derive some indications of the structure and course of race relations in a society from these ideologies of cultural difference.

In analysing ideologies of the dominant race, the most widely accepted sociological theory is that the characterizations of the subordinate race and the associated directions for action and relationship, are a function of the interests of the dominant race in the society, expressed in its own cultural idiom in a specific societal context.[15] The various processes of dehumanization may thus be associated with different patterns of relationship – extreme forms of dehumanization with the virtual denial of relationship, as in

15 In asking why the *colons* in Algeria freely used *ratons* in reference to Arabs, while Afrikaners in South Africa freely use *bobbejaan* (baboon) for Africans, one is driven to seek explanations in the difference between French urban *esprit* and Afrikaner rusticity, that is to say, in the difference in cultural idiom between French and Afrikaners, rather than in differences between the peoples so abused.

the extermination of Bushmen, or chattel slavery, and milder forms of dehumanization as in the curtailment of rights and opportunities under paternalism.

Extreme forms of ideological dehumanization may indicate a readiness for extreme violence and cruelty: they dehumanize the subject race in ideology, but they may also dehumanize the dominant race in action. The brutal suppression of the Mau Mau movement in Kenya may be an example of this. It was accompanied by the most degrading and dehumanizing conceptions of the movement as wholly evil, serving the powers of darkness, emanating from the black and bloodstained forces of sorcery, unspeakably obscene, an atavistic return to barbarism.[16] Perhaps a proliferation of dehumanizing ideologies and slogans often precedes massacres of peoples, whether of subordinate or equal status, and whether differentiated by race, nation or religion; and it may be possible to derive from the comparative analysis of the ideological context of these massacres some measures of the relationship between ideologies and the probability of violence.

Ideologies dehumanizing the dominant race presumably have the function of restructuring in some way the relationship of domination and subordination. They undermine consensus, the premise of inequality as Maquet (1961) describes it for Rwanda, or perhaps more accurately acquiescence or quiescence; they promote sentiments of equality or of superiority; and they encourage members of the subordinate race to resist domination. The extreme forms of dehumanization in terms of animal analogies and demonization seem rare. In the USA the categorization of whites as devils or pigs may stimulate a greater readiness for acts of violence against

16 See Buitenhuijs (1971), Chapter 6, 'Les Mythes Mau-Mau', in which he analyses white conceptions of Mau Mau, and the Corfield Report (1960: 9, 284). Philip Mitchell (1954), former Governor of Kenya, expressed the most intense repugnance for Mau Mau: 'obscene, orgiastic abominations' (259), 'hyenas that follow to eat the carrion' (267), etc.

them, but the characterizations do not seem to be widely held or specially significant.[17] In South Africa, during the resistance movements in the 1950s and 1960s, the characterizations were largely in terms of the political structure of white domination and the supporting racial attitudes. In Zanzibar, there was an extreme dehumanization of Arabs in African ideologies, based on charges that Arabs had been guilty of almost unspeakable cruelty against Africans.[18]

These characterizations by subordinate and dominant races may provide some indication of the structure of race relations and the imminence of violence. Further indications,

17 Gary T. Marx (1967: 107 ff.) offers some discussion of the small support for Black Muslim ideology in a survey carried out in 1964.

18 Lofchie (1965) describes how the political conflict between the Zanzibar National Party and the Afro-Shirazi Party was expressed in terms of race conflict between Arabs and Africans and comments that: 'Imagery about the cruelty of slavery was so widespread and well known among ASP supporters that party speakers did not often refer to it directly in their speeches. The ASP press played an important role in keeping this imagery alive. A stylized version of the history of slavery became a prominent editorial topic in the final weeks before the June election. One African newspaper, *Sauti ya Afro-Shirazi* ('The Voice of the Afro-Shirazis'), carried the following item as a commentary on an ASP public meeting. "Today we would like to . . . remind our African brethren who are insisting on helping the Arabs . . . [of] the actions done by the Arabs during their time alone. The Arabs made the people sweep with their breasts; the Arabs pierced the wombs of the women who were pregnant so that their wives could see how a baby was placed. The Arabs shaved the people's hair and then used their heads as places for knocking their toothbrushes. The Arabs made the people castrated like cows so that they might converse with their wives without wanting them. The Arabs made the African old men chew palm nuts without breaking them in order that they may laugh." These stories and many others like them pervaded the African villages and the rural areas. African old-timers presented them to younger fellow-villagers as personally verified experiences of extreme physical suffering under Arab overlordship. Direct person-to-person repetition of such stories endowed them with a legendary authenticity, and created an atmosphere of apprehension and terror far greater than could ever have been aroused in the more ebullient environment of an open public meeting' (209-10).

perhaps more revealing of the structure of race relations than the racial characterizations themselves, may be derived from the interaction between ideologies of cultural difference. Do the ideologies adjust, moving towards synthesis, and offering a basis for conciliation, or do they develop in dialectical opposition?

Confining comment to the situation in which the relationship between racial domination and ideologies of cultural difference is most clear, and in which cultural differences become a battleground, that is to say, white settler and colonial societies, I will take as a starting-point Fanon's (1967: 38 ff. and 1963: 42 ff.) theory of the cycle of ideological interaction. The first stage is one in which the colonized come to accept and internalize the denigration of their race and culture: 'The "inferior race" denies itself as a different race. It shares with the "superior race" the convictions, doctrines, and other attitudes concerning it.' This alienation from the colonized's original forms of existence is found in the official texts under the name of assimilation (1967: 38). In the second stage, members of the subordinate race begin to assert the values of their culture, which becomes an object of passionate attachment, while the dominant race responds by pointing out the specificity and wealth of its own values: but the colonized masses mock at these values, insult them and vomit them up. In the final stage, the stage of decolonization, the colonized decide to fight all forms of exploitation and of alienation of man. The colonizers, on the other hand, multiply appeals to assimilation, to integration, to community (1967: 43). But the logical end of the colonized's will to struggle is the total liberation of the national territory. When this is achieved, the two cultures can affront each other and enrich each other: 'Universality resides in this decision to recognize and accept the reciprocal relativism of different cultures, once the colonial status is irreversibly excluded' (1967: 44).[19]

19 Balandier (1962: 85-96) offers an interesting discussion of myths of colonization and decolonization among the colonized.

The first stage then is the long period of colonization or of white settler rule, in which ideologies of cultural difference are interwoven with political domination and economic exploitation, shaping educational policies with respect to language of instruction, content, amount and cost of education, segregation or access to the knowledge and facilities of the dominant race. If there is a qualified franchise for subordinates, then calculations of political arithmetic affect not only level of franchise but educational policy.[20]

The second stage of an assertion by the colonized of their own values is by no means sharply separated from the initial stage of cultural alienation. Probably large sections of the subordinate race were never culturally alienated and did not share in the denigration of their culture, but continued to live their customary way of life, adapting to changed circumstances. It would seem that the perspective of alienated intellectuals has been generalized as the experience of an entire race. Moreover, not all the intellectuals were alienated. Particularly in societies with an old tradition of scholarship, intellectuals continued to immerse themselves reverently in the study and transmission of traditional culture. Side by side with the alienation of a section of the intellectuals, there was thus also the persistence of traditional culture and values, adapting and modifying. But in the phase of cultural nationalism, the traditional values are glorified, romanticized and asserted with pride, in opposition to the culture of the dominant race.

In the third stage, of movement for liberation, the reactions of the dominant race are quite varied. No doubt in some cases, the rulers multiply appeals to assimilation, integration, community, as Fanon suggests. But this was certainly not the pattern in the more extreme racial conflicts on the African continent.

20 These issues of educational policy are brought out in an interesting historical account by A.M. (1963) of education of Muslims in Algeria. See also Leo Kuper (1965: Chapters 12 and 13) for analysis of the South African situation.

In South Africa, the interaction is no doubt somewhat bizarre, since it is the dominant race which encourages cultural nationalism among the different African ethnic groups, while many Africans respond guardedly to cultural nationalism or indeed recoil from it. Moreover, the response of the rulers to the African liberation movement was apartheid, and not the overtures of integration. In Kenya, the conceptions that many whites held of the Mau Mau movement, merely strengthened convictions of cultural difference. In Zanzibar, the ruling Arabs appealed to sentiments of solidarity in the possession of a common language, a shared religion and loyalty to the Sultan, but these appeals were addressed to the local Shirazi population, and not to the Mainland Africans, who were thought of as alien, and who became the main carriers of the revolution. In Rwanda, the Tutsi response to Hutu demands was in part to deny the existence of internal divisions under sanction of reprisals; it was not an appeal to integration, but an affirmation of the unity of the society, and a mobilization against subversion of that unity; and the more traditionalist response was to assert the Tutsi right to domination by reason of conquest and Hutu submission.[21] Moreover, it was the Tutsi ruling caste which sought to revive the glories of past cultures in a movement of cultural nationalism.

Both in Rwanda and Zanzibar, the relationship between the dominant and subordinate sections was complicated by colonial rule, and by the leadership of Tutsi in Rwanda and Arabs in Zanzibar in the militant movements for independence. But even in Algeria, which was presumably Fanon's model, many of the *colons* persistently resisted integration. There was a dialectic of irreconcilable ideological conflict between sections of the white settlers and sections of the Muslim population. Soustelle (1956: 70) shows vividly the nature of this dialectic, and its threat to peaceable develop-

21 D'Hertefelt (1960 and 1964) discusses the complexity of these ideologies.

ment in his discussion of the reactions to the relationship beween Muslim status and French citizenship:

On observe ici ce fait bien souvent constaté: que les positions extrêmes se rejoignent. Tandis que du côté européen des 'ultras' persistaient à refuser aux Musulmans la pleine citoyenneté sous prétexte que celle-ci aurait été incompatible avec leur 'statut personnel' islamique, du côté musulman, les extrémistes poussaient leur coreligionnaires à refuser cette même citoyenneté comme incompatible avec leur salut. D'un côté on disait: 'Pour être un bon Français il faut cesser d'être Musulman'; de l'autre: 'Pour être un bon Musulman, il ne faut pas être ni devenir Français'. La convergence des aveuglements jouait contre l'évolution paisible et raisonnable de l'Algérie. (70)[22]

In these situations of extreme racial conflict, the interaction did not conform to the pattern described by Fanon. The rulers did not respond to the militant movements for liberation by multiplying appeals to assimilation, integration and community. Or if they did make such appeals, there was also dialectical opposition between the extremes on either side, which contributed to the polarizing of relationships between large sections of each race. The issue of integration was most relevant for white settler societies. Where there were small numbers of whites, they might readily feel their future safeguarded by policies of integration. But where the white settler population was appreciable, the main ideological response was likely to be in terms of ideologies of exclusion, or of irreconcilable cultural difference. It would seem that the third phase described by Fanon serves an ideological

22 'One observes here an often-recognized fact, namely the convergence of extremes. While the European extremists persistently refused Muslims full citizenship under the pretext of its incompatibility with their personal Islamic status, the Muslim extremists pressed their fellow Muslims to reject this same citizenship as incompatible with their salvation. One side declared that "to be a good Frenchman, one must cease to be a Muslim", the other that "to be a good Muslim, one must neither be nor become French". The convergence of these blind prejudices was an obstacle to the peaceful and rational evolution of Algeria.'

function, rather than an analytical purpose. If the goal of total revolution is to be achieved, then the movement must be protected from compromise solutions. The third phase, in Fanon's formulation, is really an ideological rejection of the possibility of integration before a reversal of power and decolonization.

4.

In this chapter, I have inquired into the relationship between racial structure and ideologies of cultural difference, and I have suggested that racial characterizations in these ideologies, and the interaction between ideologies, might serve as an indication of the state of race relations in a society.

Though ideologies of cultural difference are not exclusive to racially structured societies, they seem to be almost universally present in them. I have argued that they are more closely associated with racial stratification than with the objective presence of cultural differences. However, in emphasizing the perceptions and ideologies of cultural difference, I do not wish to imply that objective cultural differences are not highly relevant.

The presence of considerable differences in culture, particularly such extremes of difference as between the cultures of industrialized societies and peasant societies, may be expected to encourage the formulation of ideologies of cultural difference in the dominant group. In the colonial expansion of the European powers, wide differences in culture were generally associated with racial differences, and they were elaborated into ideologies. In various ways, cultural differences were used as a criterion for the unequal incorporation of the races. In consequence, interpretations of cultural difference became an important issue in the struggle between the races, during the movement towards independence or liberation.

Similarly, in the USA, there was initially a close association of racial differences between black and white with extreme cultural differences, and ideologies of cultural and racial difference abounded. But race is no longer associated in the USA with cultural differences between black and white. Black nationalists argue to the contrary, and compare the situation of blacks with the situation of Africans under colonial rule. The comparison, however, serves rather to demonstrate the minor role of cultural differences. The contrast is between African societies, having distinctive cultures rooted in communities with considerable continuity, and blacks in the USA, participating in the same political and economic institutions, sharing the same language, and holding many of the same beliefs. The differences seem to me more in the nature of sub-cultural differences. They may rank high in the ideologies of black nationalists and they may be enhanced by the revival of selected aspects of African cultures. But they seem likely to remain relatively minor in relation to the common institutions; and the emphasis on cultural difference may not be persuasive to the great mass of blacks in the USA. Moreover, cultural differences are not particularly salient for the dominant race, and they are not accorded formal recognition in the structure of domination, discrimination in the USA being more nakedly racial than in any other part of the world. It seems unlikely therefore that ideologies of cultural difference will be a particularly significant element in the struggle between the races.

Clearly, the objective cultural differences between races are highly relevant for the structure of their relations. They not only influence the perception and ideological use made of cultural differences, but the very nature and extent of these differences affect the structure of the society. However, the significance attached to these differences is quite variable. At a time when cultural differences are in fact diminishing, they may become more salient to the racial sections; or minor differences may be stressed in one society, while major differences are played down in another. Cultural pluralism, the objective cultural differences between races, would thus be an unreliable guide to the nature of their relationship.

I have suggested that ideologies of cultural difference, however, may serve as an indication of the state of race relations in a society. Three main assumptions underlie this suggestion. The first is that these ideologies express the interests of the parties. In the ruling race, they are a function of domination: in the subject race, they are a function of subordination, in situations of acquiescence, resistance or revolution, and in the context of the structure, and legitimating ideologies, of domination. The second main assumption is that the characterizations of the races in these ideologies are a significant element, and that there is an association between dehumanization in ideology and dehumanization in action, or predisposition for action. Different processes of dehumanization would be associated with different patterns of relationship. The third main assumption is that the interaction between ideologies, whether moving towards synthesis or in dialectical opposition, is related to processes of change in race relations, offering possibilities of adjustment, or promoting racial violence.

The extent to which these assumptions are valid, and if so, the conditions under which they are valid, and the nature of the indications which can be derived from ideologies of cultural difference, must be tested. In some circumstances, ideologies may be of little significance. Racial massacres may perhaps take place without ideological overture. Or the ideologies may be full of blood and thunder, but pure rhetoric, or ritual, unrelated to action, or indeed a substitute for action.

Many variables will affect the significance of these ideologies. There are the variables directly related to the ideologies — the carriers of the ideologies, their numbers, social situation and organization, strength of commitment, practical directives for action, relationship to other ideologies and resources available. Then there are the variables affecting the racial pluralism of the society[23] — its demographic

23 See Leo Kuper (1969*b*), especially 473-9.

composition, economic development, mode of racial incorporation, inequalities, discontinuities and cultural differences.

Much of the discussion in this paper was related to African
societies with extreme racial pluralism – as between Europeans and Africans in South Africa and Kenya, Arabs and
Mainland Africans in Zanzibar, Tutsi and Hutu in Rwanda –
or with extreme ethnic pluralism as between Europeans and
Muslims in Algeria. In South Africa, Algeria and Kenya, the
dialectic between ideologies was especially clear. In South
Africa, there were the innumerable oppositions between
universalism and particularism, and between different forms
of particularism, as for example, policies of universal education versus tribal education, conceptions of a common
humanity as opposed to conceptions of separate destinies,
African nationalism against the apartheid cultivation of tribal
cultural nationalism, African nationalism confronting Afrikaner nationalism, and interracialism in conflict both with
apartheid and Africanism. In Algeria, the integrating policy
with reference to citizenship, was to accept Muslim status as
compatible with French citizenship: the ideological polarization was between ideologies of colonists requiring the
renunciation of Muslim status as a prerequisite to citizenship,
and Algerian Muslim ideologies declaring French citizenship
incompatible with Islam. In Kenya, the opposition between
commitment to Kikuyu culture and its denigration as
barbarous found expression in the conflict over female
circumcision for example, and in the Mau Mau movement. In
Zanzibar, ideologies polarized in conceptions of a culturally
autonomous Islamic State, a specifically Zanzibar nationalism, as opposed to Pan-Africanism and African nationalism
(Lofchie, 1965: 198-9). In Rwanda, there was the opposition
between the revival of old traditions and ideologies of
domination among sections of the Tutsi, and egalitarian and
Christian perspectives among the Westernized Hutu leaders.
As for the USA, I have suggested that ideologies of cultural
difference are not likely to be particularly significant in the

contemporary period, but there are movements of contra-culture, as for example, the rejection of Christianity and the commitment to Islam among the Black Muslims, or of black culture in opposition to white among black nationalists.

In all these societies, interests in domination or resistance are projected into the ideologies of cultural difference and the interaction between ideologies is both a part of the struggle for power, and an expression of the state of race relations. It is for this reason that the analysis of ideologies of cultural difference may often serve as an important indicator of the changing structure of race relations in a society.

2

Race Structure
in the Social Consciousness

Conflict between races in a society finds expression in different conceptions of the racial structure of that society. This applies to formulations of the structure by academicians engaged in purely objective analysis, as well as to the somewhat explicitly ideological declarations of persons caught up in political struggle and committed to specific programmes of action.

At the academic level, controversy over the utility and applicability of the concept and theory of the 'plural society' may serve as an example, among social scientists, of divergent conceptions, with different ideological implications. Proponents of the theory emphasize the sharpness of the cleavages between the racial sections and the propensity for violent change, while critics of the theory draw attention to the presence of common institutions and of interracial association, finding in these some indication of a process of, and a potentiality for, evolutionary change.[1] The controversy over the use of the term *caste* to describe white-black relations in the USA (Cox, 1948: 489-538), the acceptance or rejection of the thesis that Negroes in the USA constitute a colonized people in a colonial situation, and the affinity of a theory of polygenesis for social policies of racial differentiation[2] may serve as further examples.

1 For a general discussion of the controversy, see M.G. Smith (1969*a* and *b*) and Leo Kuper (1969*a*).
2 Banton (1967: 12-35); Birdsell (1963: 178-85). Theories of monogenesis provide a basis for such concepts as a common humanity and brotherhood of man, but they are also compatible with extreme doctrines of racial separation, as for example, South African apartheid.

At the political level, the documents presented by Nkunda-bagenzi (1961), covering political developments in Rwanda during the period 1956-61, disclose the extraordinarily diverse conceptions of the structure of relations between the country's three racial categories,[3] the dominant Tutsi minority, the large and subordinate Hutu majority, and the numerically negligible Twa at the lowest level of subordination. As commonly happens, the third category, in this case the Twa, was often forgotten in the conflict between the other races, resulting in a bi-racial conception.[4] In manifestos, Hutu leaders proclaimed their conception as one of racial subjection under Tutsi domination (Nkundabagenzi, 1961: 20-32). Some Tutsi leaders expressed the same conception, denying that there was a basis for fraternity between Tutsi and Hutu in a structure of relations which had arisen out of conquest and was always based on bondage (Nkundabagenzi, 1961: 35-6). Other Tutsi conceptions stressed unity though with acknowledgment of differentiation, as in the view that Bahutu, Batutsi, and Batwa were simply nicknames of persons sharing the common family name of Abanyaruanda, or in the slogan, *Le Peuple tripartite* (Nkun-

3 Maquet (1961: 10) writes that 'a definite physical appearance is considered typical of each group. According to the socially accepted descriptions of the three stereotypes the typical Twa is short, pygmoid rather than pigmy, with a head low in the crown, face and nose flat, cheek-bones prominent, forehead bulging, eyes narrow and slightly oblique. Hutu characteristics are woolly hair, flat broad nose, thick lips often everted, and middle stature. Tutsi are very slender and tall. They often have a straight nose and a light brown skin colour. The objective measurements of Professor Jean Hiernaux do not entirely coincide with these stereotypes.'

D'Hertefelt (1964: 219-38) has contributed an interesting analysis of the relationship between myth and ideology in Rwanda.

4 See comments of M. de Schryver, president of a work group appointed by the Belgian government, at a conference in May, 1959. 'Nous avons vu des laïcs en grand nombre et aussi des religieux, des fonctionnaires, des juges, des membres du Conseil Supérieur, le Mwami et aussi des Batwa oubliés par les deux autres races Hutu, Tutsi ' (Nkundabagenzi, 1961: 84).

dabagenzi, 1961: 31, 75). Or Tutsi leaders emphasized unity, with rejection of differentiation, based either on perceptions of present reality as in the statement by the King (Mwami Mutara) that he would have no criterion for differentiating the terms Mututsi and Muhutu, or on aspiration for the future, as in the resolution addressed by the National Council for Rwanda to the Belgian government, insisting that the terms Bahutu, Batutsi and Batwa should be crossed out in all official documents (Nkundabagenzi, 1961: 1, 37). Or conflict might be acknowledged, but the significance of racial difference for the conflict denied, as in the conception advanced by Tutsi students that the problem was social in itself, but racial in the eyes of the administration and of certain autochthonous elements (Nkundabagenzi, 1961: 107).

It is with some aspects of the diverse conceptions of the racial structure in the social consciousness that this paper deals. These conceptions are an integral part of the racial structure of a society. They influence the course of race relations, and they may serve as an index of change, of social forces stimulating sharp conflict and polarization, or contributing to harmonious adjustment and integration. There has been little systematic analysis of conceptions of racial structure, and I therefore start with a preliminary classification before exploring some of the relations among conceptions, and between conceptions and racial structure. The particular themes selected here for comment are, first, the description of conceptions in terms of criteria of differentiation, numbers of racial categories identified, and the manner in which they are characterized and structured; secondly, the interrelations between conceptions, in terms of fluidity, and of transformation from one conception to another; and thirdly, the interaction between different conceptions with reference to their varied structural bases and situational contexts.

The approach derives appreciably from *Class Structure in the Social Consciousness* by Ossowski. His systematic analysis of conceptions of class structures is illuminating for the understanding of conceptions of race structures, in terms both of similarities between the conceptions, and of unique distinctive features. It is for this reason that I develop a comparison between conceptions of class and race structures. I have retained the term 'social consciousness', though it is somewhat archaic, and I follow Ossowski's use of *social consciousness* to refer to concepts, images, beliefs and evaluations that characterize certain milieus, that are more or less common to people of a certain social environment, and that are reinforced in the consciousness of particular individuals by mutual suggestion and by the conviction that they are shared by other people in the same group (1963: 6). In the approach to the structure of race relations, I shall use the term to refer to a category that is socially defined, but on the basis of physical criteria (see van den Berghe, 1967: 6).

1.

Conceptions of the racial structure vary in the numbers of racial categories identified, and I shall distinguish two-category, multi-category and unitary.[5] Conceptions vary also in the criteria by which the categories are defined and described. These criteria may be specifically racial, in the sense of reference to distinguishing physical characteristics (such as black and white); or the racial reference may be indirectly conveyed in geographical terms, such as area of origin (e.g. Africans and Europeans, settler and native, colonist or colonizer and colonized), or by reference to such cultural criteria as level of evolution or civilization, or by group name or ethnic identity (as above, in the case of Hutu, Tutsi and Twa). The criteria may imply continuity (for example, where civilization is the defining characteristic), or

5 Two-category and multi-category are terms used by Banton (1967: 287). Alternative usages are dichotomous, trichotomous, multidivisional (Ossowski, 1963), *sociétés bi-communautaires* and *sociétés pluri-communautaires* (Quermonne, 1961: 36), or bi-plural and multi-plural. None of these terms is very elegant.

discontinuity (as between Negroid and Caucasoid); a related distinction would be that between attributes and variables. Finally, conceptions vary in the manner in which the categories are structured, ranging from conceptions which imply exclusion[6] or a relative absence of linkage, to those which portray the categories as linked, whether harmoniously or antithetically.

Two-category conceptions tend to define the racial categories in terms of attributes, that is to say in terms of qualitatively distinct and discrete characteristics, such as white and Negro, or African and European. If the defining characteristic is a variable, such as civilization, then presumably the tendency would be to treat it as an attribute, distinguishing qualitatively between the categories of civilized and uncivilized, without recognition of intervening categories. The criteria are quite varied in their reference and descriptive terminology, including racial, geographical, cultural and ethnic distinctions, as well as animal analogies.

There may be no implication in the two-category conception that the categories are in any way linked. Thus the categories European and African are not related in themselves, and would seem to represent racially exclusive categories, though this is not necessarily so, as in the Pan-Africanist extension of African identity to include all who accept African majority rule and identify with Africans (Leo Kuper, 1965: 378). By contrast, the categories of European and non-European link the entire society by a single characteristic, the quality of being (or not being) European. The change from one conception to the other may be an index of basic change within a society, as for example in South Africa, when the law prohibiting 'illicit carnal intercourse' between Europeans and Natives, was changed by the

6 Thus, to take an example from caste society, the four *varna* constitute an inclusive system; exclusion is introduced in the conception of pariah castes, and this exclusion becomes more marked in the conception of caste and outcaste.

Immorality Amendment Act of 1950 so as to prohibit such intercourse between Europeans and non-Europeans. Thereby a prohibition relating to only two of the categories within the society was extended so as to give effect to a dichotomous conception of the society as a whole, in terms of apartheid legislative planning.

The linking of categories, where this is present, may be conceived as harmonious or antithetical. The conception of white American and American Negro emphasized perhaps exclusion or lack of relationship more than unity, whereas the terms white American and Negro American stress rather the harmonious unity of being American: an analogous case would be the contrast between the terms South African Indian or Indian South African. Antithetical conceptions, such as characterization by opposites (e.g. white-black) are presumably associated with situations of domination and of conflict. The extreme form of antithetical conception would be that defined by Ossowski as the dichotomic conception, namely 'a generalization for the entire society of a two-term asymmetric relation in which one side is privileged at the expense of the other. In this conception society is divided into two correlative and diametrically opposed classes in such a way that each of these classes is characterized by the relation of its members to the members of the opposed class' (Ossowski, 1963: 31). The Marxist conception of the dialectical relationship between bourgeoisie and proletariat is a model of dichotomous conceptions in the class structure, as is Fanon's characterization of the relation between colonizers and colonized in the racial structure (Fanon, 1963: 31-4).

Quite apart from any theoretical or ideological elaboration of a dialectical relationship between the racial categories, the terms by which the categories are identified may become increasingly polarized in a dialectical relationship. Thus South African apartheid legislation, by systematically extending control over race relations in a large number of social situations, under threat of penal sanctions, increasingly weights the racial categories with new social connotations, conceived dialectically. There is an increasing range of social contexts, in which the laws define as legitimate, and presumably desirable, association with members of one's own race, but as criminal, the same acts of association when they are engaged in with members of a different race. This is a similar phenomenon to that mentioned by Ossowski (1963: 139) with reference to class, namely that the characterization of class may be more or less rich in content.

Multi-category structures. Where the social structure is conceived in more than two categories, the criteria for identifying the categories are again quite diverse. They may consist of variables, as for example, such shades of colour, as *preto, cabra, cabo verde, escuro, mulato escuro, mulato claro, pardo, sarará, moreno, louro, branco da terra* in Vila Recôncavo, Brazil (Banton, 1967: 276), or of attributes, such as Africans, whites, Asiatics and Coloureds in South Africa. They may be discontinuous, or continuous, with the possible implication in the latter case of transformation from one category to another.

As to the structuring of the categories, the conception may be of units largely unrelated. This is part of the *ideological* conception of apartheid, the racial categories being described as having their separate destinies, and a duty to develop along their own lines. Or the categories may be conceived as linked, whether harmoniously or antagonistically. The linking may take the form of a ranked order, in the conception Ossowski describes as gradation; either a simple gradation in which the relations are based on the grading of some objectively measurable characteristic, or a synthetic gradation, where rank is determined by an evaluation resulting from the comparison of incommensurable factors (1963: 42). The simple case of gradation would be one, for example, where an intermediate category, arising out of an initial two-category structure, receives recognition, such as a category of Coloureds or mestizos. Where, as in many colonies, a third category was introduced, Indians under indenture for example, this category might again occupy a distinctive position in consequence of a synthetic gradation based on such incommensurable values as colour, culture, national or geographical background and social role. Naturally, simple and synthetic gradations, and conceptions of harmony or antagonism, are likely to vary with the different situation of strata in the social structure.

A *unitary conception* of the racial structure is only meaningful, in the context of this analysis in situations where conceptions of a plural racial structure are prevalent in the society. The unitary conception, corresponding to the conception of the classless society, may consist in the simple denial of racial differentiation, as in the declaration by the Mwami of Rwanda that he would have no criteria for distinguishing Tutsi, Hutu and Twa. Or division and conflict might be acknowledged, but conceived as based on other than racial division, as for example on social differentiation (Nkundabagenzi, 1961: 107), or differences in culture or xenophobia, as in many discussions of English attitudes to coloured people.[7] Or the exorcism of racial division, and the assertion of the unitary conception, may be expressed in the emphasis on the unifying principle (that all are members of the Abanyaruanda and united in loyalty to the Mwami, or that all are Zanzibari, loyal to the Sultan).

2.

The interrelations between these conceptions are quite fluid. I have mentioned the case of a third category arising from the interaction of two categories. These persons of mixed racial ancestry may not be recognized as a category, or they may be recognized under a variety of terms, such as mestizo, creole

7 This has always seemed to me, with a different conception of the racial structure of English society, to be a somewhat esoteric rationalization for the rather common phenomenon of racial prejudice and discrimination.

or Coloured, or they may be recognized as a category by members of only one racial section (as for example, in the USA where the whites withheld status from intermediate strata recognized by the blacks themselves, such as the light in colour). Or the conception of a third category may arise as the result of the introduction of immigrants of different race. Or the recognition of the third category may be a consequence of the intersection of two-category conceptions. Thus, in the French and Portuguese colonial African territories, there was a conception of a two-category structure consisting of French or Portuguese (the colonizers) and the indigenous (colonized) peoples, and a second conception of civilized and uncivilized. From the intersection of these two two-conceptions, arose the legally recognized and privileged category of the *évolué* in French territories or the *assimilado* in Portuguese territories. Both the accommodating and revolutionary roles of the members of this category are related to the ambiguity of their position. It would seem that not all the categories arising from the intersection of two conceptions are used. Thus the intersection of black-white, and African-European, gives rise to black African, white European, and black European,[8] but not white African (though perhaps this last category begins to emerge with African political independence and a movement of whites towards the new centres of power). In the same way, the intersection of black-white and Christian-heathen, gives rise to all categories other than white heathen. From the intersection of white-Negro and rich-poor, there arises, in addition to the expected categories of rich white and poor Negro, the social problem category of poor white, conceived as a combination of incompatibles. Rich Negro undergoes a somewhat pompous transmutation to black bourgeoisie.

Fluidity is expressed also in changing conceptions resulting

8 Jordan Ngubane, an African who settled in a Swazi village, and built himself a latrine, heard himself referred to by Swazi as the black European. Black Etonian would be a similar conception, but emanating from whites.

from a process of situational selection (Epstein, 1958: 235). Thus under apartheid, members of the dominant race define the racial categories in some situations as white and non-white, and in other situations as Afrikaner, English, Bantu, Asiatic, Coloured, Malay.[9] In some contexts Africans are conceived as an entity, namely as Bantu, and in other contexts they are fragmented into Zulu, Xhosa, Sotho, Tswana and so on.

There is fluidity also in the reverse process, that is the transformation from multi-category to two-category conceptions. This may result from a process of conceptually obliterating one or more categories, as in the example given above of witnesses before the Belgian work-group in Rwanda forgetting the Twa, or in the conception of the conflict in South Africa as one between African and Afrikaner nationalism, Indians, Coloureds and English-speaking whites being consigned to distant obscurity or to oblivion. Transformations of this type are no doubt readily effected where there is a dominant cleavage, or where there was an original dichotomy. Again, transformation may arise by a process of situational selection, a range of categories, present for example when the situation is relatively permissive, being reduced to a simple dichotomy in the political sphere, or there may be a coalescence of categories, as in the Pan-Africanist conception of Africans and non-Africans, the category of Africans, however, including those non-Africans who identify with Africans.

Unitary conceptions of the racial structure may be quite unstable. There is ambiguity in them — as in the conception of diversity in unity, or of 'the people tripartite'. The racial divisions may be preserved, but expressed in other terms, thus maintaining the conception of a racially unified society, but the reality of racial differentiation. The conceptions often express the aspiration for unity, in the context of

---

9 Even the legal definitions of racial entities varied in different situations.

division and conflict, or they constitute a declaration of policy, rather than a belief in unity; and they are highly vulnerable to challenge.

3.

There would seem to be no specific social *locus* for any of these conceptions. They are carried by the most varied strata in the society. Sections of the *dominant group* in the same society may emphasize different conceptions, dichotomous or unitary. Dominant groups in different societies may have quite different conceptions of racial structures which appear to the outside observer quite similar. Different expectations may be derived by social scientists from the same social context, as for example, a diminution or a heightening of racial consciousness, consequent upon advanced industrialization.

Subordinate categories similarly hold the most varied conceptions. They may seemingly accept conceptions justifying their subordination, and resign themselves to an inferior status in the racial categorization of the society. Or sections may deny the validity of race as a basis for social differentiation, and emphasize other qualities, as did many educated and Westernized Africans serving in the role of an auxiliary elite to European colonizers. Or they may proclaim a dichotomous and revolutionary conception of the racial structure, and this whether they are a majority, as in South Africa, or a numerical minority as in the USA. The controversy between African leaders in South Africa in 1959 over multi-racialism and non-racism, with charges and counter-charges of racism, is a reflection of the somewhat kaleidoscopic conceptions which may arise within a single stratum in an emotionally charged situation (Leo Kuper, 1965: 379).

The conceptions held by a *category intermediate* between a dominant racial minority and a subordinate racial majority may perhaps be more predictable, but these also seem to run the gamut of possibilities. Members of an intermediate category may accept the conception held by a dominant stratum, though with revision of their own status within that conception, and they may reproduce the same stereotypes concerning the subordinate majority. Some sections may identify with the dominant groups in politics of accommodation or with the most subordinate categories in a protest or revolutionary struggle of the oppressed races. Others may stress claims to a special significance by virtue of qualities of character or civilization; or they may passionately reject racial conceptions of the structure of the society.

Clearly, there is no simple theory which will explain this great diversity of relationships between the conceptions held by various strata, and the situation of those strata in the structure of the society. This does not mean that we are driven back to the assumption that we are dealing with historically specific relationships. But it does mean that it is somewhat hazardous to venture general propositions.

There are further difficulties. Not much research has been specifically directed to establishing the conceptions of racial structure held by different sections, and the salience of these conceptions in their social relationships and political movements. Sometimes the evidence may be clear enough, as when a political party repeatedly proclaims a particular conception, and on assuming power, introduces legislative policies in line with that conception. At other times, the evidence as to the social basis and salience of different conceptions is by no means secure.

Moreover, conceptions may have a quite variable relationship to structure in terms of the period to which the conceptions refer. They may express nostalgia for a past golden age, or aspiration for a future Utopia, or manipulative intent, or an image of the present state of the society. There may be no difficulty in discerning the intent and time referent, as in a change of census policy in the recording of data by racial group (see Hilda Kuper, 1969: 248-9); or there may be a quite ambiguous relationship to present reality.

Indeed, the basic distinction between 'objective' structural reality and a conception of that reality, is in itself troublesome, as discussed below. While all these considerations raise obstacles to generalization, it is nevertheless possible to offer some suggestions.

Dichotomous conception, structure, context. Ossowski relates dichotomic conceptions of class to the objective structure of the society, and to circumstances which foster the image of a dichotomic structure among particular classes (1963: 34-5). He comments that revolutionaries tend to view the world in terms of a dichotomy of opposite attributes, while those who defend the existing social order are inclined to present the structure of their own society in terms of a functional scheme or a scheme of non-egalitarian classlessness. But he also shows that the same conception, as for example a dichotomic conception, may be held by representatives of both the privileged and underprivileged class, though serving mutually exclusive purposes (Ossowski, 1963: 174).

We may accept in general the proposition that certain characteristics of the 'objective' structure of a society are likely to favour dichotomic conceptions both among the rulers and the ruled. These characteristics would be such as create discontinuity between the racial categories, namely differential incorporation in the polity (as where one category monopolizes the vote and legislative power), cultural diversity raising barriers to ease of association, extensive segregation, inequality in many contexts, and a demographic situation of two racial categories, or a distribution substantially approximating a two-category structure, as for example, a dominant minority, a large subordinate majority of one racial category and relatively small numbers in other racial categories[10] (M.G. Smith, 1969*a* and *b*; Leo Kuper, 1969*a*

10 The presence of these other racial categories does not necessarily exclude dichotomic conceptions by the subordinate racial majority, since the categories may be conveniently eliminated or ignored in

and *b*). The superimposition of these discontinuities in many varied contexts may be expected to encourage a generalized dichotomic conception in the social consciousness of both rulers and ruled.

There is no necessary implication that this conception would be either revolutionary, or defensive of the status quo. It might simply be embedded in experience, accepted as part of the natural order by the ruling group, and as routine reality by subordinates. In situations of change, where members of different racial categories begin to bridge the discontinuities, or where there is a challenge to the monopoly of privilege, the ruling group, in an aggressive assertion of power, or in defence of that power, may elaborate the ideological potentialities of the dichotomic relationship by such conceptions as the inevitability of conflict, domination and subordination in the contact between races, and the imperative necessity for racial solidarity in the struggle for survival. Conversely, leaders of subordinate groups in situations of change, may elaborate the dichotomic conception in a revolutionary ideology which proclaims the dialectical structure of relationships between the races, and the inescapable necessity for violence to change a system grounded in violence.

This argument as to the influence of discontinuity in structure on dichotomic conceptions of that structure must be somewhat qualified. The 'objective' structure and the conception of the structure cannot be sharply separated. In an important sense, the conception is the structure. Thus structures of racial domination may persist for long periods, supported by sentiments of racial superiority in the ruling group, and by seeming acquiescence in, or resignation before,

---

political struggle and ideology. A somewhat related phenomenon is the strong attack on white liberals by black revolutionaries in both South Africa and the USA. This has the function of eliminating an intermediate category, namely that of whites who identify in some measure with blacks. The dichotomy, racial and ideological, is thereby preserved.

the assertion of racial superiority and the racial right to rule. But if members of the ruling group or of the subordinate race begin to question these claims, then the structure is thereby immediately modified in some measure.

Now if the challenge of new ideas arises within the society, the stimulus may come from internal changes in social conditions and relationships. There may be increasing pressure on the land, as for example in Rwanda and Kenya; or industrialization and urbanization may provide opportunity for inter-tribal co-operation in movements of African nationalism against white rule as in South Africa, or a basis for the sharpening of conflict between black and white by urban guerrillas as in the USA. The structural base, that is to say, remains a condition of primary significance.

But the ideas and support for the ideas, may also come from the outside. A conception of a dichotomic structure, as in a dialectic, or some adaptation of a class dialectic to the colonial situation or to race relations, may be introduced into a society which is by no means dichotomic in structure; and the propagation of the conception and the struggle initiated under its inspiration, may help to create within the society those very conditions of polarization by which it was characterized in the initial conception. Here then it is the dichotomic conception which in some measure creates or increases structural discontinuity in the society. A somewhat mixed case is that in which dichotomic conception and discontinuity in structure develop further and together under the stimulus of some new element, as for example, the introduction of adult franchise in Zanzibar or Guyana, preparatory to independence.

One additional complexity in the projection of dichotomous conceptions from discontinuities in structure, is that the relationship between them may be dialectical. In the same way that a dominant group may react to increasing continuity in the relations between the racial categories by emphasizing rigidity and exclusion, so too, it is precisely under conditions of mobility and increasing continuity that members of the subordinate racial category may mobilize in a revolutionary challenge to the structure of domination, and under a revolutionary ideology proclaiming an unbridgeable racial dichotomy. Sometimes, of course, the mobility and continuity are spurious, being purely token, and this is a condition which may stimulate bitter struggle in a revolution of rising, but frustrated, expectations.

Multi-category conceptions, structure, context. The relationship between 'objective' structure and conception is most complex in the case of multi-category conceptions. These conceptions seem to be favoured by both discontinuity and continuity in structure. Thus the entry of a third category, distinctive in culture, which becomes functionally differentiated, would encourage multi-category conceptions, as for example, in those British colonies where Indians entered under indenture or as immigrants, and became retail traders and artisans. Conversely, where greater racial continuity develops in a two-category structure, so that racial status becomes less of a generalized status, and members of different races begin to hold similar positions in the structure of the society, conditions may favour multi-category conceptions, based on criteria which are not racial in reference or not entirely or exclusively racial, such as culture, class, colour or some synthesis of race and other criteria. But these conditions of greater continuity may also stimulate, as we have already suggested, defensive or aggressive dichotomic conceptions among members of the dominant category, or revolutionary dichotomous conceptions among the subordinates. Clearly further conditions need to be specified.

In the interpretation of varied perspectives in class societies, there is often an assumption that upper classes are more conscious of fine class distinctions and that lower classes see the structure as comprising only two classes, those above and those below, ruling class and ruled, or rich and poor. This may be an insight into the social basis of different conceptions in class structured societies, but it would be misleading if applied to racially structured societies.

A related example of 'multi-tribalism' will serve to illustrate some of the complexity in applying a theory of the greater sensitivity of upper strata to sectional differentiation. Thus in British African colonies, particularly where the policy of indirect rule was applied, the colonial power recognized and utilized 'tribal' diversity in its government and administration. The basic conception of the structure of the society, however, was clearly a conception of two racial categories, rulers and ruled, with subdivisions within the subordinate racial category. For the subordinate 'tribal' groups, the differences between them remained significant, probably of greater significance than for the ruling race. At the same time, they developed a conception of a two-category racial structure, of rulers and ruled, attaining full expression in the struggles for national liberation, after which the internal 'tribal' differentiation regained significance.

A ruling race may be very conscious of a variety of racial categories, as in the traditional policies of divide and rule, while retaining basically a dichotomic conception of the racial structure. Though the multi-racialism is an expression of objective reality, it is related to the exigencies of rule, and does not modify the basic dichotomic conception. Where the ruling race is a numerical minority, its domination may be supported by ideologies which emphasize the unity of the dominant race and the racial or ethnic diversity of the subordinates.[11]

Multi-racialism, instead of being an instrument of domination, may however be a defensive position for a racial group which can no longer maintain its domination. An example of this would be the espousal by white settlers in British African colonies of racial parity in representation, when the introduction of an adult franchise would ensure

11 This is substantially the political situation under apartheid in South Africa, though there are many cleavages between the Afrikaans- and English-speaking whites.

African majority rule over the European and other minorities.

Members of a subordinate race are likely to be very conscious of the different racial categories in a society, both ruling and other categories, and to differentiate between them. A common phenomenon is a specially antagonistic reaction to relatively small stranger or 'pariah' racial categories. They were often introduced in colonial societies, where there was a great gulf in technology and other aspects of culture between the dominant and subordinate race; they remained separated from both the ruling and ruled race by discontinuities in political situation, economic role, religion, family life and so on, and they offered a target for racial tension. Thus, in conflict between the ruling racial minority and the subordinate racial majority, the 'pariah' or stranger racial section readily becomes a scapegoat for both these categories. Even where the subordinate majority develops a revolutionary dichotomic conception of the structure of the society, and ignores or seemingly forgets the stranger group, it is likely, when the revolutionary struggle succeeds, to return to earlier conceptions, and to settle old scores with the 'strangers' in its midst. A subordinate racial category seems unlikely to conceive the racial structure in dichotomic terms, where there is a 'pariah' racial category in the society, or where the third or other category is numerous and a rival for power, as in Guyana. Probably dichotomic conceptions prevail in the consciousness of members of a subordinate racial majority either when other subordinate categories are insignificant in numbers and social functions, or temporarily at the height of revolutionary struggle.

In analysing the conception held by third and other racial categories, in situations where there is a dominant minority, and a subordinate majority, a distinction must be drawn between 'stranger' and intermediate racial categories. A 'stranger' category, separated from the rest of the society by discontinuities in structure and culture, and affording a likely target for persecution, can hardly fail to be aware of the multi-racial structure of the society. One section may seek to align itself with the dominant race, another with the subordinate majority, and they may attack race as a criterion for social relationships, but they can hardly escape awareness of a separate identity. In an intermediate category, arising out of the intermingling of the dominant racial minority and the subordinate racial majority, and in a situation where there are continuities in structure and culture, some sections may experience a sense of separate racial identity, and perceive the society as multi-racial, while other sections identify with either the dominant or subordinate racial categories, and work essentially with a two-category conception. An example of this is given by Zanzibar, where the Shirazi conceived of themselves as Africans who had intermingled with Persians, and where there was continuity in structure and culture both between Shirazi and Arabs, and Shirazi and Africans. Okello, the leader of the Zanzibar revolution against the Arabs in 1964, explained his reluctance to recruit Shirazi by reference to the ambivalence in their situation, as follows:

The Shirazis, despite their numerical majority, were always the doubtful element in Zanzibar politics. One section identified more with the Arabs, and thus with the Sultan . . . . another section with the non-Shirazi Africans, those of mainland origin, and a third group strove to preserve its specific Shirazi identity. There were no clear reasons why people fell into one or another of these groups. (1967: 78)

Unitary conception, structure, context. A relatively high degree of racial homogeneity will encourage unitary conceptions of the racial structure, as among Englishmen and Frenchmen for example, even though small racial minorities in their countries are subject to discrimination. These societies are not structured by racial criteria, and racial exclusion was so rationalized as not to disturb the conception that racial differences were of little or no social significance. Where there has been considerable intermingling of racial groups, a unitary conception of the racial structure may serve as an ideology of the dominant group, which maintains its racial prerogatives under other rubrics.

A unitary conception, as a defensive measure, may be propagated by small dominant racial minorities, or by sections of these minorities, when there is an effective challenge to their rule, as happened in Zanzibar and Rwanda with the movement towards independence and the introduction of a universal franchise. In these societies, there was a ruler, the Sultan and the Mwami, to serve as a symbol of unity, though identified in both cases with the ruling racial minorities. A unitary conception is not likely to be influential among members of the dominant race, when they constitute a relatively large minority in an industrialized· society with marked discontinuities in racial structure, as in South Africa. The reason is that being numerous, members of the dominant group will be distributed at different levels in the economy; the sections at the lowest levels, threatened by competition from members of the subordinate races, provide a social base for extremist racial politics, expressed in dichotomic conceptions.

In the case of subordinate racial categories, continuity in racial structure may be expected to encourage unitary conceptions, under conditions where the continuity has resulted from intermingling and mobility, with consequent ambiguity in racial identification. Conversely, discontinuity in racial structure and racial discrimination are likely to foster dichotomic or exclusive conceptions, but they do not seem to exclude unitary conceptions. These may take the form of a Utopian desire that other criteria of differentiation than those of racial identity should prevail, or the belief that these other criteria are already in some measure operative. An example of this belief was provided during the colonial era by the Western-educated among the colonized peoples. It was from this stratum that there was some acceptance of the belief that cultural differentiation was replacing racial differentiation. It was however also from this stratum that leaders were later recruited in the revolutionary struggle against colonial and racial domination.

4.

This chapter has sketched some conceptions of the racial structure in the consciousness of different strata, distinguishing between two-category, multi-category and unitary conceptions, and analysing the criteria by which categories are differentiated and the principles by which they are structured. The chapter commented on the fluidity in these conceptions, and sought to relate them to varied situational and structural contexts.

Ossowski's discussion of the class structure in the social consciousness greatly influenced the approach, and I examined some of his hypotheses and conclusions in the context of the race-structured society. Clearly racial differences are of a more enduring nature than class differences, and there are very extensive social correlates of racial differences in many racially structured societies. In some critical respects relevant to conceptions, class structures and racial structures constitute different systems of stratification, however much they may overlap; and I therefore conclude this chapter by offering brief comment on an important distinction between these two systems, as it affects conceptions.

The essence of the distinction is that class structures are intrinsic to interaction in the society, whereas racial structures are in some measure extrinsic, or have a point of reference outside the interaction. Class societies, that is to say, may be viewed as arising directly out of the *interaction of the members* of the society. The concept of class refers to the results of that interaction, or describes that interaction from a special perspective at a particular moment in time. Race by contrast, is in some sense *extrinsic to that interaction*. To be sure, the racial structure is also constituted by the interaction, but the *racial differences* which are societally elaborated, *have preceded that interaction*. Race has referents that are independent of the interaction, and it was often associated, as in colonial systems, with previously existing, politically distinct, and culturally differentiated

communities. This difference between race and class structure gives race a greater salience and persistence in the
conceptions of the social structure held by both dominant
and subordinate racial groups, and increases the likelihood of
dichotomic and revolutionary perspectives in racially structured societies under conditions of social mobility and
increasing social continuity. In the class-structured society,
the power, wealth and prestige of the dominant class are
constituted by the class structure itself. Upper-class position
refers mainly to the possession of these prerogatives. Hence,
this position may largely be secured without reference to the
authority of class. The conception of a classless society or of
non-egalitarian classlessness may therefore readily offer an
ideological defence for class privilege, which is maintained
under the denial of class.

The same position can arise in a race structure where the
dominant race is small in numbers, and where its position is
entrenched by political and economic power. But race in
such a society constitutes an independent basis for power,
and there is thus a greater likelihood that racial conceptions
will be asserted in defence of the status quo. Where the
dominant racial minority is relatively large in relation to the
resources available, and there is competition for these
resources between members of different races, then 'raceless-
ness' can no longer serve as a defensive ideology. On the
contrary, the defence is likely to rest on racial difference
with an extreme assertion of racism by sections of the
dominant race. In the case of the subordinate racial majority,
race is an independent basis for exclusion from privilege, and
economic and political deprivation flow from that exclusion.
Hence the situation encourages perceptions of race as the
crucial factor in social discrimination. At the same time, the
significance of race is enhanced by the fact that it is the basis
for political challenge through the mobilization of the greater
numbers of the subordinates.

Increasing progressive continuity in the structure of the
society may be expected to encourage fluid and inclusive

conceptions of the structure, consonant with evolutionary change. But increasing continuity seems to have different consequences in the two structures. In the class society, the continuity is a product of the interaction. It may give rise to tension, and encourage class conflict, but the tension and conflict are within the class system itself. Continuity in a class-structured society is a transformation of the class system itself. In a racially segmented society, increasing continuity is again a product of interaction, and likely to occasion tension and conflict. But the tension and conflict arise not only in the sectors affected by the mobility, as in the economic or educational sectors; there is tension also between this mobility and the racial identity. This racial identity remains recoverable, and the generalized status of race persists, in appreciable measure, outside the interaction and constitutes an independent point of reference. Under these conditions, and as a result of the tension with the extrinsic status and identity of race, increasing continuity in the 'objective' structure seems more likely to stimulate revolutionary challenge and dichotomic conceptions in racially structured societies, than in class structured societies.

3

Ideologies of Violence
among Subordinate Groups

This chapter deals with an aspect of political change in plural
societies. These I define in the present context as societies
characterized by cultural diversity and social cleavage arising
from the contact of different peoples within a single political
unit.[1] The process of political change in plural societies often
takes the form of violent conflict, as in Algeria, Zanzibar, and
Rwanda, and some students believe that this is its general, if
not inevitable, form.[2] The movement towards violence is
likely to generate appropriate ideologies; and I want here to
examine some of the elements and functions of an ideology
of violence for subordinate groups in a plural society. In
constructing this ideology, I draw ideas mainly from Frantz
Fanon's book, *Les Damnés de la terre,*[3] where the ideology is
formulated with great force and clarity in the context of the
extreme violence of political change in Algeria. I rely also on
statements by African political leaders in South Africa, a
plural society in which the consummation of political change
may be equally violent.[4]

1 For discussion of plural societies, see Furnivall (1948); J.C.
Mitchell (1960); Rex (1959: 114-24); M.G. Smith (1965); van den
Berghe (1964: 11-18); and Leo Kuper (1965a: 107-30).

2 See, for example, M.G. Smith (1965: 91).

3 Quotations in the text are from Fanon (1963).

4 I have omitted, for the most part, discussion of the ideologies of
the dominant groups and the policies they pursue which provoke
subordinate groups to violence. For analysis of these aspects in South
African society, see Leo Kuper (1956 and 1965).

1.

Common elements in an ideology of violence are the declaration of the necessity for violence as the only efficient means of change, the justification of violence on moral grounds, and the rejection of nonviolent techniques; there may or may not be an idealization of violence as creative rebirth for those who use it. Inevitably the elaboration of this ideology calls for assertions as to the nature of the society that is to become the battleground of violent conflict, and as to the qualities of the dominant group which make this conflict inevitable. These assertions describe the society as polarized into the two radically conflicting groups of oppressors and oppressed; and they establish (or seek to establish) the collective destiny of the oppressed and the unyielding domination of the oppressors, thereby guarding against what are conceived to be the erosions of individualism and the illusions of concessions and evolutionary change.

The argument as to the necessity for violence rests in part on repetitive declaration:

From birth it is clear to him [the colonized] that this narrow world, strewn with prohibitions, can only be called in question by absolute violence.[5]

The starving peasant, outside the class system, is the first among the exploited to discover that only violence pays.[6]

We have seen that it is the intuition of the colonized masses that their liberation must, and can only, be achieved by force.[7]

The argument also rests, more or less persuasively, on such empirical generalizations as that the history of freedom is written in blood,[8] or on generalizations derived from the

5 Fanon (1963: 31).
6 ibid. (48).
7 ibid. (57).
8 There is much corroboration from the shelters of the academic world. See, for example, Rupert Emerson (1960: 331): 'The great issues of nationalism and self-determination have been settled not by the genteel processes of votes and majorities but by the revolutionary

many examples of violent political change in plural societies, or on such more specific generalizations as that offered by Fanon when he describes the process of decolonization:

National liberation, national renaissance, the restoration of nationhood to the people, commonwealth: whatever may be the headings used or the new formulae introduced, decolonization is always a violent phenomenon. At whatever level we study it . . . decolonization is quite simply the replacing of a certain 'species' of men by another 'species' of men . . . The naked truth of decolonization evokes for us the searing bullets and bloodstained knives which emanate from it. For if the last shall be first, this will only come to pass after a murderous and decisive struggle between the two protagonists.[9]

The moral justification for violence derives from oppression and humiliation, from the transparency of the connection between the good fortune of those who rule and the misery of those who are ruled, and from concepts of human dignity and the rights of man. But these conditions and beliefs justify radical political change, and not necessarily violence, as the instrument of that change. Violence, at any rate from the standpoint of civic order and the rule of law, must rather find its legitimation in the qualities ascribed to the plural society and its ruling group, as in Fanon's denunciation of colonialism, which he declares is not a thinking machine or a body endowed with reasoning faculties: it is born in violence, it is maintained by violence, it speaks the language of violence, and in the final stage of the movement towards national consciousness, it transforms the atmosphere of violence among the colonized into violence in action; it is violence in its natural state, and it will yield only when confronted with greater violence.[10]

The rejection of nonviolence, which is the counterpart of the commitment to violence, also finds its legitimation in the

rising of peoples and the successful waging of wars, which have carried history with them.'

9 Fanon (1963: 29-30).
10 ibid. (31, 48, 56, and *passim*).

structure of the society and the qualities of its rulers. The rejection may be defensive, implying the higher moral worth of nonviolence, and justifying the anguished choice of violence as compelled by the imperviousness of the rulers to supplication, petition, reason, argument, demonstration, and civil disobedience. It is in these terms of disillusionment with the government of South Africa, and with nonviolence in the face of its obdurate inhumanity, that leaders of the African National Congress explain the organization of *Umkhonto we Sizwe* ('Spear of the Nation')[11] for violent action. Yet even in this movement towards revolutionary struggle, there was a deliberate selection of sabotage as the initial means of violence in preference to terrorism or guerrilla warfare, which would more fiercely inflame racial hatred.[12]

In contrast with the unhappy denunciation of nonviolence in the particular circumstances of the plural society, the rejection of nonviolence may be expressed in terms of cynicism or contempt for its futility. Thus the Non-European Unity Movement ridiculed the civil disobedience campaign of 1952 for its naïve conception of racial domination in South Africa:

The Herrenvolk has made up its mind over three hundred years not to climb off the backs of the non-Europeans of its own accord and free will . . . There is no possibility of any of these laws being modified or repealed because the ruling class have had it brought to their notice that the non-whites hate these laws. They are fascists, and they know that we hate them and their laws. There is only deception and self-deception in dealing with 'Malanazis' as though they were 'democrats' and 'Christians' who will suffer pangs of conscience because certain non-white 'leaders' are in gaol. The function of leaders is to lead; the gaols are there to hinder and not help the cause of freedom.[13]

So, too, Fanon reacts to the nonviolent reformist techniques with contempt. He describes them as a practice of

11 See Leo Kuper (1965: 384).
12 Nelson Mandela (1965: 168-74).
13 Leo Kuper (1956: 152-3).

therapy by hibernation, a sleep cure used on the people.[14]
He sees nonviolence as the creation of the colonial situation,[15] functioning like the inevitable religion to calm down
the natives: 'All those saints who have turned the other
cheek, who have forgiven trespasses against them, and who
have been spat on and insulted without shrinking are studied
and held up as examples.'[16] Indeed, far from a defensive and
reluctant choice of violence, Fanon positively affirms violence. He writes that it is in and through violence that the
colonized man finds his freedom:[17] only out of the rotting
corpse of the settler can life spring up again for the native.[18]
Where Gandhi sees the realization of truth in *satyagraha*
(soul-force), Fanon finds it, for the colonized, in violence:

Violence alone, violence committed by the people, violence organized
and educated by its leaders, makes it possible for the masses to
understand social truths and gives the key to them. Without that
struggle, without that knowledge of the practice of action, there's
nothing but a fancy-dress parade and the blare of the trumpets. There's
nothing save a minimum of re-adaptation, a few reforms at the top, a
flag-waving: and down there at the bottom an undivided mass, still
living in the Middle Ages, endlessly marking time.[19]

And Sartre, in interpreting and endorsing Fanon's ideology of
violence for the colonized, declares that

he shows clearly that this irrepressible violence . . . is man re-creating
himself. I think we understood this truth at one time, but we have
forgotten it — that no gentleness can efface the marks of violence; only
violence itself can destroy them. The native cures himself of colonial
neurosis by thrusting out the settler through force of arms. When his

14 Fanon (1963: 52). He qualifies his comment with an ironic
illustration of success attendant on nationalist reform in Gabon.
   15 Karl A. Wittfogel (1957: 331), mentions passive resistance as a
response to Oriental despotism.
   16 Fanon (1963: 53).
   17 ibid. (67).
   18 ibid. (72).
   19 ibid. (117).

rage boils over, he rediscovers his lost innocence and he comes to know himself in that he himself creates his self.[20]

The ideology of violence, as I have shown, includes a characterization of the plural society. The main component of this characterization is a polarized conception, which directs violence unambiguously against the enemy.[21] The complex patterns of pluralism are reduced to the simple dichotomy of a dialectical opposition. For Fanon, it is a dialectic without possibility of synthesis, without possibility of a higher unity. The colonial world is a world of two species, a world divided into two reciprocally exclusive divisions. Between them, no conciliation is possible, for of the two divisions, one is superfluous.[22] Their roles may change: the quarry may become the hunter, the oppressed the persecutor.[23] But there can be no sharing of power. An irreconcilable conflict, an absolute opposition of interests, separates the parties. Decolonization is total, complete and absolute substitution, without transition: it is the abolition of one zone, its burial in the depths of the earth or its expulsion from the country.[24] In a world of radically opposed and irreconcilable interests, there can be no evolutionary change towards a shared society. Individualism cannot bridge the collective destiny of the parties in the struggle for freedom;[25] and concessions may merely be the cloak for a less blatant but more complete servitude.[26]

There may be, in plural societies, a necessary association, an ideological fusion, between the call to violence and the conception of polarized groups. Certainly, for a brief period,

20 ibid. (18).

21 Turner and Surace (1956: 14-20) demonstrate a similar process in violent crowd behaviour, where a clearly unfavourable symbol was required as the rallying-point for violence against the Mexicans.

22 Fanon (1963: 31-2).

23 ibid. (42).

24 ibid. (29, 33).

25 ibid. (37-8).

26 ibid. (113).

ideologies of revolutionary violence in South Africa increasingly showed this tendency, with dogmatic assumptions as to the unity of the oppressors, and the reduction of the great diversity in structure, values and function within each of these categories to a crude dichotomy of violence.[27]

2.

I have described the call to violence and the associated characterization of the society as ideology, thereby assuming that the ideas are to be interpreted as expressing the needs and desires of those who proclaim them, rather than as offering an analysis of the objective structure of the plural society and its potentiality for peaceful change. But the ideas may nevertheless quite accurately portray dominant tendencies within the society while at the same time serving sectional interests in a revolutionary challenge to the structure of rule. There may be an extreme polarization between the ruling and subject groups, and violence may indeed offer the only possibility of political change. Instead of assuming the ideological function of the ideas in question, it becomes necessary to examine them in the social context to which they refer.

The empirical evidence hardly sustains the generalization that decolonization is always a violent phenomenon. In the recent struggles for independence in Africa, there has certainly been extreme violence in some territories, as in Algeria and Kenya, or presently in Angola and Mozambique; but in most African territories, decolonization, as distinct from the aftermath of decolonization, has been attended by relatively little violence. The violent phenomenon was colonization rather than decolonization, and even then, not all colonial rule in Africa was imposed by violence.

A Marxist might argue that there has been little or no decolonization in Africa; that the contemporary independ-

27 See Leo Kuper (1965: Chapter 23).

ence of African States is appearance, not reality; that the
reality is the persistence of colonialism in the masked form of
neo-colonialism; and that Westernized African elites, the new
incumbents of the old colonial posts, fulfil functions analogous to those of their colonial predecessors. But this shifts the
basis of the argument and finds the necessity for violence in
communist revolution, while conceding that important
changes in the relations of the races within the plural society
and in the whole structure of the plural society may be
effected without violence.

A more cogent argument as to the generality of violence in
the process of decolonization is that decolonization must be
seen as a global process. From this perspective, the colonial
power occupies a field with colonial possessions on the
perimeter and engages in a struggle with other powers for
position in a changing world situation. The violence that acts as
the catalyst of change is not violence within a particular
colonial territory, but violence directed from any point on the
colonial perimeter, and the violence, or threatened violence, of
international conflict. Viewed in this way, as in Fanon's *Pour la
révolution africaine*[28] there can be little doubt of the violence
of decolonization, though differences in its incidence between
the French and British empires show that violence is not simply
a function of the process of decolonization.

The empirical evidence for the inevitability of violence is
more convincing in the case of settler societies than in
colonial societies. There are many differences between them
which have relevance for the probability and intensity of
violence, such as the very permanence of the settler population and its determination to persist in the enjoyment of
numerous vested interests. There is the intense involvement
of the settlers in their relations with the subject groups, since
privilege and indeed survival may be precarious in the close

28 Fanon (1964). See 'Décolonisation et indépendance' (119-25),
'Lettre à la jeunesse africaine' (135-40), 'La guerre d'Algérie et la
libération des hommes' (167-72), 'L'Afrique affirme son unité et définit
sa stratégie' (177-81), and especially 124, 135, and 171.

immediacy of their living together. Fanon asserts a direct
relationship between the size of the settler group and the
extent of violence, arguing that the violence of the colonial
regime and the counter-violence of the native balance each
other and respond to each other in an extraordinary
reciprocal homogeneity, and that 'this reign of violence will
be the more terrible in proportion to the size of the
implantation from the mother country'.[29] The relationship is
probably more complex. A larger number of settlers would
be associated with greater economic development and greater
interdependence between the groups. This interdependence is
likely to inhibit the outbreak of violence; but if violence does
break out, then it may be all the more intense, destructive,
and inter-suicidal by reason of the dependence of the groups
on each other.

Perhaps of greatest significance is the contrast in constitutional status. The line between settler and colonial societies is
not easily drawn, since colonial status may be associated with
a substantial settler class as in Algeria and colonial societies
may have many of the characteristics of settler societies (the
so-called 'settler colonies' as distinct from the 'exploitation
colonies'). Yet even in these 'settler colonies', the different
constitutional status of the colony has the significant
consequence that it immediately involves a third party, the
colonial power itself. To be sure, the colonial power is a main
protagonist, and it may in fact heighten destructive violence
by engaging its relatively great military resources in the
conflict. But its role in an era of decolonization may be very
different, and may include elements of mediation. In the
metropolitan centre, a measure of detachment from deep
emotional involvement in the conflict is possible, or at any
rate groups in the metropolitan centre may achieve this
detachment and function in much the same way as a third
party to encourage a nonviolent adjustment of interests.
Certainly this third-party role was a significant factor in the
resolution of conflict in Kenya, and may still prove so in

29 Fanon (1963: 69).

Rhodesia, though this becomes increasingly unlikely.

In the conflicts of settler societies, however, no third party with a possible mediating role is automatically involved. The United Nations might so function, but for the Cold War which wages international peace through local dichotomies of violence, as in Korea and Vietnam. As Fanon observes, 'today, peaceful coexistence between the two *blocs* provokes and feeds violence in the colonial countries . . . Between the violence of the colonies and that peaceful violence that the world is steeped in, there is a kind of complicit agreement, a sort of homogeneity.'[30] If this observation has any validity for colonial countries, in which the colonial power has the opportunity and responsibility to resolve conflict, it will be all the more valid for settler societies, in which independent status offers a freer field for the masked play of international war. In the context of the Cold War, the intervention of third parties in the conflicts of a settler society seems likely to foster a polarization of the society into two hostile camps, corresponding to the strategic needs of the great powers.[31]

The theoretical argument for the necessity of violence as the instrument of change rests on assumptions as to the nature of man and society. I will accept, for purposes of this discussion, the assumption that men have to be forced from positions of dominance, that they will not voluntarily relinquish or share the power they have once enjoyed. I will accept and indeed make the case that there are many special circumstances in plural societies which render ruling strata extraordinarily tenacious of power and exclusive in their exercise of power. These societies often take the form of domination by a minority of different race and culture with more highly developed technology.[32] The domination is

30 ibid. (62-3).

31 Diversification of international structure, consequent on Chinese international intervention, seems likely to affect the external presssures for polarization.

32 For a characterization of colonial society, see Balandier (1955: Chapter 1). M.G. Smith specifies domination by a cultural minority as one of the characteristics of plural society.

deeply embedded in the political and other institutions of the society and supports elaborate and strongly fortified structures of privilege. Rationalizations that dehumanize the subject peoples and glorify the civilizing mission of their overlords justify ready recourse to repression and force. The use of force is encouraged also by greater development of political institutions, the generation of disproportionate political power as compared with economic and other institutional power. Particularly in white settler societies, the monopoly of power, the appropriation of scarce resources, and the contrasts in life situations suggest a dialectical opposition of interest between the groups. But even accepting all this, these assumptions and generalizations would only establish the need for great pressure to bring about political change; they do not prove that violence is the only efficient means for that change.

At this point, the argument for violence may move to the assertion, as by African leaders in South Africa, that nonviolence has proved ineffective. It does not follow that violence will therefore be effective, though this is always assumed. Nor is it easy to determine whether the possibilities of nonviolent action were fully explored, let alone exhausted. There are questions of cost, of the threshold of nonviolence, and of the structure of power. Men vary in their tolerance of suffering and readiness for self sacrifice. Hence a subjective element enters into the assessment of the extent to which such techniques as civil disobedience have been fully tried out; the answer is relative to the leaders' perception of tolerable cost. Then too, among the mass of followers, the threshold of nonviolence may be low in the sense that their culture inclines them towards impatience with nonviolence.

Other circumstances, in the conditions of the plural society, may contribute to the same result and indeed foster an easy recourse to violence. These conditions would be such as contribute to the formation of mass society,[33] as, for example, abrupt discontinuities in culture and authority, and

33 See discussion of W. Kornhauser (1960), particularly Part 2.

between rural and urban centres; the agglomeration and insecurity of many new townsmen in slum and shanty; and the incitement of hardship, humiliation, and brutality. In consequence, the leaders may find that they have little latitude for experimenting with nonviolence, and the repressive and violent exercise of government authority may offer them even less. It is to be understood then that they might conclude that they had exhausted the possibilities of non-violent political change when, from the perspective of Gandhian *satyagraha*, they had merely initiated preliminary campaigns.

If the society is polarized, then it may be reasonable to infer that political change will be abrupt, revolutionary, and presumably violent. Polarization implies a division into two camps — the oppressors and the oppressed — with few relationships that transcend group barriers and restrain conflict by the ties of cross-cutting loyalties.[34] Interests are in dialectical opposition[35] and values antithetical; the subject peoples deny legitimacy to the social order and the rulers respond with increasing repression. Social cleavages are superimposed[36] so that domination in political structures coincides with domination in other institutional structures. The dichotomy of values is pervasive, unresolved conflicts cumulate, and minor, seemingly isolated issues quickly escalate to the level of the total society. There is no neutral ground of detachment from the struggle, which drives all strata into opposing camps; there is no appreciable intermediate area of living which might serve as the foundation for a more inclusive system of relationship.

Clearly, most plural societies do not conform to this pure

34 See Gluckman (1963: Chapter 1) and Lipset (1960: Chapters 6, 7), for discussion of consequences of cross-cutting loyalties and cross-pressures.

35 See Fanon's discussion (1963: 66).

36 Dahrendorf (1959: 213-18), deals with the relationship between the intensity of conflict, and the superimposition of group conflicts and issues of conflict.

type of polarization: it represents revolutionary ideology
rather than sociological analysis. Perhaps the closest approxi-
mation is to be found in the early stages of conquest and
consolidation of power. Later, as the plural sections coexist
within the same society, relations of interdependence and of
common interest begin to mitigate the extreme enmity and
to modify the sharp division. These integrative relationships,
varying with the nature of the society and its mode of
production, may be fairly negligible in an 'exploitation
colony' and more extensive in an industrialized 'settler
society', as in South Africa. Here, the stark simplicity of a
model of polarized relationships quite distorts the complex
reality of racial hatreds, which vary in intensity, expression,
and direction among different racial groups and social strata.
In its exclusive concern for cultural conflict and racial
cleavage, it ignores the effects of shared knowledge and
understandings, of common religious beliefs, of interdependent participation in an exchange economy, and of
social relationships across racial barriers; and it projects, as
present reality, social perceptions that derive from an
operational blueprint for revolution.

3.

These ideologies and the social perceptions they crystallize
may serve as an index of the probability of violence. They mark
a qualitative change in relations which seems to precede the
outbreak of violence; they may of course be the agent of that
change. This is not to say that violence necessarily follows the
dissemination and wide adoption of revolutionary ideologies
within a plural society. And conversely, violence may erupt
quite spontaneously, without ideological overture. Indeed, the
relationship between ideology and violence may be reversed,
the ideology emerging from the violence, not the violence from
the ideology.

The rulers may contribute to the probability of violence
by their ideological reactions to the threat of violence. They

may declare that these people understand only the moral persuasion of force, which must be firmly used for preservation of law and order.[37] They may refuse concessions, since these would seem to reward violence; they may also believe that concessions are a delusion, leading not to an adjustment of interests but to the eventual subordination of the rulers themselves. Being convinced of the absolute incompatibility of different sections of the plural society, and therefore of the impossibility of social synthesis, they perceive the alternatives as either to rule or to be ruled. There is thus an almost exact correspondence between the ideologies of revolution and of counter-revolution, expressing dialectical opposition and reflecting a long history of ideological exchange. For theorists who believe that by the inescapable pragmatism of all action, force and the threat of force unavoidably breed more force,[38] the reproduction of ideologies of violence is merely a particular expression of this more general process.

A quite different response to the threat of violence is by way of 'concessions', and these may in fact reduce the probability of violence; much of the movement to independence in the British African colonies has been in this form, that is to say, in the form of evolutionary change. There are certainly many contrary examples of 'concessions' that proved to be quite illusory and served simply as devices for maintaining domination. But these historic events (such as manipulations of a qualified franchise) cannot be translated directly into universal laws. It is necessary to specify the conditions that exclude the possibility of evolutionary change by means of concessions. No doubt, these conditions are most likely to be found in settler societies.

Since the violence threatens the very existence of the plural society, the response may be a series of measures designed to knit the society more closely together. This has

37 This is presumably a rationalization by the rulers for their inability to legitimate their authority.

38 See, for example, H.H. Gerth and C. Wright Mills (1946: 334).

been the response of the South African government, regardless of its much advertised policy of apartheid (separation) which professes quite the contrary. The government has in fact used a mixed strategy of violence, 'concessions' and 'integration'. Violence is long established in South Africa as an appropriate traditional technique for the governance of people of different race; and I think it probable that, but for the hostile reaction of outside powers to the Sharpeville massacre, the government would have sought a solution by holocausts of violence. As to 'concessions', the most important are the Bantustans, in which Africans are promised self-rule. These concessions seem to be the very epitome of the concessions ridiculed in the revolutionary ideologies: their promises appear to be illusory, merely a decoy to fragmentation and continued domination. But this is not certain. Underlying the belief in the illusory nature of concessions is the assumption that the initiative rests entirely with the dominant group. Where subordinate groups have some possibility of initiative, as in the Bantustans, the consequences of concessions are indeterminate, depending on the way Africans use them, and not only on the plans of the government. The Bantustans may or may not offer a base for a challenge to white domination.

More immediately significant than these 'concessions', if they can possibly be described as such, are the means by which the government seeks to bind the society more firmly together. Gluckman, in *Custom and Conflict*,[39] demonstrates from Nuer society the principle that the greater the interdependence between groups, the greater the likelihood of institutional mechanisms for resolving conflict. There is certainly great interdependence between the races in South Africa, resulting from long years of contact and from high levels of economic growth and industrial development, which draw increasing numbers of all races into a common exchange economy. This economy rests largely on non-white labour and is therefore particularly vulnerable to racial

39 ibid. (Chapter 1, especially 15 ff.).

conflict. In these circumstances, the government has not met the threat of violence by the creation of institutional mechanisms for resolution of conflict, and few of these mechanisms have developed spontaneously outside the framework of government. Instead of resolving conflict, the government's policy is to contain conflict and to 'integrate' the plural sections or, more specifically, to coerce them into togetherness.[40] The government generates more political power and greater capacity for violence; it elaborates authority structures for more total control; and it creates special structures for ordering the parts within the preordained whole.

I have argued that few plural societies show the polar structure ascribed to them in ideologies of violence. There is generally tension between the ideological image and the social reality. For this reason, violence is often directed initially within the group itself. A whole vocabulary emerges to stigmatize those who do not conform to the brutal dichotomy of violence. In terms of graphic abuse, it distinguishes different categories of nonconformist; at the same time it exposes them almost equally, the altruist and the non-racist as well as the spy and the informer, to indiscriminate retribution.

A like process engages the rulers. Though at all times they direct aggression outwards, they also pillory their own dissenters. They may rely more on due process and resort less to summary procedure, but as the conflict escalates, they too ultimately silence their nonconformists. There is nonconformity within each of the groups and interrelationship between members of different groups. It is not the society that is polarized, it is the ideology; indeed it is one of the functions

40 There is a problem in the use of the word 'integrate' to describe such societies as the apartheid society of South Africa. 'Integration' suggests to many sociologists a unity based on consensus and not a unity that rests largely on regulation and force. Perhaps 'integration' might be used where cohesion rests largely on a consensual basis, and 'regulation' where its basis is mainly coercive.

of the ideology to polarize the society. Where the plural divisions are of different race, then the ideology of polarization becomes racism.[41]

If the goal is a polarized society, then violence would seem to be an efficient means to that end. It easily multiplies in a plural society, where the intermingling of peoples affords lavish occasion for violence; it deeply engages the personalities of the parties; it spreads sentiments of exclusive solidarity and silences moderation; it recalls ancient wrongs and heightens present anguish; it inflames hatred and inspires sacrifice.

For these reasons too, violence may be an efficient means for awakening an apathetic populace, for heightening political awareness, and for fostering political action. Plural societies often, perhaps generally, take the political form of minority domination, and sometimes these minorities are very small. In these circumstances, the subject population, if resolute, might readily effect social change by nonviolent means. This is probably true for Rhodesia, and perhaps even for South Africa, though this is much more doubtful. It is not so much that the nonviolent techniques are ineffective in themselves, as that the subordinate groups are not ready for effective political action of any kind, violent or nonviolent. Given much quietude, apathy, and confusion among the people, the leaders are likely to despair of building an effective organization for nonviolent action, particularly under continuous harassment by the authorities. Understand-

41 Fanon attacks racism in many of his writings (see, for example, 1963: 115-16, 126-7). See also Fanon (1965a: 147-78), in which he counters group stereotypes by showing the active collaboration of European and other non-Arab Algerians in the revolutionary struggle. But it is difficult to avoid the racism where dominant and subordinate groups are of different race, and the tenor and the emotional thrust of the general argument in his essay, 'Concerning violence', in *The Wretched of the Earth* (1963) are in fact a powerful call to racism. For a brief discussion of Fanon's work and reactions to it, see Gordon (1966: 121-32). See also A. and V. Zolberg (1967: 49-63), for a different interpretation of Fanon's political ideology.

ably they may turn to violence, which then becomes also a method of political campaigning and organization.

Where the commitment is in any event towards violence, and where nonviolence is felt to be repugnant, the problem becomes one of military strategy, which, under the present conditions of the Cold War, will include the assistance or intervention of a third party. Where, however, the commitment is to peaceful resolution of conflict, and racial or other internal war is perceived as incitement to atrocity and by no means ennobling, then there is a real dilemma in relation to such countries as South Africa. Perhaps it is not true, or only partly true, that the society is so polarized and so devoid of middle or bridging structures as to exclude the possibility of nonviolent, evolutionary change. Perhaps it is not true, or only partly true, that given the character of the rulers and their imperviousness to morality and reason, only violence can prevail. Perhaps it is not true that the possibilities of nonviolence have been fully explored, and perhaps the ineffectiveness of the nonviolent campaigns stems in part from political unpreparedness.

Suppose all this is granted (and it would be questioned by many observers), there is still the agonizing problem of immediate and intense suffering under a rigidly maintained system of domination. Violence does seem to offer some better prospect of relief. In any event, the parties are moving towards the atrocity of violence. But it seems unlikely that violence will be effective in bringing about political change, unless outside powers assist the revolutionary parties. So too, it seems unlikely that peaceful political change can be brought about by forces internal to the society: in this case also, there will be need for outside intervention. If it is indeed true that effective violent and nonviolent action both presuppose active intervention from without, then presumably the final arbiter of South Africa's fate will be the great powers themselves, and the choice between violence and nonviolence will be largely determined by their international relations.

4

On the Theme
'Black is Beautiful'

1.

These are reflections on the contribution which might be made to the nonviolent restructuring of race relations by changes in the social consciousness of the racially subordinate. I shall concentrate on that aspect of social consciousness which relates to the redefinition by the subordinate race of the characteristics of its own group, the characteristics of the dominant race, and their interrelations. This process of deliberate redefinition is expressed symbolically in the theme 'black is beautiful' and black politicians and writers in the USA have developed a quite specific theory of the strategy and role of redefinition.

Huey Newton, one of the leaders of the Black Panthers in the USA, comments that, until recently, unenlightened black people defined the white man by calling him 'the Man', which he says carried the implication that the black man did not even define himself as man. Now, he continues, we define the omnipotent administrator, along with his security agents, as less than a man because *we* define them as pigs:

I think that this is a revolutionary thing in itself. That's political power. That's power itself. Matter of fact what is power other than the ability to define [a] phenomenon and then make it act in a desired manner? When black people start defining things and making it act in a desired manner, then we call this Black Power.[1]

1 Huey Newton (1968: 10-11).

Eldridge Cleaver (1969: 54-5) reports that Stokely Carmichael of the Student Nonviolent Co-ordinating Committee would cite *Alice in Wonderland* in his public talks:

'When I use a word' Humpty Dumpty said in a rather scornful tone, 'it means just what I choose it to mean, neither more nor less.' 'The question is,' said Alice, 'whether you *can* make words mean so many different things.' 'The question is,' said Humpty Dumpty 'who is to be master, that's all.'

Stokely would tell his audience that one of the most important aspects of the struggle for Black Power was the right to define. Black people have been the victims of white America's definitions (black people are inferior, Negroes, Niggers) and by reacting to these definitions, blacks allowed themselves to be put in a bag which white America controlled. One of his favourite examples, eliciting a hysterical response, was that, during the civil rights movement, when black leaders would say 'We want to integrate', white people would define integration as meaning that blacks wanted to marry their daughters. By reacting to this definition, 'No, we don't want to marry your daughter', they were backed against the wall, and placed on the defensive, losing the force of their indictment of white America. Blacks must not react to white definitions: they must demand the right to define themselves.

The right to define implies the power to originate perspectives, to determine the issues, and to establish the field of confrontation:

The revolutionists insist on redefining their situational culture in a way that liberates them while it imprisons the whites ... What redefinition means to the black revolutionists is that the whites will have to bargain on black terms and understand the world as constructed by blacks ... Blacks seem to believe that there is some truth in the old adage, 'the namer of names is always the father of things'. To be defined by whites is to remain a slave, and slavery is anything but a pleasant memory to the black race. Thus his rhetoric shows new assertiveness, movement, aggressiveness, as he refuses to allow the white man to define his identity (A.L. Smith, 1969: 8-9).

These formulations of the theory of revolutionary definition and redefinition are by blacks in the USA, but similar approaches are widely diffused throughout the Third World. In South Africa, there is the beginning of a movement of black consciousness, concerned with cultural nationalism, autonomy of blacks in their own movements, and emancipation from the imprisoning notions bequeathed through white control.[2] The South African example is particularly interesting, since South Africa must surely be the most oppressive system of race relations in the world, and theories of the possible contribution of a radical social consciousness in the restructuring of race relations would receive a very severe test in this extreme situation of racial domination. I shall therefore keep the South African situation before me as a sort of acid test, but I shall refer also to the USA and somewhat marginally to other systems of racial domination.

2.

The call for a changed social consciousness is characteristic of revolutionary social movements, and perhaps of all social movements whether directed against class exploitation, cultural repression, caste exclusion or racial domination. It is, of course, quite central to the theory of class struggle, in which the working class is exhorted to reject the false consciousness

2 In a paper by B.S. Biko, Chairman of the racially exclusive South African Students' Organization (1971), there is the anticipated reference to Aimé Césaire ('no race possesses the monopoly of beauty, intelligence, force, and there is room for all of us at the rendezvous of victory'), inevitably a quotation from Fanon, and intimations of the writing of Amilcar Cabral, former leader of the liberation movement in Guinea-Bissau, though there may not have been direct exposure. The theme 'black is beautiful' does not appear, since it could not have been greatly in doubt among Africans in South Africa, but most of the other themes are there, though without the technical analysis of definition and the revolutionary implications of redefinition. Biko argues that the South African movement of black consciousness has its roots in African nationalism, and is not derivative.

induced by the indoctrination of ruling class definitions, and to acquire a true consciousness of its class situation and revolutionary role.[3]

In theories of the post-industrial society or corporate State, a changed social consciousness may be conceived as a revolutionary force in itself. This is the conception advanced by Charles Reich in *The Greening of America*. He argues that all orthodox liberal and radical thinking about social change or revolution rests on two main approaches to translating consciousness into effective action: a liberal approach based on the use of existing legal, administrative and democratic procedures, and a radical approach based on the assumption of power through either electoral politics or violent revolution. Neither of these approaches, however, can succeed against what he calls the corporate State; but there is a third and effective approach, through a simple change in consciousness. 'Consciousness is capable of changing and of destroying the Corporate State, without violence, without seizure of political power, without overthrow of any existing group of people' (1970: 327). Since the corporate State depends on a special consciousness, that of the willing producer who desires status, and the willing consumer who desires what the State makes him want, the corporate State will vanish with radical change in social consciousness.[4]

Reich's argument is directed generally to the corporate State, as he characterizes it, and more particularly to the 'democracy' of the USA. It is in this context, and under a variety of conditions he specifies, that the case is made for the thesis that consciousness is prior to structure (1970:

3 'Material force,' Marx writes, 'must be overthrown by material force; but theory, too, becomes a material force once it seizes the masses' (1970: 137).

4 Reich (1970: 13, 15) defines consciousness as 'a total configuration in any individual, which makes up his whole perception of reality, his whole world view ... It is the whole man; his "head"; his way of life. It is that by which he creates his own life and thus creates the society in which he lives.'

362), and that the coming revolution will originate with the individual and with culture, and change the political structure only as its final act.

Contemporary concern over the role of cultural repression in advanced industrial capitalist society has been stimulated by the work of Marcuse. Implicit in this perspective is the conception of the revolutionary force which would be exerted by a liberated consciousness. In his lecture, 'The end of Utopia' (1970: 74), Marcuse argues that the development of consciousness, 'this idealistic deviation', is one of the chief tasks of revolutionary materialism under conditions where the material, technical and scientific productive forces exist for a free society. There is, of course, in Marcuse's exposition, none of the facile optimism of Reich. Quite the contrary. The highly industrialized societies muster a concentration of power against which even the freest consciousness appears ridiculous and impotent. Transformation of needs must precede the transformation of society, and for new revolutionary needs to develop, there must first be a felt need to abolish the mechanisms that reproduce the old needs (1970: 84). Understandably, Marcuse cannot imagine how the state of almost total indoctrination and co-ordination can turn into its opposite in an evolutionary way (1970: 80).

Gandhi, in the course of his campaign against untouchability in the caste system, bestowed on the untouchables the name *Harijan*, meaning 'children of God'. 'The new name was intended, it was said, to give new dignity to the Untouchables and to impress on caste Hindus the need to admit these unfortunates into the Hindu fold' (Isaacs, 1965: 39). Here was a process of naming designed in part to transform the social consciousness of the outcaste, but the new baptismal name became merely a synonym for the untouchables, without transforming the caste system. There were other experiments in outcaste nomenclature (see Isaacs, 1965: Chapter 2), but the results hardly encourage optimism in the magical power of the renaming of names.

It is in the field of race relations, that emphasis on the

significance of a changed social consciousness is most marked
at the present time. Scholarship, exhortation, campaigns are
directed to transforming social consciousness, in what is
often described, I think somewhat erroneously, as a search
for identity. Members of a subordinated race surely know
their identity perfectly well. They are attacking the social
definitions which prevail in their societies, and which
rationalize their deprivation of freedom and autonomy. The
issue is one of social redefinition and racial liberation, not of
a search for identity.

3.

The concept, colonization of the mind, corresponds in Third
World writing, to false consciousness in the field of class
analysis, and to cultural repression in the analysis of post-
industrial society. Some of the most powerful statements of
this process come from the West Indies.

The characterizations of Frantz Fanon are widely known
and used. Equally powerful and scorching denunciations of
alienation under colonization and slavery are made by the
Haitian writer, in exile, René Depestre. In 'Les Fondéments
socio-culturels de notre identité' (1969) he writes that one of
the principal consequences of colonial domination is the
depersonalization of human beings in the three continents of
Africa, Asia and Latin America. Colonization, in establishing
by violence the cultural unreality of the subjugated peoples,
in petrifying their cultures in an immense ghetto of history,
deprives the colonized of all identity. The colonizer declares
that the colonized is not only inferior, but an object, and his
function is reduced to that of an object. Depestre prefers the
term 'zombification' to alienation for this process.[5]

5 'Ce n'est pas par hasard qu'il existe en Haiti le mythe du *zombi*,
c'est-à-dire le mort-vivant, l'homme à qui on a volé son esprit et sa
raison, en lui laissant sa seule force de travail. Selon le mythe, il était
interdit de mettre du sel dans les aliments du zombi, car cela pourrait
réveiller ses facultés créatrices. L'histoire de la colonisation est celle

Added to this subjection of consciousness, the process of cultural assimilation renders the colonized hostile to himself.[6] In consequence, the African, Asian or Latin-American foundations of his life appear as unworthy of the human species. The colonized forms a terrible image of himself, and denies not only his unique qualities of culture, but also in certain cases, his appearance, colour, and the reactions of his sensibility. Colour is made into an insurmountable obstacle between the generic being of the black and his realization in history.

Depestre does not distinguish clearly between the consequences of colonization and slavery. He assimilated, perhaps deliberately, the two historical situations, seeing in slavery a more intense expression of 'zombification'. Slavery is anti-identity, accelerated depersonalization. The black man reduced to slavery becomes the man of coal, the man of oil, combustible man, and the use which is made of his labour creates forces external and hostile to him, such as sugar, coffee, indigo, spices, cotton and other commodities abundantly available on the colonial market. This incredible process of reification and assimilation implies the total loss of identity, the psychological annihilation of being, a generalized 'zombification' (1970: 21-2).

The main elements in the colonization of the mind are the denigration of the culture of the subordinated race, the denigration of the subordinates themselves, the idealization of the culture and qualities of the dominant group, the consequent justification of rule, and the enlisting of the

---

d'un processus de *zombification* généralisée de l'homme. C'est aussi l'histoire de la qûete d'un sel revitalisant, capable de restituer à l'homme l'usage de son imagination et de sa culture.'

6 'Pour l'homme engagé dans cet implacable circuit acculturatif, le fameux: "Je est un autre", d'Arthur Rimbaud devenait "*Je* est un sous-produit anglo-saxon, *Je* est un sous-produit latin, *Je* est une ombre congelée au soleil conquerant de l'Occident chrétien".'

motivations of the conquered in this process.[7] The more extreme denunciations of the colonization of the mind describe it as entailing the destruction of the culture of the colonized, and the loss of their identity. But this is greatly exaggerated; it is a perspective of Westernized intellectuals, perceiving their own dilemma as the experience of 'their people'. Amilcar Cabral, in his paper 'Le Rôle de la culture dans la lutte pour l'indépendance' (1972) argues that in fact the masses maintain the indestructible character of their cultural resistance to foreign domination. The return to the source, or cultural renaissance, is not a problem posed for the masses; they are themselves the source of the culture, its bearers, and at the same time solely capable of preserving and creating the culture. For Africa at any rate, a distinction must be drawn, in his view, between the situation of the masses, who preserve their culture, and that of the indigenous colonial elite, more or less assimilated, uprooted and cultur-ally alienated.[8]

Cabral's comments provide a valuable corrective to the alienated intellectual view of the colonization of the mind. But Cabral's own perspective is no doubt shaped by the

7 Daniel P. Kunene (1968: 19) uses the term 'deculturation' to describe this process. He defines deculturation as 'the process whereby, at the meeting of two cultures, one consciously and deliberately dominates the other, and denies it the right to exist, by both directly and indirectly (a) questioning its validity as a culture, (b) denigrating it, (c) making its carriers objects of ridicule and scorn, and thus (d) leading finally to the questioning thereof by the very people whom it has nurtured and given an identity and a positive being.'

8 Depestre, who expresses this perspective of the intellectual elite, nevertheless stresses the continuity of cultural resistance: 'De toute façon il reste que le perspective assimilationiste a échoué lamentablement, et que les cultures de nos peuples, pour mutilées et stagnantes qu'elles étaient, pour mystifiées, dévitalisées, zombifiées qu'elles étaient, du fait de la colonisation, ont gardé, malgré tout, à titre de souvenirs et d'espérances, "ces grandes reserves de foi, ces grands silos de force" dont parlait Aimé Césaire, ou au moment décisif, le décolonisation peut récolter des armes spirituelles et morales' (1969: 5).

special conditions in Guinea-Bissau. Certainly in some areas of Africa, there has been considerable penetration of the masses by the colonizer's culture. And the enlisting of the motivations of the colonized has sometimes been quite remarkable. Thus the loyalty of the Algerian people to the French, and the heroism of their soldiers in the service of the French during the Second World War, seem almost incomprehensible in the context of the whole history of the colonization of Algeria and against the background of the French massacre of Algerians at Setif on 8 May 1945. It seems astonishing that, during a period of militant campaigning in South Africa, one of the resistance songs of the African National Congress *Mayibuy' Iafrika* ('Let Africa Return'), should have carried as a refrain, the missionary perspective, 'While We Were Still in Darkness'. And then there are the African theodicies, which read like a theological justification of white domination.[9]

4.

Since colonization of the mind is conceived as an extensive appropriation of the psychological resources of the subordinate races, the process of decolonization ranges widely over almost all fields of human thought and social interaction.

The basic redefinition is of the racial qualities of the subordinate, the quality of being black for example, as in *négritude* or black soul. It is ironic that Senghor's theories, in which the conception of *négritude* has been most elaborated, should come under sharp attack precisely at a time when they have great cogency for blacks in the USA, and there is a Third World movement of racial redefinition.

For Senghor (1971: 5) the 'problematique de la négritude' lies in discrimination against blacks and denial of their civilization. Objectively, he sees *négritude* as a fact, a culture, a complex of values of the peoples of black Africa, and of

9 See Chapter 1.

black minorities in other parts of the world. Subjectively, it is the acceptance of the fact of their civilization, and its projection into the future. Initially, *négritude* developed as a reaction to white racism, as dialectical opposition to the cultural values imposed by whites; but later, Senghor conceived it as part of a synthesis at a higher level, namely the contribution of blacks to the civilization of the universal — a change in conception related to changing social conditions, and having some significance for the quality of race relations.

Even severe critics of *négritude* may concede that it served a progressive function at one time.[10] But their main criticisms are that in the contemporary setting it is neither revolutionary nor attuned to the situation of independent African States and problems of development: 'La recherche de l'identité, le retour sur soi même, l'inventaire du passé, tout cela ne suffit pas. Les chants ouolofs ne multiplieront pas la production du blé à l'hectare.'[10a] Or they may draw a distinction between revolutionary forms of *négritude*, which combine the revolutionary thought of our age with recognition of the singularity of the black experience, and Senghor's theory of *négritude* which Depestre (1970: 29-30) describes as having become a dangerous dogma, a new form of alienation, which serves as a cultural foundation for the neo-colonialist penetration in Africa and America, an invention of new myths which seeks deliberately to conceal the

10 For example, Adotevi (1969*a*: 74-5), a most extreme antagonist of *négritude*, writes that it should be considered 'as a primitive period necessary to the African renaissance . . . at a time when the whole world was given over to racialism . . . at a time when the whole of humanity raised voice in competitive cacophony, there was a single pistol-shot in the middle of this concert — négritude. It shook a few consciences and brought a few Negroes together, and this was a good thing.'

10*a* Depestre, quoted in Guillaume and Lagroye (1969: 259): 'The search for identity, the return to self, the inventory of the past — these are not sufficient. Not all the Wolof chants in the world will increase the per hectare production of wheat.'

economic and political factors which have conditioned the situation of blacks.

Redefinition implies that the initial definitions establish the arena of confrontation, so that the ruling race continues to originate ideology for the ruled. From this point of view, *négritude* may be seen as pure negation, or as a trap, which continues black subordination.[11] The problem is to transcend the initial definitions.

The redefinition of the characteristics of the subordinate race, the reaffirmation of the value of its culture, and the reappropriation of its history, are all closely related. The qualities of the culture have to be entirely reassessed. Characteristically, national liberation movements are generally preceded by a cultural revival. Cabral (1970: 3, 6) asserts that to take up arms to dominate a people is, above all, to take up arms to destroy, or at least to neutralize, to paralyse, its cultural life:

For, as long as there continues to exist a part of these people retaining their own cultural life, foreign domination cannot be sure of its perpetuation. At any moment, depending on internal and external factors determining the evolution of the society in question, cultural resistance (indestructible) may take on new forms (political, economic, armed) in order fully to contest foreign domination ... If imperialist domination has the vital need to practice cultural oppression, national liberation is necessarily an *act of culture*.

Cabral (1970: 4,5) views culture as an essential element in the history of a people: it is simultaneously the fruit of a people's history and the determinant of its history. Imperialist domination violently usurps the free operation of the process of development of the *productive forces*. It thereby negates the historical process of the dominated people, as well as its cultural development. The reappropriation of

11 'Les Nègres ont jusque'ici vécu en esclaves, dans la mesure même où ils se définissaient toujours, non par rapport à eux-mêmes, mais d'abord et avant tout par rapport au Blanc' (Yambo Ouologuem, quoted in Guillaume and Lagroye, 1969: 253).

history is the assumption by subordinate peoples of control over their historical and cultural development.

History must be rewritten to express the new perspectives. The history of a people no longer begins with the act of their being discovered by the invaders. Instead, invasion is relegated to the status of an episode in a long history. The perspectives are now those of the dominated. The conquered emerge as subjects and as actors, not as objects of action. The villains of colonial history are transformed into the heroes of liberation. New themes become salient, above all the continuity of resistance under alien domination.[12]

5.

The characterizations of the dominant group permeate all the institutions. They are embedded in education, history, anthropology, political theory, theology, grammar, and these have to be purged, as it were, and redefined. There is a great debunking of the ideologies of the dominant group. The justifications of colonial rule, as a civilizing mission, are seen in the context of ruthless exploitation and violence. Violence itself is redefined, so that indoctrination, or high rates of infant mortality, become acts of violence.[13] Political conceptions which seemed somewhat extravagant when first launched, are now well established in the rhetoric of redefinition, as for example the characterization of blacks in the USA as a colonized people.[14] Through the prism of redefinition, the benevolent aid which former colonial powers feel they are giving to the underdeveloped countries of the world is refracted into neo-colonialism, that is the continuity of colonial exploitation through and in complicity

12 See Gordon (1971) for a discussion of many of these problems.

13 I am indebted to Anne Bailey for this insight.

14 The differences between colonial rule and the situation of blacks in the USA are certainly as pronounced as the similarities, but the identification is argued persuasively and provides an additional ideological basis for linking blacks in the USA with the Third World.

with, indigenous politicians and bourgeoisie. The wealth of industrialized nations is viewed as related dialectically to the impoverishment of the underdeveloped countries, based on the exploitation of their labour and natural resources. Argument begins to be advanced that the former colonial powers have an obligation in international law to effect restitution.

The religious institutions are a major field for redefinition, concerned as they are with basic values and interpretations of the human condition. They offer much scope for redefinition, in the past because of difficulties in effective surveillance of the religious observances of the subject race, and at present because of the diminished salience of religious beliefs for social control.

There are many manifestations of changed social consciousness in the reactions to conversion to Christianity. Most dramatic are the Messianic and millenarian type movements, holding out the promise of a reversal of roles in this world or the next, and the independent churches emancipating themselves from racial domination in the governance of the church. In much the same way as the reappropriation of history implies initiative and control over the future, so these religious movements may be viewed as a restoration of a group consciousness impaired by foreign intrusion, the assertion of cultural continuity and at the same time the resumption of initiative in the orientation to the future.[15] For many years, the role of Christianity in colonial domination has been under mounting attack – the contrast between other-wordly preoccupations for the colonized converts, and the sturdy pursuit of very mundane, material interests by the colonizing Christians; the inculcation of attitudes of submission in many denominations with the chilling threat of hell-fires; the rubbing-off on the white intruders of some of the reverence for the Almighty,

15 See Bastide (1972) for a discussion of these issues, and the evolution of Messianic movements from movements of revolutionary opposition into movements of salvation.

colonization and Christianity, missionaries and whites, having come together appreciably as a package-deal with the denigration[16] of traditional culture as barbarous and given over to pleasures of the flesh. Alioune Diop comments that

because the authority of Western culture and Western institutions outstripped ours where the expression of faith was concerned, it succeeded in converting African Christians into a people without soul or visage, a pale shadow of the dominating pride of the Christian West. At the very heart and centre of the Church in Africa, we have in fact witnessed the mutilation of the African Personality, and the trampling of human dignity in Africa. (Quoted in Harry Sawyerr, 1969: 81-2)

The reactions, to be sure, are very mixed and it is precisely Christian conviction that has been a stimulus to scholarly theological redefinition. Again there are the problems of continuity and control over the future:

By a miscarriage of purpose the Church has succeeded in preaching to, and in teaching, Africans about a strange God whom they have somehow come to identify as the God of the white man. But what has happened to the God as known to their forebears — the God who is the foundation of their traditional beliefs? (E. Bolaji Idowu, 1969: 13)

What is the continuity between African religions and Christianity? What is the revelation of God for all races? What are the special contributions different peoples may make, as they take control over their religious evolutions — such African contributions, for example, as vital participation, or ritual expression of the relationship between departed and living Christians? (Vincent Mulago, 1969: 157, and John S. Mbiti, 1969: 183)

These scholarly redefinitions are somewhat related to the development of a black theology, though this development is more specifically political, and may include a call for the

16 I have retained the word 'denigration', since it illustrates one of the points made in this chapter, the pervasive penetration of Western culture, if one may use the term, by conceptions which have a racist connotation. I am grateful to my friend Max Gluckman, for drawing my attention to the derivation of the word — to blacken thoroughly.

use of institutional power to fulfil the purposes of religion among black people. Predictably its main expression is among blacks in the United States, with some reverberation among Africans in South Africa.

The justification for a black theology is the special suffering of the black man. At the National Seminar on Black Theology in Roodepoort, South Africa, in March 1971, the participants accepted that the fundamental experience of black people in South Africa was the negative and debilitating effect of their blackness. 'They experience themselves as black, and this experience makes it hard for them at all times to experience themselves as men.' It is this experience which legitimizes the 'theologizing around the black religious experience'. When a black man's religious experience is integrated into his whole experience of life, then it becomes integrated into his experience of suffering, poverty and oppression. 'Black' was a legitimate theological concept, denoting not so much pigmentation as the condition of the oppressed and the poor (Ntwasa, 1971: 2).[17]

This conception of blackness as suffering may be given a Messianic cast, as in the discussion by Washington of the *Politics of God* (1969). Black people in the USA are chosen people, chosen as the 'suffering servants' in the kingdom of God. 'The "curse" of being a Negro' is really a blessed symbol, that of God's paradoxical instrument as the means of his grace for all men' (1969: 171). 'All mankind is in a state of deprivation and the Negro is the servant of release from this bondage of human separateness – this deprivation – being as he is externally the most deprived . . . Like the Jew

17 There was disagreement as to whether prior stress should be placed on the blackness of black people, in order to build up a conscious sense of pride and dignity in blackness, as a necessary step in the full acceptance of their own humanity, or whether the prior affirmation should be that of humanity. When humanity 'becomes the central affirmation of any and every man, then they are free to accept any other man with his particular racial characteristics, and thus also free to accept joyfully and positively their own blackness'.

before and with him, the Negro will receive no reward until all are healed' (1969: 159-60).

The ramifications of these redefinitions, rooted in a changed philosophy of life and human relations, are almost infinite. There is heightened sensitivity to particular structures of race relations, such as paternalism or liberalism. New vocabularies of vituperation emphasize the changed perceptions. New symbols express the changed consciousness, as for example the Afro hair style in American black-white relations, or the Jewish skull-cap (*yarmulka*) in response to antisemitism, and old symbols of domination come under sharp attack. The very categories of thought are subjected to critical examination. There is the potential for a thoroughgoing, radical and creative critique of Western thought, and more immediately of the cultural biases in the social sciences. At a general level, these redefinitions may be seen as part of a broad revolutionary movement for the deracializing of human society, a sort of intellectual and moral fumigation of the Western ethos. At the level of a particular society, they appear to be an essential element for the restructuring of race relations.

6.

In thinking of a change of social consciousness as a strategy in the challenge to systems of racial domination, there is a preliminary question to be answered, whether all forms of social consciousness are possible. This conception of possible social consciousness is discussed by Lucien Goldman (1971: 8-24) who distinguishes between 'conscience réelle' and 'conscience possible'. He suggests, by way of example, that a rigorous inquiry into the social consciousness of Russian peasants in January 1917 would probably have established that the great majority were loyal to the Czar, and did not even envisage the possibility of the Russian monarchy being overthrown, while at the end of the year this 'conscience réelle' had radically changed. The overthrow of the Czar was a form of possible social consciousness. At the same time, Lenin considered that it was impossible to make the peasants accept the doctrine that it was better to work the land co-operatively than under private ownership, and he therefore formulated the slogan — 'the land to the peasants'.

For an analyst to determine the forms of possible social consciousness seems a most intractable problem. Virtually all forms of consciousness are possible to the leaders, who can take ideas from any part of the world, or in other ways creatively transcend their own experience. But the question is what forms of social consciousness are possible for the strata they represent (class or religious or ethnic or racial group) and are likely to be a significant factor in social change. It may be quite misleading to project possible forms of consciousness from present attitudes, as shown in the example given by Lucien Goldman; nor can an answer readily be given on the basis of an analysis of the social structure of the local situation.

Even determining possible social consciousness retrospectively is most difficult. The fact that a particular form of social consciousness was expressed in action at many different levels during the course of a revolutionary struggle by no means excludes other possibilities. Looking back at the Algerian revolution before the final stages of OAS terrorism, can one really say that the situation was such as to have excluded the possibility that the majority of the Muslim population would accept the conception of an integrated Muslim-French Algeria? Certainly a plausible case can be made against the ultimate acceptability of the proclaimed French policy of assimilation (see Dunn, 1972: Chapter 6), but might not even this have been a possibility if the Popular Front government in 1936 had passed the Blum-Violette proposal by which many categories of Algerian Muslims could have combined French citizenship with the retention of their status under Islamic law, and if elections had been conducted with integrity and reforms implemented?

Compounding the difficulties of analysis and prediction is the fact that revolutionary or counter-revolutionary action

changes the probability that certain forms of social consciousness will prevail. When the Algerian revolution was
launched by a handful of revolutionaries, the demand for
independence hardly seemed a possible form of social
consciousness in the sense that it would attract a mass
following under the conditions which prevailed in 1954. And
polarized conceptions of the structure of Algerian society
only became increasingly persuasive as a result of the struggle
itself. In South Africa, one of the forms of the government's
strategy of counter-revolution was to establish Bantustans, a
sort of lesser galaxy of tribal satellites, to wither in the
splendour of the South African sun. It seemed inconceivable
that the tribal consciousness which these Bantustans were
designed to embody, would be in the least persuasive, and
African leaders rejected the new tribalism with scorn. But as
the Bantustans are established, with African involvement in
their administration, this narrower social consciousness
becomes increasingly a possible form of social consciousness.

The problem is even more complex, since not only local
changes, but changes in the international scene, are relevant
for changes in social consciousness. Ghanaian independence
in 1957 was a catalyst for changing political conceptions
among African leaders in South Africa. Whereas previously,
the demand was for a sharing of power, there was now
introduced the quite feasible goal of an early conquest of
power. A new rhetoric developed, appropriate to African
majority rule, and an exclusive form of nationalism. It
seemed to fire African imagination, from which one might
infer that this form of social consciousness was embedded in
the situation. But is this something an African leader could
readily have foreseen, before the event?

In theory, it seems easy enough to meet the requirement
that the changed social consciousness, which the leaders seek
to create, should be possible, in the sense that it emerges
from the structure of the situation and is likely to move
masses of men. In practice, meeting the requirement is so beset
with difficulty, that politicians are driven to explore different

possibilities in action, sometimes to the point of experimental frenzy. For purposes of the present discussion, I certainly do not know how to establish the possible forms of consciousness in a given society. I will however assume that sentiments of dignity and self-respect are widely present among subordinate racial groups, and that the sort of elaborations of these sentiments, and the strategies connected with their realization, discussed above, are possible forms of social consciousness in the societies with which I am dealing.

7.

The relationship between change in social consciousness and transformation of a society may be viewed at different levels – individual, institutional and societal. The most idealistic position is that which stresses change in individual consciousness as an effective agent of societal change. Emphasis on purification of the individual was an important element in the thought of Gandhi, though it was hardly the force on which he relied in the struggle for independence. Nehru, in his autobiography (1962: 521 ff.), expresses ambivalence towards this aspect of Gandhi's thought: 'Gandhiji wants to improve the individual internally, morally and spiritually, and thereby change the external environment. He wants people to give up bad habits and indulgences and to become pure.' But how is this to be accomplished when the whole system encourages man's predatory instinct? And how can individual change be socially effective in transforming an oppressive system? Is it realistic to anticipate that autocratic Indian princes and rapacious landlords will become, by a process of individual conversion, the trustees of the very people they exploit? In the context of Nehru's socialist perspective, the type of social consciousness Gandhi desired would not be possible for the great majority of peoples under the conditions of capitalist society, nor would privileged strata voluntarily relinquish their vested interests. The main target of attack must be the system itself.

Change at the intermediate level between the individual and society may seem more feasible than direct change at the societal level, where there is a great concentration of power in the State. The movement would be from change in individual consciousness through institutional changes to a restructuring of the society. This strategy has seemed particularly attractive to varied strata in the advanced industrial society or corporate State. R.D. Laing, in a discussion of 'The obvious' (1968: 16), comments that

> in our society, at certain times, this interlaced set of systems may lend itself to revolutionary change, not at the extreme micro or macro ends; that is, not through the individual pirouette of solitary repentance on the one hand, or by a seizure of the machinery of the State on the other; but by sudden, structural, radical qualitative changes in the intermediate system levels; changes in a factory, a hospital, a school, a university, a set of schools, or a whole area of industry, medicine, education, etc.

The basis is presumably a change in individual consciousness but directed at strategic aspects of the values and structures of intermediate systems. It is a strategy of revolution at the micro-level.[18]

Attack at the societal level is represented by such revolutionary movements as national liberation movements. Change in consciousness, being an integral part of the resistance, depends for its effectiveness, as a weapon in societal change, on the effectiveness of the action. In many of the discussions of the post-industrial society, there is perhaps some plausibility in the conception of a change of consciousness being in and of itself a vehicle of societal change, since it is the consciousness of the children of the affluent, the social consciousness of ruling strata, that is usually in question. But even then, action would be necessary

---

18 Galtung (1969: 11) describes the New Left as having made a lasting contribution by directing attention to revolutions at the micro-levels within organizations in addition to revolution at the national and international levels.

to make the redefinition effective. Institutions are not simply the behaviour and ideas of individuals. In situations of racial domination, it seems almost inconceivable that a change in social consciousness of the subordinate race could be an effective agent of change at the societal level without specific action and struggle directed to that end. This places the emphasis rather on the actions and campaigns, whereas I am wanting to analyse the potential contribution of a change in social consciousness of the subordinates to change in structures of racial domination. So I shall concentrate on this aspect, rather than on the campaigns and strategies of resistance.

Two general propositions seem specially relevant. The first asserts that systems of domination rest in some measure on consent. This is a popular theme in anarchist thought: 'Let the most oppressed people under heaven once change their mode of thinking and they are free' (quoted from Godwin in Apter and Joll, 1972: 56). Narayan Desai (1969: 61) following in the tradition of Gandhi, takes the same stance with reference to the Indian Peace Brigade: 'Exploitation is perpetuated only when it is accepted by the exploited. So when the exploited people refuse to accept exploitation, it becomes almost impossible . . . The prime thing is the individual and social decision that they are now going to be courageous. This is how socialization of courage begins. ' [19]

The second proposition is the rather obvious one that if a party to a social relationship modifies his behaviour, the

19 The level of application to which Desai refers is that of village structure. Reinhold Niebuhr (1932: 237) writing at the time that the Nazis were rising to power, expressed the role of consent in social power much more cautiously: 'All social power is partially derived from the actual possession of physical instruments of coercion, economic or martial. But it also depends to a large degree upon its ability to secure unreasoned and unreasonable obedience, respect and reverence. In so far as reason tends to destroy this source of its power, it makes for the diminution of the strength of the strong and adds to the power of the weak. The expropriators are expropriated in another sense beside the one which Marx analysed.'

social relationship is thereby changed. Thus Reich (1970: 358) argues that since students at a university are part of the organization, they have the power to alter the structure by changing their own role within it, even if no one's thinking is changed, but their own.

8.

Now what consequences might be expected to flow at the national level from a change in social consciousness among the subordinates, which asserts the values of their culture and being, which affirms the principle of racial equality and which rejects all forms of discrimination?

In the past, the answer to this question was often sought in the effects on the consciousness of the dominant group. Thus it was commonly argued that by a change in the consciousness of the subordinates, the convictions of the rulers are challenged, and an important element of power, their moral certitude, is thereby undermined. Certainly this seems to have happened in the field of race relations in the USA. Blacks have been able to make effective in the wider society their consciousness of the injustices under which they live, and the position of blacks appears to be in process of rapid transformation. There were however many favourable circumstances — the American role in international affairs, African independence, mounting international criticism, some influence of the American ethos of human equality and democracy, and *de jure* political equality.

The situation is quite different in South Africa. There the constant and routine experience of domination nurtures profound delusions of grandeur among the white minority.[20]

20 These are much more intense and inflated than the narcissistic sentiments described by Depestre (1970: 26) for the USA, where 'l'opinion terrible que le Noir a trouvée de lui-même dans le miroir de l'entourage blanc et l'opinion "narcissique" que le Blanc a trouvée de lui-même dans le miroir de son hégémonie socio-économique sont des images de la même misère spirituelle qui doivent être effacées pour que puisse se réaliser dans l'histoire américaine l'unité de l'espèce humaine'.

Rationalizations, exalting whites and dehumanizing blacks, legitimize the possessions and good fortune of the ruling race. Segregation interstimulates and mutually reinforces, as if in collective rituals, extreme sentiments of racial superiority. Under these conditions of legally constituted inequality, almost impenetrable barriers seem to be raised against an effective impact from the ethical judgments of the subordinates. For these new movements of redefinition, however, the target is not the barricaded conscience of the rulers. It is in their own changed racial consciousness that members of the subordinate race seek a source of direct power for the challenge to racial domination.

Now the proposition that the oppressed consent to their own oppression, infuriates many of those who live under extreme oppression, as in South Africa. They argue, with great truth, that the instruments of domination are the denial of the elementary political rights of association, speech and movement, penal sanctions, violence and terror. There is nevertheless, even in the extreme case of South Africa, some consent, or acquiescence. The most obvious measure of this acquiescence are the numbers of the subordinate group working the instruments of their own oppression, as for example Africans in the Bantu Affairs Administration or in the South African Police Force. Or a further measure might be provided by the pass laws controlling freedom of movement. The South African economy is so greatly dependent on African labour, that Africans could destroy the pass system, one of the corner-stones of the structure of domination, by the refusal to carry passes.

The problem is not merely to withhold acquiescence, but to render the withholding socially effective. If this could be achieved in South Africa, then non-co-operation in the administration of oppression would become possible (though the administrative positions are relatively well rewarded), the pass laws could hardly be enforced, and the dependence of the economy on African, Coloured and Indian labour might be used increasingly as a source of pressure for political change. Clearly all these campaigns would call for immense courage and sacrifice. It is difficult for those of us who have not lived under oppression to appreciate the terrifying nature of these demands.

For Gandhi, emancipation from fear of the dominant group could be achieved by participation in nonviolent resistance. For Fanon, the catalyst of revolutionary courage was physical violence against the oppressor. Clearly both conceptions have validity. In the process of the nonviolent resistance movements, Indians experienced a remarkable liberation from fear. And in Algeria, the dialectic of violence and counter-violence proved a great recruiting agent for the Algerian liberation movement.

Suppose, however, that there is so much repression and such concentration of power that subordinates fear to expose themselves by direct confrontation to the certainty of savage reprisals. It may still be possible, at an intermediate level, to socialize courage and to express and reinforce a changed social consciousness, by falling back on the principle that where a person is a party to a social relationship, he may modify that relationship by a change in his own role. For this purpose, three aspects of social relationships need to be distinguished, namely the extent of interaction, the degree of interdependence of the parties, and the symmetry or assymmetry of their roles.

Where there is no relationship at all, no interaction, the possibilities of redefinition are great, but as far as effectiveness is concerned, it may be somewhat like a retreat into fantasy. The relevant situations are those where there is interaction. The more marginal situations in which there is little interaction, provide freer scope and may serve as a training ground. Thus the independent or segregated churches in South Africa, like the mosques of the Black Muslims in the USA, offer a base for developing, testing and expressing the new racial consciousness. So too art forms might be a vehicle for new consciousness, comparable to the Negro spiritual, or contemporary pop music in the USA, or revolutionary theatre. Voluntary relationships, such as pure sociability, and of course casual contacts, provide a testing ground for new patterns of race relations. In the USA, a startling demonstration of redefinition rendered effective in action, is provided at interracial student meetings where black university students originate interaction and define the issues, thereby eliminating expressions of white patronage and paternalism.

Where the relationship is totally asymmetrical, in the sense that the subordinate is far more dependent on the relationship than the dominant, this would clearly not be an appropriate context for action. For example, university education for Africans is of little significance for the apartheid government in South Africa, but it is highly significant for Africans. It is difficult, under these conditions, for African students to restructure the segregated universities of which they are a part, by redefinition of their role. The government does not hesitate to send the students home, thus obliging them to beg for readmission, or to replace them by other students, or indeed to close down the university.

The greater the interdependence on both sides, as for example the economic relationships between black and white in South Africa, the greater the potential for effective redefinition. At the same time, the dominant group reacts with the greatest repression precisely in those situations where its most valued prerogatives depend on the maintenance of the old definitions. The attack in these vital sectors calls for careful preliminary training and testing in the more marginal or voluntary contexts. In much the same way, that guerrillas undergo training in arms, in the making of explosives, in strategy and discipline, so too there is a need for preliminary training in campaigns to redefine race relations and to render the redefinitions socially effective.

9.

I have dealt only with the redefinition by the subject race. But, in the process of struggle, the ruling group reacts to these redefinitions and a dialectical process of polarizing ideologies may result. Or the dominant group may respond by more inclusive definitions, which incorporate the subordinates, as in the emphasis on national unity, a common religion, or loyalty to the ruler. At times, the expressions of this process are very clear. Categories of classification are changed from one census to another, as if the conflict between racial and other groups could be exorcized by the naming of names. Or myths of origin are reinterpreted in ideological interchange.[2][1]

I have suggested that the thoroughgoing critique of the racial definitions of the dominant group, both explicit and implicit, is a necessary element in the deracialization of human society and in local movements of racial liberation. The important contribution in movements of 'black consciousness' is the emphasis on the consciousness of the subordinates, in place of the customary preoccupation, particularly in liberal thought, with consciousness of the dominant group. For the subordinate group, decolonization of the mind is part of the process of emancipation from domination.

However, unless there is action to make the redefinitions effective, they are not likely to be significant for radical restructuring of the society. The strategies and consequences will naturally vary with different systems of domination. The discussion of theories of change in the corporate State or post-industrial society were included because of the significance they assigned to the role of social consciousness. But these theories deal with the characteristics of advanced industrialized societies. They tend to assume racial homogeneity, or at any rate they do not bring racial division into focus. Instead, their main concern is usually with such privileged strata as technocrats or university students, potential recruits to leading positions in the society. These are strata

21 This is discussed in Chapter 1. The revolution in Rwanda provides exceptionally rich material for analysis of processes of redefinition by dominant and subordinate groups. See d'Hertefelt (1960 and 1964).

whose changed social consciousness might more readily have effect on the structure of the society.

Many circumstances, such as its international situation, render the contemporary USA more open to racial mobility and equality. The civil rights movement, violence in the urban ghettos, new definitions of race relations, and militant strategies to render the redefinitions effective in intermediate structures, have all contributed to this end.

South Africa, by contrast, becomes continuously more rigid in its racial structure. This is particularly true at the level of the central political institutions. Under these conditions, it is difficult to see how change in the intermediate systems of relationship can become effective at the level of the central structures of power without a general confrontation. Moreover the regime, being totalitarian in character, exercises a wide range of controls over these intermediate institutions, and over social relationships generally. Nevertheless there is scope for expressing a militant social consciousness, and for effecting change in the quality of social relationships, at intermediate levels, and the socialization of courage is a necessary preliminary to any effective general confrontation.

PART TWO:

REVOLUTIONARY CHANGE

5

Continuities and Discontinuities in Race Relations: Evolutionary or Revolutionary Change

1.

This chapter discusses the significance, for evolutionary or revolutionary change, of continuities and discontinuities between groups in the culture and structure of a society. Theories of evolutionary change stress the significance of continuities in culture and structure. These theories are appreciably influenced by Durkheim's theory of change in the forms of solidarity, and increase in its strength, with the progressive division of labour, as societies move from the mechanical solidarity of segmented structures to the organic solidarity of functional and structural differentiation and interdependence. Theories of revolutionary change emphasize discontinuities, as in the Marxist conception of revolution arising from the polarization of classes; or the discontinuity in the situation of the *déclassé* may be seen as shaping individual propensity for revolutionary action (Olson, 1963: 531); or conditions conducive to political 'extremism' may be found in the detached situation of certain occupational groups, such as longshoremen, lumbermen and dockworkers (Lipset, 1960: 87-8); or an explosive mixture of continuity and discontinuity may be seen as a stimulus to revolutionary action, as in theories of status incongruity or status disequilibrium (Galtung, 1964).

The theories derive initially from the context of Western industrial societies, experiencing the impact of class conflict, not race conflict, the societies being for the most part racially homogeneous. What then is the significance of these theories for racially plural societies which incorporate the racial sections on a basis of inequality (Kuper and Smith, 1969)?

Are the effects of continuities and discontinuities similar in class-structured racially homogeneous societies and in racially plural societies?

In considering this problem, I shall use the revolutions in Zanzibar and Rwanda as case studies. Both these societies included racial sections, which had lived together for centuries and might therefore be expected to have established continuities in culture and structure. In neither, however, was the division of labour much advanced. I shall therefore include some reference to an earlier study of continuities and discontinuities in South African society, in which there was the beginning of a revolutionary movement in the period 1952-64 (see Chapter 6).

By continuities and discontinuities, I refer to the social distance between racial sections. Are persons of different races incorporated, as members of their racial sections, on a basis of inequality, or are they incorporated as individuals on a basis of equality? Are they segregated or assimilated, culturally differentiated or homogeneous, and is there inequality or equality in access to, and distribution of, power, status and material resources (Leo Kuper, 1969*b*: 473-9)? Thus the dimension of discontinuity-continuity is conceived broadly, and not specifically as expressed in the division of labour and its consequences.

2.

The analysis by Durkheim of the social consequences of the progressive division of labour has inspired many of the theories of evolutionary change in class and race relations. The polar types in Durkheim's theory are, at one extreme, the relatively undifferentiated segmented society characterized by mechanical solidarity, in which segments may readily detach themselves, since they are substantially self-sufficient, and, at the other extreme, the functionally differentiated and highly specialized society of organic solidarity, in which there is so great an interdependence that the detachment of a part threatens the disruption of the whole. This is a conception of the progressive division of labour as stimulating, and as expressing, a more integrative and enduring solidarity.

Durkheim's thesis is readily translated into a persuasive theory of evolutionary change. With the progressive division of labour, individuals are detached from their original segments and drawn together in relationships transcending the segmental divisions. As these new horizontal relationships increase in number and diversity and scope, the original vertical segmental divisions become less salient and largely dissolve in the interdependent structures resulting from differentiation and specialization.

The process may be viewed theoretically as one of continually progressive evolutionary change. Alternatively both ends of the continuum in Durkheim's theory may be seen as excluding the possibility of revolution, the potential for revolution being located at some point in the process of change. In the latter approach, the segmented society, with its vertical divisions, may be portrayed as pre-revolutionary. The advanced industrial society (or post-industrial society), on the other hand, may be conceived as post-revolutionary, characterized by a great continuity of most diverse statuses, interwoven in complex mosaics of interdependence. The rationale for this conception is that the society has transcended the possibility of revolution, either because it lacks the stratified social basis for class revolution as a result of continuity and interdependence, or because the 'modernized' society has in addition the capacity to respond effectively to social pressures for change. As for revolutionary potential, this is located at a stage in the progressive division of labour, varying with such factors as the nature of the initial structure, the degree and rate of economic change, the extent of mobility, subjective reactions, and indeed a host of other variables.[1]

1 See the discussion by Germani (1966: 364-94), in a somewhat analogous context, of the variables affecting the social and political consequences of mobility, including radical opposition.

A third approach to the relationship between the division of labour and revolution, combines the perspectives of Durkheim and Marx. Thus Gluckman associates the progressive division of labour with varying tendencies to different forms of civil strife, as for example feuding in simple segmented societies; irruptions of segments or rebellious war in segmentary States (Gluckman, 1969: 402); and revolution as well as rebellion, where there has developed a closely interwoven network of economic dependence (Gluckman, 1965: 164).[2]

Durkheim's theory was developed in the context of a racially and ethnically homogeneous society, and it dealt with movement from the homogeneity of the segmented society to the heterogeneity of the functionally differentiated society, as a result of processes internal to the society. It is applied, however, to the very different situation of ethnically and racially plural societies.[3] Gluckman (1969: 402), for example, sees as inherently unstable those societies in which vertical divisions between territorial or ethnic segments are inadequately crossed by the development of links of 'organic', utilitarian, economic interdependence, and he comments that without that interdependence, civil war is endemic in the system. The general expectation in the application of Durkheim's theory to racially or ethnically plural societies is that conflict between the original sections will decline as horizontal structures of relationship increasingly cut across the vertical racial or ethnic divisions. This is the theoretical basis for the prediction of evolutionary change to racial integration and democratic participation in South African society, if economic growth is sustained.

2 Gluckman uses revolution in the sense of changes in the structure of power, and rebellion in the sense of changes in the incumbency of positions of power.

3 The term 'plural society' is used here to refer to societies characterized by racial and/or ethnic cleavages. For a general discussion of the concept, see Kuper and Smith (1969: Parts 1 and 4).

3.

Some indications of the role of continuities and discontinuities may be derived from the analysis of the revolutions in Zanzibar and Rwanda. In the case of Zanzibar, there is a wide range of interpretations, the major conflict of interpretation being between those who view the revolution as a struggle of the oppressed classes against the class of oppressors, the Arab oligarchy, and those who see it as a revolution by Africans against Arabs.[4] In the case of Rwanda, the social structure was less complex than in Zanzibar, and less calculated to stimulate in its interpreters the projection of their own personality inclinations. The range of interpretations is therefore more limited, perhaps involving different emphases, on caste or class or race, rather than sharply divergent interpretations. In both situations, the difficulties of interpretation are heightened by the interweaving of racial and economic differentiation.[5]

In the Protectorate of Zanzibar, comprising Zanzibar and Pemba Islands, the four main racial and ethnic segments at the time of the revolution in 1964, were the Shirazi, Mainland Africans, Arabs and Asians. The Shirazi were the oldest established and the most numerous section. They had arrived from the mainland of Africa many centuries earlier, and they claimed to have intermingled with Persians who had migrated to Zanzibar in about the tenth century. They most nearly correspond to indigenous African groups. However, membership of the Shirazi included ex-slaves, who had been brought to the islands, and descendants of slaves (Middleton and Campbell, 1965: 15-20). The total population of the Protectorate, according to the 1958 Census, was some

4 The most authoritative accounts of the background to the Zanzibar revolution are to be found in the studies by Lofchie (1965 and 1969).

5 See Chapter 7 for a discussion of the relations between economic and racial differentiation in Zanzibar and Rwanda, and problems of interpretation.

299,000, that is, over 165,000 on Zanzibar Island and almost 134,000 on Pemba. In 1948, Shirazi constituted over half the population on each of the islands. Probably, this proportion had not greatly changed by 1964.

The second largest section was of Mainland Africans, representing relatively recent migration from the mainland, and including many migrant labourers.[6] Mainland Africans comprised almost one-fifth of the total population in 1948, a fourth of the population on Zanzibar Island, and about one-eighth on Pemba.

Arabs, of varied origin, had settled on the islands over many centuries, but more particularly after 1830, when the Sultan of Oman decided to locate his capital on Zanzibar Island (Lofchie, 1969: 287). In the eighteenth and nineteenth centuries, until the establishment of the British Protectorate of Zanzibar in 1890, the island was under Arab rule, and the British continued to support the Sultan and the Arab ruling oligarchy. The Arabs were the third largest section, comprising about a sixth of the total population, less than one-tenth of the population of Zanzibar Island, and over one-fourth of those living on Pemba. There were thus almost three times as many Mainland Africans as Arabs on Zanzibar Island. On Pemba Island, on the other hand, Arabs were more numerous than Mainland Africans, a ratio of over two to one.

There have been Indians on the islands for many centuries. They were a small population, 6.1 per cent of the total in 1958, essentially urban, and the great majority lived on Zanzibar Island.

The crude, stereotypic view of Zanzibar prior to the revolution emphasizes the discontinuities between the sections. Arabs are categorized as the ruling stratum, the senior bureaucrats, the large plantation owners, Indians as merchants and financiers, and Africans, both Shirazi and Mainland, as fishermen, cultivators and labourers. There were certainly marked discontinuities in power, in occupation and

6 ibid.

in education. Lofchie (1969: 293-309) presents tables, based on a survey in 1948, which give quantitative measures of social structure — land-ownership, occupational status, and access to higher education — 'to illustrate the close coincidence between racial community and economic class in Zanzibar' (1969: 302). Certainly the owners of the large clove plantations were Arab and Indian, the upper professional and upper middle occupational categories (such as owners of large commercial firms, top professionals, administrators, teachers, newspaper editors, and retail shopkeepers) were mostly Indian, but also Arab, and much higher proportions of Asian and Arab schoolchildren were in the upper standards of the schools.

But there were also many continuities in economic position. The economy was little developed, resting largely on the marketing of cloves, subsistence agriculture and fishing, with some employment by government and in commerce, but little in industry. Inevitably, there was poverty among all sections, and many Arabs, Indians, Shirazi and Africans shared the same class situation. It is clear from the tables presented by Lofchie that there was a considerable overlapping in landownership and occupation. The great majority of Arabs (5,515, or 92 per cent of Arab landowners) owned small plantations, with less than a thousand clove trees, being in the same economic situation as the Shirazi landowners; or if the level of the small plantation is taken as less than 250 trees, then 3,630 Arab owners (60 per cent) were in the same landowning stratum as 20,275 (91 per cent) of Shirazi, Mainland African and Comorian owners. In the distribution of non-agricultural occupations, the upper stratum was Indian, and the upper middle was appreciably Indian, but the great majority of Indians were in the middle strata of skilled manual workers and of uncertified clerical and administrative personnel, and in the lower middle stratum of vendors, peddlers and semi-skilled workers. The Arabs constituted the top-ranking government administrators, they were appreciably represented in the upper middle and middle (non-manual) occupations and little represented in the skilled manual category, but the overwhelming majority (8,000, or 82 per cent of Arabs in non-agricultural occupations) were concentrated in the lower middle and lower categories (semi-skilled workers, peddlers and labourers) in about the numbers that would be expected in terms of their proportion of the total population. Mainland Africans were concentrated in the manual occupations (skilled, semi-skilled and unskilled), but they were also represented in the upper middle and middle (non-manual) occupational levels. Shirazi were distributed over a wide range of occupations, but most heavily in the lower middle and lower occupational categories. In education, relatively few Shirazi children were in the highest classes of the schools, but the proportion for Mainland Africans was almost commensurate with its proportion of the total population, though appreciably below that of Indians and Arabs (see Appendix, at the end of this chapter).

What then is to be said of the pattern of discontinuities and continuities? The discontinuities were marked at the level of the Arab oligarchy, as Lofchie demonstrates, and at the level of professionals and merchants, mostly Indian. There was discontinuity also in occupational patterns, most of the cultivators and fishermen being Shirazi, and most Mainland Africans being employed as labourers in Zanzibar City or as squatters or seasonally on clove plantations. And finally the presence of an Indian middle class contributed to discontinuities between the racial sections at the upper occupational level, by impeding the upward mobility of other sections (Lofchie, 1969: 300).

At the same time, there were marked continuities, in the sense that many persons of different races followed similar occupations and shared roughly the same life situation. Common occupational and life situation may have the most varied consequences, dependent on a great many factors. They may provide a basis for common interests and for class action, as when workers are massed together in large industries, but they may inhibit, or at any rate not be conducive to, communal action if the workers are in the separate work situations of small-scale business and domestic labour, as in Zanzibar, or if they are in competition for wage employment, or for the same urban market for agricultural produce.

In addition to continuities in economic situation and education, there were continuities in culture and in group composition. Lofchie (1965: 71-2), in discussing factors making for integration, emphasizes common language and religion, Swahili being the common language, and Islam the main religion. More than 95 per cent were Muslim in 1948 (Lofchie, 1965: 71-2), the great majority being of the Sunni denomination. Almost two-thirds of the small Asian population were either Muslims of the Shia sect or Hindus; and there was a substantial section of Ibadhi Muslims among the Arabs, most of the Arab elite being Ibadhi, not Sunni. About 2,000 of over 57,000 Mainland Africans were Christians. However, adherence to Christianity may have been understated (Lofchie, 1965: 72), and there was a widespread stereotype of Mainland Africans as a Christian group (Lofchie, 1969: 307-8).

Some continuity in group composition resulted from interbreeding between the races, and the acceptance of persons wishing to identify with a particular racial section. Lofchie (1969: 296-7) shows how large numbers of Swahili (persons of mixed Arab-African descent and Islamic faith) changed their identification to Arab in the period 1924-31, with some measure of acceptance. This avenue of movement into the Arab section by self-identification was difficult however for Africans, and Lofchie (1969: 298) argues first, that upwardly mobile individuals accepted into the Arab elite group reinforced the racial aspect of political domination and the social division of labour, and secondly, that not enough people were involved in change of identification to alter the racial character of social stratification. However that may be, it is clear that there was some continuity, or fluidity, in group composition, between Arabs, Shirazi and persons of mixed Arab-African descent.

Probably relatively precise measures could be given of many aspects of continuity and discontinuity, where extensive census and other population data are available. This was not the case in Zanzibar, and the difficulties are increased by the fact that the categories of African and Arab were combined in the 1958 Census. Given this paucity of data, there may be greater validity in statements of relative continuity between sections. Thus, it seems clear that the maximum continuity was between Arabs and Shirazi on Pemba Island, and that the maximum discontinuities were on Zanzibar Island, between Mainland Africans and Arabs, and Mainland Africans and Indians.

On Pemba Island, a different experience of Arab settlement from that on Zanzibar Island was expressed in the historical belief among Pemba Shirazi that they had entered into a voluntary relationship with Arabs, and that they had not been subjected to an enforced subordination (Lofchie, 1965: 170, 244-5). There were always Shirazi as well as Arab plantation owners on Pemba, there was more social acceptance, intermarriage and concubinage between Arabs and Shirazi than on Zanzibar Island, and by reason of kinship ties, men from outlying parts could move to the clove areas and take part in the clove industry as small growers (Middleton and Campbell, 1965: 35-9). In addition, there was a common language and religion. In relative terms, these constituted relations of greatest continuity between sections.

Maximum discontinuity characterized the relations on Zanzibar Island between Mainland Africans and Arabs. Many of the Africans had been born on the mainland of Africa, and there must have been appreciable numbers of recent immigrants among them. Mainland Africans tended to be the poorest section of the population. They were employed predominantly in the towns, either in domestic services or in manual work as government labourers; those engaged in agriculture were usually squatters on land to which they had no permanent rights (Lofchie, 1965: 83). The great majority of Africans lived in the Ngambo ('the other side') section of Zanzibar City and in its peri-urban environs, in coral houses roofed with petrol tins, under conditions in invidious contrast to those prevailing in Stone Town, the essentially Arab and Indian section of Zanzibar City. The conspicuous consumption of wealth by the small Arab elite would be particularly visible in Zanzibar City (Lofchie, 1965: 77, 87, 88). Middleton and Campbell (1965: 19-20) describe Mainland Africans as largely Christian or pagan, and comment that they were cut off from much of the social life of the country because few of them were Muslims. The evidence of the censuses is quite to the contrary, but it may be misleading. Certainly almost three-fifths of the small Christian population in 1948 was Mainland African (Lofchie, 1965: 72). To these discontinuities must be added the discontinuity in milieus between Africans from countries on the mainland struggling for independence, and caught up in nationalist and Pan-Africanist movements, and Arabs dominating an island enclave off the East Coast of Africa in an era of emancipation from colonialism. Finally, there was the historical cleavage resulting from the Arab role in the slave trade.

Sharp discontinuities in culture and milieu, and in political and historical roles, were the basis of the great discontinuity between Indians and Mainland Africans. Also the main traders and financiers were Indian, and they seem to have been perceived, or stereotyped, as a wealthy trading class, though only a small proportion of Indians belonged to this class.

4.

The discontinuity between the racial sections in Rwanda is immediately conveyed by the frequent description of the traditional society as a caste or feudal society. Its origins were in about the sixteenth century, when waves of immigrant pastoral Tutsi began to establish their domination over the agricultural Hutu and the Twa, by a combination of peaceful means and conquest. The central region was the area with the longest record of continuous contact between Tutsi and Hutu, and it constituted the 'core area' of traditional Rwanda (Lemarchand, 1966*a*: 601). In the north, Tutsi control was not firmly established until the 1920s (Lemarchand, 1966*a*: 599), with the assistance initially of the German, and later of the Belgian, administration.

The traditional system of Tutsi domination rested on the structure of the State and on the system of clientage. Power was vested in the divine king, the Mwami, and it radiated from him to the court, the territorial administration of hill chiefs and chiefs of province, and the military organization, in final analysis the source of restraining power. This State structure was in the hands of Tutsi (Maquet, 1964: 555). The system of taxation and of clientage supported the State structure of domination. Taxation fell unequally on Hutu and Tutsi, the former being required to provide agricultural produce, heads of cattle and services, while the latter made less onerous contributions, consisting of pastoral products. Under the system of clientage, the clients rendered services and produce in exchange for protection and the use of cows. Maquet (1964: 557) writes that by means of this double mechanism of taxation and feudal obligation, the Tutsi stratum appropriated the surplus of agricultural production.

The discontinuities then, in the traditional system, lay in the monopoly of power, wealth and privilege by the Tutsi, and in their domination, as a pastoral warrior stratum, over a peasant, serving population. This domination was supported by the German administration, and by the Belgian administration, until shortly before the revolution. As a result, sharp discontinuities persisted in the structure of the society. It was these discontinuities which Hutu intellectuals stressed in the Hutu Manifesto of 24 March 1957, which acted as a preamble to the revolution. Hutu leaders declared that the sources of conflict lay in the political monopoly by the Tutsi race, a political monopoly which, given the structure of the society, became also an economic, social and cultural monopoly, to the great despair of the Hutu, who saw themselves condemned eternally to the role of subordinate manual workers (Nkundabagenzi, 1961: 22-3).

This picture of discontinuity is a broad structural stereotypic view of the relations between the Hutu majority (about 85 per cent of the population of two and a half million at the time of the revolution) and the Tutsi minority (about 14 per cent).[7] It ignores the many continuities between the sections. As in Zanzibar, power and wealth were the prerogative of a small oligarchy. The mass of Tutsi had no access to power, nor prospect of power. The country was poor, the economy little developed, and based mainly on subsistence agriculture and herding. Foreigners controlled industry and commerce, and these sectors, and agriculture, provided very limited and modest employment for workers and peasant labourers (see Chapter 7). There was only a small professional stratum. Inevitably, many Tutsi lived under the same economic conditions as the overwhelming majority of Hutu. A survey of the standard of living of sample populations of Hutu and Tutsi, excluding however chiefs, sub-chiefs, and functionaries and bureaucrats living in the urbanized zones, showed little difference in the value of subsistence production and monetary revenue, but somewhat greater differences in the production of milk and the distribution of cattle (Leurquin, 1960; see Chapter 7). There was clearly appreciable continuity in standard of living and economic situation.

Continuities in culture must be added to the continuities in standard of living. Maquet (1964: 554) characterizes these continuities as inclusion in a political unity under the authority of the same sovereign, a common language, the sharing, in very large measure, by Hutu of the Tutsi system of values oriented to cattle, and participation in the same economic system. There was some interbreeding, but, in contrast to Zanzibar, without intersectional mobility by

7 I have omitted reference to the small number of Twa.

self-identification and affiliation. The main discontinuities were between Tutsi elite and Hutu, and between Tutsi and Hutu generally in terms of the collective prerogatives appropriated by the Tutsi collectivity. These discontinuities naturally dominated the perspectives of Hutu political leaders in the early stages leading to the revolution.

It was in this context of continuities and discontinuities in structure and culture, that the revolutions took place in Zanzibar and Rwanda, and the problem is whether it is possible to analyse the consequences, for the revolutionary process, of these continuities and discontinuities.

5.

The revolutions in Zanzibar and Rwanda followed very different courses, and they resulted in very different social systems, but they shared in common the expunging of minority racial domination from the structure of the society.

In Zanzibar, on 12 January 1964, about a month after independence, there was a nine-hour revolutionary struggle, confined to Zanzibar Island, in which a small revolutionary force captured the police armouries in the African quarter of Zanzibar City, occupied the radio station and seized the capital. They were led by a Mainland African, John Okello, and they were overwhelmingly Mainland African. It was Okello's deliberate policy to recruit his supporters largely from Mainland Africans. The force included a nucleus of policemen, and again, in recruiting these policemen, Okello was especially interested in men from the mainland; he felt that Zanzibar Africans (i.e. Shirazi) could not be trusted, since they were strongly connected with, and even related to, Arabs on the island, and might well be spies (Okello, 1967: 119).

On the days immediately following the revolutionary seizure of power, violent mobs came out into the streets of Zanzibar City. Their precise composition is not known but they must certainly have been appreciably Mainland African, since large numbers lived in Zanzibar City and its environs (Middleton and Campbell, 1965: 21): they would also have included many Shirazi, more particularly Hadimu Shirazi. There was no revolutionary struggle on Pemba Island.

Arabs were the target group. No reliable information is available of Arabs massacred. Okello (1967: 160) gives a figure of 11,995 enemy and soldiers and persons killed, and 21,462 enemies and stooges detained, as compared with six of his soldiers and 1,631 African civilians killed. Lofchie (1969: 325-6) writes that several thousand Arabs on Zanzibar Island lost their lives, and that the total decrease in the Arab community attributable to loss of life, repatriation and emigration probably amounted to about 10,000 persons. There was looting and burning of Arab and Indian shops and some Indians were killed. Many Arab properties were expropriated.

The inheritors of the revolution were the Afro-Shirazi Party and Umma. Both these parties had been established in the period of sharp political conflicts preceding independence, conflicts Lofchie (1965: 269) describes as characterized by elemental and irreducible racial fears. The Afro-Shirazi Party had attempted to unite Mainland Africans and Shirazi (Lofchie, 1965: 10). Umma was a small radical party, Marxist in ideology, non-African in composition (Lofchie, 1965: 277): it had seceded from the Arab-dominated Zanzibar National Party in 1963. It was a revolutionary party, but there is no way of knowing whether Umma, and the Afro-Shirazi Party, would in fact have organized a revolution against the coalition government of the Zanzibar Nationalist Party and the Zanzibar and Pemba People's Party.

The *Zanzibar Gazette* carries declarations of the policies of the revolutionary government. Presidential Decree no. 5 (25 February 1964) declared the People's Republic of Zanzibar a democratic State dedicated to the rule of law. Presidential Decree no. 6 (25 February 1964) proclaimed that a primary objective of the Zanzibar People's Revolution was to end all economic, social or legal privileges and disabilities which had in the past divided various citizens, and to promote equality, reconciliation and unity: it declared every citizen equally entitled to the rights, privileges and protections of citizenship in so far as duties and obligations of citizenship were assumed, but reserved the power to legislate for special relief or other preference to economically, culturally or socially under-privileged categories. It would seem that the government is developing a socialist programme, with aid from Chinese and Russian communists. Large numbers of Indian civil servants have been replaced by Africans, Indian properties are being expropriated, and Indians are leaving the islands. As to the Arab communities, their power was destroyed in the early period of the revolution.

The Rwanda revolution was more protracted. Luc de Heusch (1964: 424) conceived that the conflict was initially social and thereafter political and that, finally, increasingly, it took a trend towards racial conflict between those described throughout the country as the 'longs' in opposition to the Hutu, the 'shorts'. Lemarchand (1966a: 609-10) draws a distinction between the central region and the northern region, suggesting that the revolution expressed social conflict in the former, and ethnic conflict in the latter.

Prior to the revolution, there had been a slow process of economic change under Belgian rule. Demographic pressure on resources increased as the result of a decline in death rates. The growth of a monetary economy, with the development of cash crops, mining, industry and trade, gave rise to a stratum of wage earners, a rural proletariat. Small numbers of Hutu, educated through the Catholic missions, entered the professions. Reforms introduced by the Belgian administration, and particularly steps taken in 1954 for the progressive abolition of the cattle-leasing contract *(ubuhake)*, had begun to modify the traditional rights of Tutsi patrons over Hutu clients. The economy, however, still rested essentially on subsistence agriculture and pastoralism, with exchange of products, in a traditional system of subordi-nation and clientage.

The catalysts of revolution were the tentative steps taken by the Belgians to democratize the society, and the struggle for power in the movement towards independence. The immediate preamble to revolution was the Hutu Manifesto of 1957. At this time, however, there does not appear to have been a developed 'class consciousness' among the mass of Hutu,[8] though there was an oral popular literature of tales and proverbs which expressed an irony and a realism toward the Tutsi (Maquet, 1964: 558-9), and the cult of Kubwanda presumably symbolized the questioning of the social order (de Heusch, 1964a: 133-46). In the year following the Hutu Manifesto, two Hutu political parties, Parmehutu and Aprosoma, were established. Tutsi leaders responded by founding, in 1959, a Tutsi party, UNAR, with some Hutu participation. This received support from the newly appointed Mwami, who became identified with Tutsi interests. About the same time, Tutsi progressives and Hutu founded a party, RADER, with the goal of reconciling the two enemies.[9] Tutsi-Hutu conflict led to an assault by Tutsi on a Hutu sub-chief, Hutu and Tutsi reprisals and counter-reprisals developing into a Hutu *jacquerie* and a civil war in which rival bands organized for massacre. There began a large scale emigration of Tutsi to Uganda and Tanganyika, and the traditional structure disintegrated in violence. Order was restored by the Belgian administration.

In 1962, after Parmehutu electoral victories and a referendum, the Republic of Rwanda became independent. The government took repressive measures against the opposition parties, both the Hutu party, Aprosoma, and the Tutsi dominated party, UNAR, on grounds of conspiracy with the representatives in exile of the old regime. There were

8 See comments by de Heusch (1964b: 99) on the 1956 elections to the electoral college. The above account mostly follows the articles by de Heusch (1964 and 1964b).

9 D'Hertefelt (1960: 114-35) analyses the political developments immediately prior to the revolution, commenting upon the policies of the political parties. See also d'Hertefelt (1960a: 403-38) and Lemarchand (1962: 333-57).

commando raids by Tutsi over the borders and Hutu reprisals, those following the raid in December 1963 being described by de Heusch (1964: 425) as a veritable genocide. He comments that the Tutsi exiles were divided into at least two factions, one of which resolutely condemned the military incursions across the borders, and that, inside Rwanda, UNAR had broken its ties to the monarchy, and declared its desire to collaborate with the Republic, while the leaders of both UNAR and RADER continuously condemned the Tutsi terrorist raids. Nevertheless, 'according to the technique of amalgamation',[10] all Tutsi were considered to be in solidarity with the extreme wing of the Tutsi exiles. This offered 'le plus malencontreux des prétextes à la politique d'extermination des Tutsi' (de Heusch, 1964: 424).[11]

This was a revolution then of the Hutu, of peasants in mass movements, of militant strata of rural proletariat, and of intellectuals in positions of political leadership. It received much support from the Belgian administration and the Catholic Church. Targets of the revolution were the Tutsi, apparently without discrimination. It is impossible to know how many were massacred. United Nations sources gave an estimate in 1964 of 150,000 refugees in neighbouring territories. These included not only Tutsi but also Hutu serfs who accompanied them into exile. Hutu now hold the positions of power in a one-party State under a government committed to rapid economic and social change, with technical assistance from the West. The constitution passed in 1961, proclaims Rwanda to be a democratic and sovereign State, and asserts the equality of all its peoples, without discrimination by race, clan, colour or religion. Private property is declared inviolable, and all communist activity and propaganda are forbidden.

In practice, the democratic idealism of the constitution is

10 'Selon la technique d'amalgame' (de Heusch, 1964: 424).

11 Roux (1969: 48-62) gives a more sympathetic account of the government's difficulties, referring to the inadequate armed forces, poor communications and complicity of Tutsi within Rwanda.

modified by the persistence of traditional structures in 'the thermidorian syndrome'. Lemarchand (1966) comments that the Hutu leaders made use of the clientage form of relationship, within their own group, for revolutionary purposes; that these types of traditional relationship persist after the revolution in structures of patrimonial power deriving from the President (in much the same way as patronage devolved in the past from the Mwami); and that they persist also in other networks of client relationships, such as the party, the bureaucracy and technical assistance, and in the revival in the north of traditional Hutu structures of clientage based on land tenure. Also at variance with egalitarian norms is the growing discrepancy of income and perquisites between high-ranking civil servants and government officials on the one hand and Hutu peasants on the other, a discrepancy between the new 'ruling class' and the masses undoubtedly wider than at any time during the old regime (Lemarchand, 1966: 322).

Lemarchand (1966: 318) concludes that the ideological guidelines of the revolution have had relatively little effect on Rwandese society, and that the eviction of the Tutsi caste from its dominant position has not been accompanied by major changes in the structuring of roles. However, he qualifies this conclusion by reference to changes in the functions of clientage, and to changes in political structure consequent upon an electoral system with a popular vote, and the introduction of a National Assembly and a 'mass' type of political party.

6.

Continuity and discontinuity were clearly relevant to the course of the revolutions in the two societies. In Zanzibar, the main conflict was between Mainland Africans and Arabs, sections set apart by maximum discontinuity. There was considerable discontinuity between Arabs and Hadimu Shirazi, and this was also a relevant factor. The Hadimu were the section of Shirazi most exposed to expropriation of land,[12] which resulted in an exodus from the fertile areas occupied by Arab plantation owners. Hadimu Shirazi had felt the direct impact of Arab domination and incessant demands for labour (Lofchie, 1965: 40-7). At the same time, there was continuity between Africans and Hadimu in Zanzibar City, where Hadimu migrants became socially and politically assimilated into the Mainland African community (Lofchie, 1965: 250).

On Pemba Island, there was great continuity between Arabs and Shirazi, and this was expressed in the voting behaviour of Pemba Shirazi, and their intermediate and vacillating position in the political struggle. It would seem that their non-involvement in the revolution was related to these continuities. In the case of Mainland Africans, there was more continuity between them and other sections in general mode of life on Pemba Island than on Zanzibar Island, but probably also more social exclusion. Lofchie (1965: 250) writes that on Pemba 'the Mainland African, not the Arab, is more commonly regarded as an alien and an "unknown stranger" '. The fact that Mainland Africans on Pemba Island did not engage in revolutionary violence may be explained quite simply in tactical terms. They were a smaller population than the Arab, and could not count on Shirazi support. In the settlements they established in some of the more remote parts of the north of the island, they formed a series of small communities, each isolated from the others by residence and tribal origin (Middleton and Campbell, 1965: 20). Communications were poor and there was no central focus of power, which the revolutionaries might capture.

In Rwanda, the relevance of continuities may be seen in the varied patterns of revolutionary struggle in different regions. Lemarchand (1968a: 27, 41)[13] mentions strong

12 This is somewhat controversial. See Lofchie (1965: 44-7).
13 See Lemarchand (1966a: 592-610) and d'Hertefelt (1960a: 419).

pro-monarchical sentiments among the Hutu of Western Rwanda, matching the traditional acquiescence of Pemba Africans (Shirazi) to Arab supremacy, and he relates the recent and harsh conquest of the northern Hutu, and the persistence of traditional Hutu authority, to the higher pitch of revolutionary fervour, and the restorative rather than innovative goals, in the north. Peasant *jacqueries* erupted above all in the north (de Heusch, 1964*b*: 108; d'Hertefelt, 1960*b*: 452). Marcel d'Hertefelt (1960*a*: 438) shows that in the 1960 elections, that is after the Hutu *jacquerie*, the revolutionary party drew support from the Hutu, and the traditionalist party from the majority of the Tutsi, but in certain regions also from the Hutu. These continuities, however, or the founding of RADER by Tutsi and Hutu with the object of promoting reconciliation, affected only the course of the struggle for power, and not the final reversal of the power relations between the two groups.

Both revolutions brought about the downfall of dominant racial minorities, but in other respects the results of the revolutions are very different. In Zanzibar, there is a radical restructuring of the society along communist lines, while in Rwanda many of the traditional forms of relationship and authority persist. Perhaps the internal structures of the revolutionary sections, the continuity or discontinuity between leaders and followers, may be relevant. In Rwanda, the intellectual leaders of the Hutu revolt were socially distant from the masses; in Zanzibar, leadership seems to have arisen from the strata which were active in the revolution.

7.

What suggestions then may be derived, from the foregoing

discussion, as to the role of structural and cultural continuities and discontinuities in racial revolutions? Are there grounds for the argument that racial revolutions are distinctive, and that theories of evolutionary and revolutionary change in class structured societies may be somewhat misleading when applied to revolutionary conflict between racial groups?

In retrospect, revolutions often seem inevitable,[14] but in Zanzibar the continuities between Shirazi and Africans, might well have provided a central core for evolutionary change. In any event, in both Zanzibar and Rwanda, the division of labour was quite rudimentary, and Durkheim's theory is concerned with a division of labour moving progressively towards a system of complex, differentiated, interdependent structures. The significance of continuities should be tested in more economically developed societies, such as the racially plural and industrialized societies of the USA and South Africa. Perhaps, under these conditions of greater economic development and interdependence, continuities may more effectively resist revolutionary impulses.

There are obvious difficulties in the application of models derived from Durkheim's theory to the integration of racially and ethnically plural societies, and there are many examples of predictions, based on conceptions of the organic solidarity of interdependence, or of cross-cutting relations, but not fulfilled in situations of racial or ethnic conflict. Thus Himmelstrand in 1966, at a time immediately preceding the Hausa-Ibo conflict, derived from a modified Durkheimian model a prognosis favourable to ethnic integration in Nigeria. Or by way of further example, Le Tourneau (1957: 112, 126), in an analysis of the Muslim cities of North Africa, attributed the greater harmony of relationships in Algeria to

14 The analyst who asserts the inevitability of a revolution which has already taken place thereby claims to demonstrate his own capacity for accurate prediction, albeit that the demonstration is *ex post facto*. There is frequently also an ideological implication in the assertion.

the fact that the French settled inside the Algerian cities, instead of in separate cities as in Morocco; he was obliged to add a footnote[15] regarding the fragility of the inter-ethnic relationships, since the revolution overtook publication.

The application of models derived from Durkheim's theory may be more appropriate to class structures than to racial structures. Class relations are appreciably constituted by the division of labour; they are intrinsic to the social system, arising out of the process of interaction. Race relations, on the other hand, have an extrinsic reference, apart from the interaction,[16] and are less fully defined by the division of labour. To be sure, race relations are also substantially constituted by interaction within the society and they are also substantially intrinsic to the society; and there is generally a very clearly defined discriminatory division of labour, which is fundamental to the structure of race relations. But there is still an extrinsic point of reference, the racial difference preceding the establishment of the society, and being associated, in the great majority of cases, as in European colonization, with cultural differences and pre-existing settled communities: and the content and salience of race relations are generally more extensive and persuasive, ramifying more widely outside the division of labour, than class relations.

The implications of these differences are that revolutions are more likely to be endemic in racial structures than class structures; and that the progressive division of labour, and continuities and interdependence in other social aspects, are less likely to reduce revolutionary potential. The rationale for these implications is as follows.

The horizontal structures of relationship which cut across the initial vertical segments in the homogeneous society of Durkheim's theory, may coincide with them in the racially

15 [9 *bis*] 'Les événements survenus depuis 1954 ont montré la fragilité de la cohabitation algérienne' (1957: 126).
16 See Chapter 2.

plural society;[17] and they may do so, even where the social division of labour is far advanced. Thus in South Africa, where the division of labour is highly advanced, the vertical segments were transformed into politically dominant and subordinate strata. There are, to be sure, many deviations in South Africa from patterns of horizontal exclusion, outside the political domain, as in overlapping of occupational and educational achievement. But continuities in the division of labour do not necessarily modify exclusion and discrimination in other sectors, and South African society has been characterized for a generation by a dialectical opposition between increasing continuity in the economy and increasing rigidity in the political structure,[18] presumably a situation of heightening revolutionary potential.

The first problem then is that the vertical divisions may be transformed into horizontal racial divisions, disconnected coexistence becoming an interdependent structure of domination and subordination. These horizontal divisions would correspond appreciably to class divisions, conceived purely as structures. However, in class structures, the horizontal divisions largely replace the vertical segmentary divisions, whereas in racial structures of this type the horizontal divisions are superimposed upon the initial segmentary divisions. The second problem, in the derivation of a model of evolutionary change from Durkheim's theory, is that at the stage of the horizontal division of the society into a system of stratification, upward mobility has different

17 This corresponds to Weber's description in *Wirtschaft und Gesellschaft* (1922) (see H.H. Gerth and C. Wright Mills, 1946: 189): 'A "status" segregation grown into a "caste" differs in its structure from a mere "ethnic" segregation: the caste structure transforms the horizontal and unconnected coexistences of ethnically segregated groups into a vertical social system of super- and subordination.'

18 The continuing discrimination against blacks, and the extent to which they are excluded in the USA is a further indication of the way in which racial division may persist with the most highly advanced division of labour. For discussion of this aspect, see Chapter 6 and Blumer (1965).

consequences for class structured and racially structured societies.

In the class structured society, upwardly mobile individuals are more likely to be lost to their initial class. In the racially structured society, the upwardly mobile member is still identifiable by the criterion of race. If *upward partial mobility* (Germani, 1966: 372 ff.), in the sense of an incongruity between upward mobility in some statuses, such as occupation or education, and barriers to mobility in other statuses, such as access to power and social acceptance, stimulates revolutionary attitudes, then these are much more likely to develop in racially structured societies, because of the persistence of racial identity, the wider ramifications and more extreme discontinuities of racial status, and the greater likelihood of partial mobility and status incongruity.

A situation which might be expected to generate revolutionary potential at an early stage in the division of labour, is the upward mobility of a small section, say an educated elite, frustrated in aspirations for complete mobility, and having available for revolutionary mobilization, a subordinate racial majority. Even where the division of labour is greatly advanced, and there has been much mobility and increasing continuity, the mobile individuals in systems of race relations are more readily recovered, and may be drawn back into revolutionary struggles by the most deprived strata, as is perhaps the situation in the USA. Racial identity provides lower strata with greater opportunity to recover or neutralize members of their race who are seeking to assimilate or conciliate in a process of upward mobility.

APPENDIX

Tables 1, 2 and 3 below give ratios for landowning, occupation and education, between the proportion of a population to the total population, and the proportion of that population in a particular landowning, occupational and educational category to the total numbers in each of those categories. A ratio of 1 indicates that the presence of a population group in a particular category corresponds to its proportion of the total population. This may serve as a crude measure of some socio-economic inequalities between the populations.

TABLE 1.

LANDOWNING (1948)

Number of clove trees on shamba*	Arabs	Asians	Shirazi	Mainland Africans
3,000 or more	4.07	5.11	0.00	0.00
1,000-2,999	3.32	1.00	0.37	0.81
250-999	3.07	0.85	0.63	0.42
50-249	0.86	0.05	1.37	0.51
less than 50	0.95	0.02	1.23	0.80

* The measure used, for value of the landowning, is the number of clove trees on plantations.

TABLE 2.

OCCUPATIONAL LEVEL OF POPULATIONS
IN NON-AGRICULTURAL PURSUITS (1948)

Occupational level*	Arabs	Asians	Shirazi	Mainland Africans
Upper	0.25	15.70	0.00	0.00
Upper middle	1.54	9.70	0.12	0.39
Middle (non-manual)	1.54	5.46	0.51	0.61
Middle (manual)	0.36	5.72	0.22	2.17
Lower middle	1.01	0.77	1.00	1.11
Lower	0.80	0.15	0.68	2.24

* Upper level is composed of top professional men, senior administrators and owners of large commercial concerns; upper middle level – auxiliary professional workers, retail store owners; middle level – non-manual, uncertified professional workers, clerical personnel and manual skilled labour; lower middle level – vendors, itinerant peddlers and semi-skilled workers; lower level – unskilled manual workers.

TABLE 3.
EDUCATION (1948)

Educational level	Arabs	Asians	Shirazi	Mainland Africans
Standards I-VI	1.80	1.28	0.74	1.00
Standards VII-IX	1.77	6.77	0.24	0.74
Standards X-XII	1.86	7.67	0.06	0.86

Sources: Lofchie (1965: Tables, 5, 6, 8; 1969: Tables, 3, 4, 5), derived from Batson's survey (1948) and figures for numbers in the different population sections.

6

Political Change in White Settler Societies: The Possibility of Peaceful Democratization

White settler societies are notoriously repressive and undemocratic; indeed, among systems of race relations, they are the very embodiment of racial domination and discrimination. We often assume that transformation of their political structures must be violent, and in revolutionary perspectives, the Algerian war represents the prototype of liberation from white domination. It seems impossible to conceive of *internal* social processes in white settler societies which might *contribute** to evolutionary change from racial conflict and oppression towards consensus and democratic participation. Yet, it is precisely this impossible conception that I examine in this chapter, and with particular reference to that most extreme of white settler societies, South Africa. If my conclusions are not encouraging, they may nevertheless invite thought beyond the platitudes of violence.[1] I say 'platitudes of

---

* I should emphasize the use of the word 'contribute' in the statement of my problem, namely, whether internal social processes in white settler societies might *contribute* to peaceful democratization. In posing the problem in this form, I am assuming that, in such societies as South Africa and under such conditions as prevailed there in 1966, when this chapter was written, internal social processes *in and of themselves* would be ineffective means to evolutionary democratic change, and that, in any event, in the contemporary world there is inevitable external involvement in the politics of white settler societies.

1 In *An African Bourgeoisie* (1965), I analyse the increasing commitment to violence and the social pressures towards a race war in South Africa; in Chapter 3 I have commented on some functions of ideologies of violence.

violence', since there is an exhaustive literature demonstrating the inevitability of and necessity for a violent resolution of conflict in white settler societies, and resting on a few axiomatic propositions, such as that the history of freedom is written in blood, which may perhaps be a little misleading both in general, and in the particular case.

My purpose then is to comment on some processes of change in white settler societies as they bear on the possibility of peaceful democratization. I shall take two processes of change. The first is a process of individuation. In terms of social structure, it is a process by which individuals, in certain of their roles, become detached from the original racial matrix and enter into new relationships across racial lines, creating new interracial social structures, formal and informal. In terms of culture, it is a process by which individuals come to share many of the same basic institutions as well as a common language. In political terms, individuation may take a form in which members of the subordinate group are progressively incorporated into the political system on the same basis as the white settlers themselves. The means to this fuller political participation may be a qualified franchise, acquisition of elements of the culture of the dominant group qualifying for citizenship, and democracy extending through incorporation of acculturated individuals. Or the stimulus to extension of rights and to progressive incorporation may derive from common participation in religious, economic, and other institutional structures, and from interracial association and shared interests transcending, at certain levels, the racial cleavages.

The second process, at the collective level, is a process of group confrontation and accommodation, in which there is initially an increasing reliance on the collective organization of racially defined groups, a heightened awareness of racial identity, and a more intense hostility. Politically, it is a process by which the organized power of the subject racial group exacts the right to equal participation. The right to participate may be expressed at an individual level through such means, for example, as universal adult franchise, the distribution of power between the different groups guaranteeing individual participation in representative government; or participation may rest on some communal or consociational basis. But before turning to these processes of change, I must define the main characteristics of white settler societies and describe some of the mechanisms that sustain them.

1.

The term 'white settler society' places the major emphasis on racial difference, on the racial identity of the dominant group, and on the permanence of its settlement. In fact, racial difference (or the imputation of racial difference) is not a prerequisite to the establishment of plural societies, nor are plural societies the exclusive creation of white settlers. Conditions of social cleavage, cultural diversity, and ethnic hostility may be found where the plural sections are of the same race (as in Cyprus) or where the dominant minority is of other than the white race, as in the black settler societies of Liberia and, until recently, of Rwanda.[2] M. G. Smith (1969c), offers much evidence to support his conclusion that 'mere identities or differences of race have no uniform implications for the modes of consociation in such mixed societies'.

Clearly, racial difference has no intrinsic significance. The social consequences derive from the associated cultural meanings and not from the fact of racial difference. There are no doubt unique features in the white settler societies of Africa, but their source is to be found in the conditions of European colonization, in the political philosophies or ideologies of the colonial powers, and in the manner in which structural use was made of racial identity in the constitution

2 See Maquet (1961); Merran Fraenkel (1964); and J. Gus Liebenow (1964: 448-81).

and government of colonial and white settler societies. It is by reason of cultural emphasis and structural elaboration that racial difference now appears to assume independent significance as a major determinant of social relations in white settler societies.

Permanent settlement is, of course, a crucial aspect of white settler societies. Maunier[3] distinguishes between colonies for exploitation, where climate does not permit permanent European settlements, and habitable colonies whose temperate sky is favourable to a European population. A more useful criterion is the intensity of settlement, to which he also refers. In terms of intensity of settlement, we may distinguish colonies of exploitation with a sprinkling of relatively transient administrators, traders, missionaries, and so on, from settler societies with an appreciable settler population.

It is difficult, however, to define what constitutes an appreciable settler population, and perhaps not useful to make the attempt. On the one hand, absolute numbers are relevant.[4] Thus, in Kenya, there were scarcely enough white settlers to sustain claims for dominion status on the South African model, though no doubt the presence of many Indian settlers contributed to the frustration of their ambitions. On the other hand, relative numbers are important, relative, that is to say, to such factors as size of indigenous population, mode of production, level of economic development, and means of control and of warfare. Mercier refers to the appearance of racial competition as indicating that the European group has reached a numerical threshold beyond which opposition to the African group will rapidly become more and more violent.[5] Perhaps this numerical threshold might serve to distinguish white settler societies from societies with white settlers.

3 Maunier (1949: 8).

4 See Georg Simmel's discussion of absolute and relative numbers in 'On the significance of numbers for social life' (1950a: 97-8).

5 Mercier (1965a: 291).

In any event, however this problem of definition is resolved, it seems clear that settler numbers have significant consequences for the structure of the societies they dominate. Large numbers are likely to be associated with greater economic development, diversification of occupational and class structure, increasing competition between members of different plural sections, the aggressive protection and promotion by settlers of their many vested interests, and extensive occasion for interpersonal contacts and relations. Very small numbers may effect little penetration of the society and constitute an almost irrelevant superstructure.

Settlement implies the expropriation or other acquisition of land from the indigenous population, or at any rate the enclosure of land by the settlers. One thinks immediately of the Southern Rhodesian Land Apportionment Act of 1931, which reserved less than half the colony's land for Africans and declared a roughly equal area open to European settlement;[6] the reduction of African landholdings in South Africa to 12 per cent of the total area, or 13.7 per cent if the Native Land and Trust Act of 1936 is fully implemented;[7] the reservation for European settlement of the fine agricultural lands in the White Highlands of Kenya;[8] the large holdings of good land by French settlers in Algeria in contrast with the meagre holdings and the many landless

6 Herbert J. Spiro (1963: 369). There was a small revision of this allocation of land in 1961. See Patrick Kealey (1963: 341-2).

7 Leonard Thompson (1966: 40).

8 Roland Oliver and J. D. Fage comment that small proportions of the populations were affected by settlement or land concessions in areas north of the Zambezi. As to Kenya, they write that among the Kikuyu 'it is likely that those directly affected constituted less than one per cent. Most of the land alienated in Kenya was taken from the pastoral tribes – the Masai, the Nandi, and the Kipsigis. All that white settlement did to the agricultural peoples was to block their natural expansion into land previously held at the spear's point by the pastoralist' (1962: 201-2).

peasants of the Muslim population;[9] or, to cite a parallel from Arab colonization, the acquisition by Arab settlers on Zanzibar Island (in contrast with Pemba Island) of practically all the arable soil, African settlement being confined to remote areas of poor agricultural land.[10]

It is in relation to land that dialectical opposition between native and settler populations is particularly marked. As a direct consequence of white settlement, local peasants are more narrowly confined in their areas, and subjected to a continuously increasing pressure of population on land. The affluence of the white farmlands and the abundance of their produce stand in sharp contrast to the erosion and infertility of the peasant holdings. It must seem to the peasants that settler wealth is the cause of their own poverty. If peasants are indeed the only revolutionary class in colonial countries, as Fanon asserts,[11] then presumably they are conditioned by this dialectical relationship with the scttlers and by their isolation from the interdependence of industrial and urban life.

Constitutional status is certainly relevant to the characterization of white settler societies. Hilda Kuper (1964) follows Moreira in defining the colonial situation broadly as arising 'whenever one and the same territory is inhabited by ethnic groups of different civilizations, the political power being usually exercised entirely by one group under the sign of superiority, and of the restraining influence of its own particular civilization'.[12] Accordingly, she uses the word 'colony' for the genus and distinguishes within it

9 Nevill Barbour (1959: 217-18, 241-5). Basil Davidson writes: 'The situation on the eve of the great insurrection of 1954 was that fewer than one thousand European landowners possessed about one-seventh of all cultivable land outside the barren southern regions, while more than half a million peasant *families* had no land at all' (1964: 39).

10 Lofchie (1969).

11 Fanon (1963: 48).

12 Hilda Kuper (1964: 149-50).

countries where white settlers monopolize power (the Republic and Southern Rhodesia), countries under authoritarian metropolitan control (the Portuguese provinces), countries in which white settlers act on advisory bodies and are jockeying for greater power (Swaziland), and countries where whites have been more restricted in their ownership of land and where metropolitan control is modified by recognition of African interests (Basutoland and Bechuanaland).

This broad approach emphasizes what is common to situations of white domination, while insistence on independent status as a criterion of white settler societies would limit the applicability of the term in Africa to the single case of South African society.

At the same time, independent status is a significant variable with extensive consequences for the political structure of the society and its processes of political change. Both colonial (dependent) societies and white settler (independent) societies may be described as political societies by reason of the very great dominance of the political over other institutions. Perhaps it would be more precise to describe them as characterized by statism, in the sense that the State is dominant in all (or most) sectors of the society.[13] They are in fact constituted by their political institutions and to an appreciable extent they are held together by political regulation. Moreover, the close association between political institutions and settler interests stimulates the settlers to a more intense political involvement in the independent societies. This is true also in the dependent societies as settlers strive for independent status and exercise appreciable *de facto* political control. In the dependent societies, however, the political institutions are an extension of the political institutions of the metropolitan power and derive their strength from this source; outside of self-governing colonies, there is less need for internal elaboration of political institutions. By contrast, in the independent society there is

13 See the discussion of statism in colonial societies in Coleman and Rosberg (1964: 662).

extensive elaboration of the political institutions which sustain settler domination and regulate a great diversity of plural structures and relationships in the interests of that domination. The independent settler society is heavily weighted with political structures generating abundant political process and power.

It is particularly in times of political change that the presence or absence of a colonial power is likely to be a crucial factor. Where there is conflict between white settlers and the indigenous population in a dependent society, the colonial power may add to the destruction by engaging its own military forces in the struggle, as in Algeria, but it may also act in some measure as a mediating third party, as attempted recently in Southern Rhodesia. In independent white settler societies the lack of this mediating role of a third party may increase the probability of civil war and the intensity of exposure to the conflicts of the Cold War.[14] Since I attach so much significance to constitutional status, I will define white settler societies in a pure sense as characterized by independent status; but since I do not wish to be confined to the single case of South Africa on the African continent, I will include in the concept, though in a marginal way and for purposes of analysis, colonial societies with 'appreciable' white settler populations.

White settler societies are further characterized by extreme cultural pluralism. In contrast with racial pluralism, cultural pluralism has intrinsic significance in the sense that objective consequences flow from the fact of cultural difference, regardless of the meanings attached by the actors. At the same time, these meanings are of great social significance. They are particularly responsive to changes in the structure of power, as can be seen in African movements from denigration

14 This greater exposure to the Cold War is perhaps exaggerated, since presumably the countries in whose sphere of influence the white settler society falls would immediately assert a prior right to intervene, in much the same way as the colonial power.

of traditional culture to apotheosis of African personality; and they have played an important ideological role in the political struggles of white settlers. We need to separate the ideological uses of cultural pluralism from its necessary consequences.

Interpretations of cultural difference have been quite central in the philosophies and ideologies of colonization. They sustained the belief in the civilizing mission of the colonial powers, who saw themselves as carriers of the higher values of white civilization to the culturally inferior peoples of Africa, and therefore as justified in exercising domination. They entered into the conception of mandated territories and of trusteeship over subject peoples. They influenced theoretical differences between the French policy of assimilation, with its overriding emphasis on French culture, and the British policy of differentiation, with its greater recognition of traditional African cultures.[15] They provided the rationale in white settler societies for a qualified franchise under such formulas as the vote to all civilized persons, or for total exclusion from democratic rights, on the ground of incompatibility between democratic process and cultural heterogeneity.[16] Indeed, the rationalizations of cultural differences extend over the whole field of social relations: in labour relations, to justify taxation or low wages under a civilized labour policy or forced labour;[17] in commerce, to restrict competition and to control and expropriate;[18] in residence, to segregate, to discriminate in provision of amenity, and to exclude from desirable localities; in religion, to segregate and to discriminate in ministerial stipends and ecclesiastical amenity; and so on, *ad infinitum.*

This pervasive ideological use, however, in no way affects the validity of inquiry into the necessary consequences of

15 Current scholarship increasingly shows the varied and overlapping policies and practices of these colonial powers.

16 See my discussion of 'White ideologies', in Leo Kuper (1956).

17 C. W. de Kiewiet (1942: Chapter 9); James Duffy (1963: 131-2).

18 See Leo Kuper, H. Watts and R. Davies (1958: Chapter 1).

cultural pluralism, though it is difficult to isolate these consequences or even to specify accurately the nature of the cultural differences. Social scientists have often equated the cultural differences in Africa with evolutionary models, again an ideological intrusion, European cultures being represented by the evolved forms of *gesellschaft* and African cultures by the more primary forms of *gemeinschaft*. This comparison, while misleading in many ways,[19] correctly emphasizes the significant aspect of differences in institutional specialization as characteristic, for the most part, of the contact between European and African societies. Balandier, in his analysis of the colonial situation, draws attention to the contrast between 'a rapid-pace mechanized, Christian culture with a powerful economy imposed on slow-moving and radically non-Christian cultures devoid of complex technology, and with a backward economy'.[20] The contrasts can readily be elaborated further. They refer, however, to a system level of analysis, the unit being the cultural system or the institution, and it is important to relate this mode of analysis to the social situation in which contact takes place, as Balandier emphasizes.[21]

On the ground, as it were, and in the context of individuals relating to one another, the cultural incompatibilities may seem very different. Granted that individuals are representative of their cultures, they may practise very selected aspects. The mode of life of the Trekboers in South Africa was more like that of the pastoral Bantu peoples they met than one would suppose from analysis of their respective cultural systems. Moreover, individuals may have a relatively flexible approach to diversity of cultures. To some extent, they may shuttle between cultural sections or they may adopt many elements of a strange culture as a whole, as in mission stations where Africans acquired within a single generation a European language, Christianity, monogamy,

19 Leo Kuper (1967).
20 Balandier (1965: 54).
21 ibid. (46 ff.).

Western education, brick homes, a professional occupation and new forms of community life. At one level there is contact between cultural systems as affected by institutional incompatibility, reciprocal modification, and the growth of new institutions. At another level there are the varied reactions of individuals, conservative or eclectic or mobile, and the redistribution of populations in some measure between cultures, by processes of individuation. In any analysis of cultural pluralism it is necessary to relate these different manifestations.

Cultural pluralism in white settler societies is associated with differential incorporation, to use the term by which M. G. Smith (1969c) distinguishes inter-ethnic accommodations in plural societies. He describes this as obtaining when the structure of the inclusive collectivity prescribes differences in the modes of articulation of particular corporate components. It is quite characteristic of both white settler and colonial domination that there should be a movement of other groups into the societies, by slavery or indenture or free migration. Hence the component sections often include groups other than white settlers and African peoples as, for example, Indians in Kenya or South Africa; and to these must be added sections of mixed parentage. Corresponding to the overriding dominance of political institutions, the mode of differential hierarchical incorporation is essentially political, and the elaboration of differentiation in other structures rests ultimately on political controls. Some groups may be so loosely related to the main structure that they can best be described as inarticulated.

Between the component sections, and related to their differential incorporation, there are social cleavages or discontinuities; and these I select as a final characteristic of white settler societies. I have commented on them in a paper entitled 'Structural discontinuities in African towns: some aspects of racial pluralism' (1967). In particular, I emphasize extreme social distance arising from the convergence of many sources of power in the dominant group; race as a primary basis for stratification, pervading the general structure of the society and all special differentiated structures; and the interaction between the general and special systems of stratification as a further source of extreme social distance, expressed in discontinuities in the wage and employment structure of industry, in stipends and amenity in religion, and in extensive segregation of social relationships. Nevertheless, there are social continuities in white settler societies and many social relationships that cross racial boundaries. They are less marked, however, than continuities of culture, which easily diffuses between groups. In effect, racial, cultural, and social pluralisms have different boundaries, and this non-alignment is a major source of tension in white settler societies.

2.

If I ask what sustains systems of white settler domination, the plain answer seems to be that in Africa they are not sustained. Outside of Algeria and South Africa, there were too few white settlers, either absolutely or relatively, to constitute an effective force. Among the former British territories in Africa, the only independent State with a substantial white settler population (more than 3 million in a population of over 16 million) is South Africa. In Southern Rhodesia, at the end of the Second World War, there were 82,386 whites, in Northern Rhodesia/Zambia 21,907, and in Kenya 24,900; by 1960 these populations had grown to some 223,000 in Southern Rhodesia, 76,000 in Northern Rhodesia/Zambia, and 67,700 in Kenya.[22] That is to say, at the beginning of an era of decolonization and militant African nationalism, the white settlers of these countries were about numerous enough to people small country towns, and in the period of constitutional change, many of them were in fact

22 Figures are from L. H. Gann and Peter Duignan (1962: Appendix).

recent migrants. The decisive roles in the political transformation of the British colonies to independent African States were those of the metropolitan power and of African political movements. I assume this will be true also for Southern Rhodesia, and that the attempt to achieve and maintain independence under white settler domination will prove abortive. In the Portuguese territories of Angola and Mozambique, the domination of the small white settler populations[2][3] seems equally tenuous; in the postwar period, metropolitan power is no guarantee of white settler domination. Independence under settler rule appears to be a necessary, if not sufficient, condition for the persistence of white settler societies.

South Africa is the only example of a relatively enduring white settler society in the British (and Dutch) colonial world. To some extent, we may view South African society, for purposes of analysis, as representing a point in a process of change through initial occupation, followed by intensive settlement and exploitation, to constitutional independence and the development of a seemingly petrified structure of white domination. There were many similarities, for example, in race relations in colonial Kenya, Southern Rhodesia, and South Africa. The diffusion of patterns of white settler domination between the territories, particularly between South Africa and Southern Rhodesia, contributed to these similarities, but they were mainly a consequence of the structure of the situation. This becomes clear from any comparison of white settlers in territories formerly under English dominion with those under French. Though accounts are given in very general terms and may not deal with significant differences in detail, there are many obvious correspondences in white settler structures, attitudes, and relationships as they emerge in, say, Mercier's account of

---

23 According to ibid. (168-9), there were about 160,000 white settlers in Angola in 1959, and about 80,200 in Mozambique in 1957.

Dakar,[24] or Bourdieu's discussion of Algeria,[25] or studies of English and Dutch settlers in the south. At the same time, care is needed in analysing these different settler situations as if they constituted a series. South African settlers had attained independence many years before the growth of strong African nationalist movements, and the difference in constitutional status is quite fundamental.

There is no mystery about the means by which white settlers in South Africa have maintained their domination. They have a preponderance of strength and a monopoly of political power which they have used to build a system of domination resting on the manipulation of social cleavages and cultural diversity. But before examining this system, I want to comment briefly on relations within the white group itself: that is, between the Afrikaans- and English-speaking sections in South Africa.

These sections were of very different culture. Leonard Thompson describes the Afrikaner and British sections as two successive fragments from pre-industrial and industrial societies, respectively, and shows how the Afrikaner fragment suffered a cultural mutation in its isolation from Western thought while the British, though adapting to South Africa, remained loyal also to Great Britain and its culture.[26] Whether the institutions of these two fragments were absolutely incompatible in any objective sense, I do not know. Certainly, many members of both groups saw themselves as representatives of widely different cultural traditions and indeed of different racial stocks, and there was much mutual repugnance and disdain, and much contempt for, and humiliation of, the Afrikaners by the English. Their different roles in the development of South Africa added to these contrasts and antagonisms. The Afrikaners remained embedded in farming and large sections became greatly impover-

24 Mercier (1965b: 163-78).
25 Bourdieu (1962: especially Chapter 6).
26 Leonard Thompson (1964: 178-218).

ished, while the English pioneered in industry and commerce, and prospered.

From this, marked structural discontinuities resulted between English and Afrikaners in most aspects of life, whether measured by distributions between town and country, or in the ecology of the towns, or in income or occupational structure, or by education or prestige. But the discontinuities were not absolute in the sense of excluding individual mobility or social community between the groups, and there were always sections that intermingled, acculturated, and intermarried. Moreover, there was no differential incorporation in the constitutional domain, the Act of Union providing common political institutions for whites.

Political party divisions were primarily between parties of exclusive Afrikaner nationalism, asserting a divisive pluralism of conflict within the white group, and parties of English and Afrikaner integration; but lines of political cleavage have never coincided precisely with ethnic differences. In a very real sense, Afrikaners constitute the political class in the Union (now Republic) of South Africa, and throughout its history they have provided leaders and rank-and-file support for both government and opposition, for exclusive Afrikaner nationalism as well as for white integration.

Now one would probably have predicted a general trend of increasing support for the party of white integration, and a progressive merger of English and Afrikaner by a process of individual mobility. Certainly there were continuing differences in class structure between them, expressed in new forms as large numbers of Afrikaners entered the lower levels of urban employment in competition with African workers; and these differences provided a social basis for distinctive ethnic and racial policies. But on the other hand, there were many circumstances to encourage integration. There were common political institutions affording effective means for evolutionary political change. There was rapid industrialization of the country and opportunity for occupational mobility. There was urbanization, an increasing mutual acculturation, a rising standard of education, and a narrowing of the discontinuities between English and Afrikaner.

On balance, there seems to have been a conjunction of circumstances favourable to integration. This is, of course, difficult to assess with confidence. In any event, it was precisely at this stage that the plural divisions between English and Afrikaner, and the collective principle of ethnic organization, were vigorously reasserted in the systematic fostering by many Afrikaners of social cleavage and cultural diversity, and in the establishment of a wide range of parallel ethnic organizations. For more than two decades, from the celebration in 1936 of the centenary of the Great Trek, Afrikaner nationalism fostered a passionate ethnic sentiment of ingroup idolatry and of outgroup rejection. Relations between English and Afrikaners became fiercely hostile, though always mitigated by many counterpressures of persisting inter-ethnic association and loyalty. In the period immediately prior to and during the early years of the Second World War, the organization of storm troopers among Afrikaners and the general mood of Afrikaner nationalism threatened a violent resolution of conflict. Indeed, the threat of violence between sections of English and Afrikaners finally abated only in 1961, when South Africa became a republic under Afrikaner hegemony.

Whether English and Afrikaner now draw together, it is difficult to say. Certainly, the English accommodate to Afrikaner power and become increasingly committed to the Afrikaner political ideology of apartheid. There appears to be a growing measure of white integration, reflected in political beliefs, the acknowledgment of Afrikaner prestige, and the continuous restratification of Afrikaners into entrepreneurial and managerial positions. But no precise answer is possible without detailed research to determine whether impressions of integration are well grounded and whether integration extends to a wide range of situations. There may be increasing identification in the public domain giving rise to what outside observers like to describe as the monolithic structure of white domination, while cleavage nevertheless persists in the private domain. At the level of English-Afrikaner relations, there may be a continuing and perhaps intense hostility, but at the level of African-European relationships, there may be a relatively high unity of purpose and effort between English and Afrikaners. If, however, the two groups are indeed progressively integrating at the present time, then the process has been a strange dialectic between increasing fission and growing fusion. No doubt, a common life situation in relation to non-whites served to restrain too great a polarization between the white sections (though this hardly seemed to be true in the 1930s and 1940s), and common political institutions provided the means for substantial change in the structure of power and of inter-ethnic accommodation, with little violence.

By contrast, there never were effective common political institutions for white and non-white. The qualified franchise exercised by Africans and Coloureds in the Cape Colony was not without political significance and might have been a means for evolutionary change to a democratic society by a process of individual mobility. But though retained in the Union constitution, the Cape franchise was not extended to the country as a whole. In consequence, it immediately declined in political significance for evolutionary change. After having been exercised for many years and after protracted political struggle, the franchise was finally rendered totally ineffective when constitutional guarantees proved inadequate to prevent its abolition for the African, and its emasculation for the Coloured. In effect, at the level of the constitution or of the public domain, non-white affairs were moved from politics to administration.

Non-whites are now increasingly governed by State departments of African, Coloured, and Indian affairs which insulate them from direct political involvement. They are separated by this system of separate incorporation, which in fact relates them in different ways to the total society. For Africans, there are further systems, both of separate incorporation as ethnic subgroups under Bantu authorities or in Bantustans, and of differential incorporation, in urban areas, white rural areas, and African ethnic areas. In urban areas, the mode of incorporation of Africans into industry may perhaps be likened to the compulsory enrolment of Lozwi into the age-regiments of their Ndebele conquerors, accompanied by political and social inequality and proscription of inter-marriage.[27] In the white rural areas, though the position of African farm workers cannot be described as serfdom, there are bonds to land and master, and the system is perhaps not so remote from the domination of the Tutsi over the Hutu in Rwanda. In the African ethnic areas, Africans are incorpor-ated as collective units, under collective domination through appointed representatives, in contrast with the many personal structures of authority on white farms and in urban areas; the system is perhaps comparable to the domination by Tswana over peoples defeated in war.[28] If there is a close relationship between cohesion and mode of incorporation, then Africans must indeed be greatly fragmented.

The history of the South African franchise, including as it does some manipulation of the African franchise even in the days of the Cape Colony, is often taken as proof of the illusory nature of a qualified franchise in white settler societies, and of the impossibility of evolutionary change by this means. This conclusion, though very plausible, neverthe-less goes beyond the evidence. It must be qualified by reference to the special conditions of the South African franchise: that it was not fully institutionalized in South African society and that the constitutional guarantees for its circumscribed role were not backed by effective power, presumably the organized power of Africans and Coloureds.

Indeed, if there had been a more adequate franchise, albeit qualified, and if Africans and Coloureds had been more politically organized, the changes taking place within South

27 See M. G. Smith (1969c).
28 ibid.

African society and promoting new interracial structures might well have contributed to democratic growth by evolutionary means. I refer to (1) the extensive industrialization of the country, continuously drawing population into the towns and into a common exchange economy, until almost one-third of the African population is urbanized; (2) the increasing economic interdependence of the races and the increasing dependence on non-white labour, which constitutes the great majority of the industrial labour force; (3) the emergence of a small but growing class of African professionals, university graduates, and businessmen; (4) the affiliation of a majority of the total population to common religious denominations; and (5) the growing practice by large numbers of all races of many elements of a common culture. The potential significance of these changes for individual mobility and racial integration may be measured by the large number of laws passed since 1948 which seek to prevent the evolution of a common society by the counter-assertion of the collective principle of racial or ethnic identity as the basis of all social organization and the determinant of life chances.

Abolition of the African franchise effectively removed a common institution by which individual mobility might have contributed to collective restratification on a non-racial basis. It established an absolute monopoly of power and raised the collective principle of organization as a barrier to individual mobility across racial lines. Through control of the public domain, separation is now systematically imposed not only on racial contacts in public life, but on almost all contacts in the private domain accessible to regulation. By the same means, the government seeks to maintain structural discontinuities through regulation of the system of stratification, attempting to ensure that in no circumstances should non-whites exercise authority over whites, providing for wide discrepancies in wage levels and life chances, and generally reinforcing structural separation by pervasive racial discrimination. So too, through control of the public domain, and under conditions in which the populations were continuously moving towards greater cultural uniformity, the government seeks to recreate cultural diversity. For this purpose, it relies on segregation of racial and ethnic groups, on local and regional racial and ethnic organization, and above all on a plural system of education to foster ethnocentric sentiment and cultural diversity. Its policy is to fragment non-white groups and to align social cleavage and cultural pluralism in a self-sustaining system. But the system is far from self-sustaining; on the contrary, it is increasingly sustained by force and repression.

The result is seemingly paradoxical. As the races grow more and more interdependent in the urban and industrial economy, and as increasing contact offers greater opportunity for association, in almost the same measure, the government passes and implements laws against interracial association and enforces separation in an ever-extending range of relationships. But the paradox is only a seeming one. There is too much interdependence to sustain the threat of severance or divisive conflict. In fact, apartheid restructures the society by an elaboration of intercalary institutions and structures, which bind together, as with hoops of steel, the units-in-separation.[29] Whether the process is likely to be a continuous and increasing binding together until the groups suddenly explode in violence, a revolution through integration, or whether this binding together may generate more gradual processes of change, I do not know.

3.

I now return to the main problem and inquire what processes

---

29 I have analysed a variety of structures for the maintenance and bridging of structural discontinuities in 'Structural discontinuities in African towns' (1967). I describe intercalary structures as structures inserted, or forming, between the dominant and subordinate racial groups, which serve both to separate and to co-ordinate their activities.

might contribute to a relatively peaceful democratization of white settler society, as I have sketched it – *in extremis*, as it were. I examine first the individuating processes, such as acquisition of the culture of the dominant group by members of the subordinate group or mutual acculturation of individuals of different race, and association between them across racial divisions, creating new interracial structures in the economic, political, religious, educational, and recreational spheres. These are the individuating interracial processes by which sharp distinctiveness between groups becomes blurred, initially at the margins and later more pervasively: lines of structural cleavage and cultural pluralism increasingly diverge; individual status and group status no longer precisely coincide; and interracial solidarities begin to modify and fragment the initial racial solidarities. These are the processes by which roles become diversified; and individuals are released from their original collective affiliation in certain of their roles and affiliate with members of other collectivities. These are the processes that liberals value in the belief that men may transcend the material and group conditions of their lives and that their actions are not simply functions of their social situations. These are the processes valued also by many churchmen, concerned as they are with individual salvation and change of heart. And I should add that these are the individuating processes so contemptuously dismissed as of negligible significance for change in white settler societies by such a weight of authoritative opinion, and with such a weight of seemingly supportive evidence, that it is almost embarrassing to mention them. Yet *naïveté* is perhaps as valid a basis for inquiry as the absolute conviction of certainty; and it is all the more necessary to raise questions about convictions of this type, since they may have grave consequences for the probability of violence in plural societies, actually contributing to the events they predict, and thereby demonstrating, not the inevitability of violence or the necessity for it, but quite the contrary, that men have a capacity for self-determination.

Revolutionary leaders often portray the society in terms of an absolute polarity between white settlers and native peoples. They describe the groups as virtually two orders of humanity ranged in absolute dialectical opposition; between the collective destiny of the oppressed and the unyielding collective domination of the oppressors, they find no middle ground for individuating interracial processes; and they see evolutionary change as an illusory device for more complete, if less blatant, servitude.[30] These descriptions may have some validity, but their function is not to contribute towards academic discourse and analysis. They are ideologies, like Marxist ideologies of the polarization of society into bourgeoisie and proletariat, and they create or seek to create in the future that which they portray as immediately present. The relevance of these revolutionary ideologies for my argument lies, not in their characterizations of white settler society, but in the fact that their emergence counteracts the individuating processes, which indeed become a special target for attack.

The scholarly argument for denying significance to association and cultural assimilation of individuals of different race rests on conceptions of the structure of white settler society, and on assumptions about human nature in general, or white settler nature in particular. As to the structure, two aspects are stressed: first, the relation between collective categorization or organization and interpersonal interaction, and secondly, the relation between the type of change, such as assimilation of culture or occupational mobility, and the basic principle of differential incorporation, such as racial or ethnic identity. Some references to the literature will clarify the argument. M. G. Smith in an earlier paper writes that cultural uniformities, or intersectional personal association, cannot directly erode or transform the corporate structures for the reason that sectional divisions and relations are based on other principles, such as race or exclusive corporate

30 See Chapter 3.

solidarity; in a plural regime, he argues, individual qualities are irrelevant for the determination of social identity, which is ascriptive and corporate in base and significance.[31] So too, Pierre Bourdieu in *The Algerians* (1962) stresses the structural aspects when he comments that the colonial situation is the context in which all actions must be judged, and that in this context it would appear that even the most generous actions, including harmonious interpersonal relations between individuals of different groups, have harmful consequences.[32]

Herbert Blumer is presumably arguing to much the same effect when he concludes that industrialization, far from changing the patterns of racial discrimination prevalent in the society, actually adapts to them, nestling inside the established order, and that political pressures and change are necessary to transform racial discrimination in industry.[33] At a somewhat different level and in a different context, Ezekiel Mphahlele proceeds from similar assumptions when he declares that the Church in South Africa

with its emphasis on the value of the individual personality, has continued stubbornly to bring outmoded standards to the situation; a situation where a powerful *herrenvolk* has for three centuries done everything in the interests of the *volk*. Where persons have been oppressed as a race group, the Church has sought safeguards and concessions for the individual, evading the necessity and responsibility of group action.[34]

The argument that the structure of the situation divests the individuating processes of significance for evolutionary change needs to be supplemented. It is not logically complete in itself; it does not explain why these individuating processes cannot result in action to restructure the situation. It is at

31 M. G. Smith (1969*b*).
32 ibid. (148-9).
33 Blumer (1965: 220-53).
34 Quoted in Leo Kuper (1965: 207).

this level that the argument may be supplemented by assumptions as to the nature of man and of human groups. Perhaps I can make some of these assumptions explicit. To explain the motivation of man, I shall take a quotation from a discussion by Robert Michels of leaders:

> The consciousness of power always produces vanity, and undue belief in personal greatness. The desire to dominate, for good or for evil, is universal. These are elementary psychological facts.[35]

For explanation of the nature of human groups, I shall turn to the Austrian sociologist Ludwig Gumplowicz, who viewed the State as characterized by the domination of one social group over another and by the incessant struggle for power between social groups:

> In its political actions each social group is a perfect unit. It opposes other social groups on behalf of its own interest solely and knows no standard of conduct but success. The struggle between social groups, the component parts of the State, is as inexorable as that between hordes or States. The only motive is self-interest.

Moreover, since each social group in its political actions is a perfect unit, the individual is again without significance:

> Though there are always individuals who deviate first one way and then the other, they, like meteoric stones which are loosened from their orbit and fly off in all directions, are abnormal, and do not influence the behaviour of the group as a whole.[36]

Perhaps most social scientists would deny the universality of these motivations to power and strife. Some may accept them only as characteristic of societies other than their own, or more particularly of white settler groups. They may discern, as does Mannoni,[37] a specific settler mentality, a

35 Robert Michels (1962: 206).
36 Ludwig Gumplowicz (1963: 227).
37 O. Mannoni (1956).

'Prospero complex' of pride, neurotic impatience, and the desire to dominate, deriving only in part from the colonial situation itself. Or they may derive the settler qualities from the social situation, from the nature of interracial interaction within the society, and from the mutual incitement of prejudice and discrimination,[38] and find the psychological roots predominantly in structural determinants. Pierre Bourdieu, for example, argues that the rationale of the colonial system renders conversion of the dominant group impossible:

The destruction of the colonial system cannot be the result of a conversion of minds which would induce the members of the dominant society solemnly and collectively to give up the privileges they hold in order, by a conscious choice, to 'integrate themselves' willingly into the dominated caste or to 'integrate it' into their caste, which would mean the same thing if we ascribe to the words their full meaning. This conversion can only be the act of a few 'traitors to their caste'. The whole rationale of the colonial system tends, on the contrary, to make this sort of collective suicide impossible.[39]

But whatever the derivation of the social and psychological attributes, they are seen as a reinforcement to the collective barriers against the individuating processes of change.

My comments on these theories can only be impressionistic. I see the individuating processes as potentially significant in bridging the plural divisions. It is for this reason that they are often denounced in white settler societies. They create new interracial structures and solidarities and they undermine the sense of colour, of racial exclusiveness, on which domination depends. Now, by significance I do not mean to imply that the individuating processes in and of themselves can resolve racial pluralism in white settler societies. It is not enough that the original racial cleavages should be overlaid with numerous interracial relationships and functional differentiations. Though the new relationships effect continuous change in the structure of the society in

38 See Leo Kuper (1965*b*: 237-47).
39 op. cit. (150).

many different spheres, these changes must still be transposed to the collective or public domain. This follows from the mode of differential incorporation of the ethnic and racial groups. Where ethnic differentiation is purely *de facto*, it is presumably directly transformed by a *de facto* coming together. But in white settler societies there is *de jure* incorporation of racial and ethnic differentiation in the constitution of the State, and in its elaborate, centralized, political and administrative structures. If the individuating processes are to contribute effectively to the transformation of divisive pluralism, then they must act directly on the central political system. And it is precisely at this level that the obstacles are most formidable, since the central political system is the basis of settler domination. Certainly, Marx's concept of the State as the executive of the ruling class describes its role in independent white settler societies.

Characteristically, the franchise becomes the battleground, as settlers seek to exclude other groups from its exercise. Of Algeria, Barbour writes that 'in 1936, the proposed Blum-Violette reforms which would have given French citizenship to 30,000 Muslims were brought to nought by the resignation of the Algerian Mayors; meanwhile the project had, it seems, raised real enthusiasm among the Muslims for acquiring French citizenship. Its rejection was the final death-blow to assimilation.' He comments that the Statute of 1947, providing *inter alia* for the creation of an Algerian assembly, did offer hope of a peaceful solution, but was never sincerely or completely applied, the elections of 1948 being 'managed' by the administration with the apparent intention of excluding 'extremists', while other provisions remained a dead letter, in consequence of which 'the Muslims rebelled in desperation'.[40] In Rhodesia, the elaborate complexities of the constitution and the unilateral declaration of independence from the metropolitan power reduce to the simple formula of a white settler struggle to control electoral and

40 op. cit. (222-4).

legislative power. In South Africa, opposition by the northern provinces limited the non-white franchise from the very inception of union, and thus prepared the way for its virtual abolition. But it is important to note that much of the struggle over the franchise in South Africa was between different sections of the white electorate, which at no time formed a 'perfect unit';.and it is interesting to speculate what the course of race relations might have been if Afrikaner-English tensions had sharpened to the point at which the English would have sought a political alliance with Africans, or if the metropolitan power had still retained the right to intervene during the recent constitutional struggles.

The difficulty goes beyond the fact that interracial solidarities must be transposed to the central political system if they are to be effective means for change in the differential incorporation of the races. Control over the political system gives the dominant group the power to maintain racial cleavages, at least initially, notwithstanding the social pressures towards 'deracialization'. The government responds to conditions that generate interracial solidarity by increasing the rigidity of racial differentiation in the political sphere, and it opposes the individuating processes in other spheres by reasserting the collective principle of racial identity, in the extreme case through systematic legislation and penal sanctions.

The dialectic between the individuating interracial processes and the collective racial processes is clearly charted in the many South African apartheid laws that seek to reverse trends towards non-racial integration. This is of special interest because South Africa is the most highly industrialized of the African territories, and it is often assumed that industrialization will encourage change towards democracy. It raises the standard of living of white settlers and provides them with more abundant and secure opportunity for rewarding employment. This greater prosperity for whites does not entail deeper misery for non-whites, since the relationship of the races in the industrial process is not dialectical. Non-whites also advance in living standards, albeit unequally, and begin to move to higher occupational levels, thus reducing the discontinuity in white and non-white occupational structures and providing some basis for shared interests, transcending race. These are changes that might perhaps be viewed as conducive to a diminution in racial extremism.

At the same time, industrialization heightens the competition between the races. The South African government's policy of racial job reservation is evidence of the competitive pressure caused by the increasing movement of non-whites into occupations calling for higher levels of skill, not only manual but also entrepreneurial and professional. This competitive pressure may be expected to grow with continued industrialization. Now it is experienced in a situation in which white settlers control the political system. If the white sector of employment in the economic system is abstracted and represented as a hierarchical structure, I assume that it will be broadly based, comprising that majority of white settlers which follows manual, minor clerical, and administrative occupations or engages in small retail trade. It is this majority that feels the increasing pressure of non-white competition and the need for protective racist policies. But since white working class and petty bourgeoisie constitute a powerful force in the political system, including a majority of voters, they are certain to attract political leaders and supporters from other strata to their racist ideologies, which in any event have a wide independent appeal.

This then is the basis for the dynamic movement in South Africa towards more extreme racism. As the economic process generates competitive pressures, so counteracting political processes are released in an attempt to restore equilibrium by increasing the racial repression of the system.[41] As I see the position in South Africa, industrialization gives rise to

41 See van den Berghe (1965c: 183-216).

tension between the political and economic systems, and this tension is resolved by an increasingly rigid emphasis on racial differentiation. These may well be only the early consequences of industrialization, and continued industrial growth may release democratizing tendencies, but the extensive discrimination against Negroes in the highly industrialized society of the United States should temper too easy an optimism.

Given white settler domination with independent status and the numerical predominance of Africans, the system of parliamentary representative government seems highly resistant to democratization and calculated to inflame ethnic and racial antagonism. There may ·be more flexibility and a greater potential for evolutionary change in structures of domination based on tributary relations or on serfdom.

At this stage, the introduction of a qualified franchise in South Africa would hardly resolve any of the major conflicts in the society. It might serve to incorporate more fully a small section of non-white bourgeoisie, but it would not effect a redistribution of land or of wealth and the masses would continue in their exclusion and impoverishment. Yet, even the reintroduction of a political mechanism, quite traditional in the constitutional history of South Africa, would constitute revolutionary change. There is a fundamental difference between the structures of the economic and political systems. The economic system, under the process of industrialization, tends increasingly towards continuity in structure. The political system, on the other hand, is quite discontinuous, in the sense that it consists of two absolutely distinct orders: there are white voters who are subjects of political and administrative action, and, with token exceptions, non-white non-voters who are objects of political and administrative action. Change in the economic sector can proceed gradually, almost imperceptibly. Political change in the principle of racial exclusion, even if it should take the seemingly evolutionary form of progressive admission to the franchise, would constitute revolutionary change, more particularly since many white settlers would immediately project the qualified franchise, and the demographic ratio of the races, into a plural society under African domination, and no doubt many African political leaders would do the same. The parliamentary system in racially divided societies is calculated to intensify the politics of race.

There is the same disjunction between the individual processes of structural change and the political processes; indeed, the relations between economic and political change, discussed above, are a particular expression of this disjunction. Under present constitutional arrangements, it is difficult to discern a political basis for action which might relate the individuating processes to constitutional change. Political parties based on white voters with non-white participation are not in themselves likely to be effective agents of political change. Political parties of non-whites with some participation by white voters may be more effective. Both are, of course, proscribed. It would seem that only large-scale movements of racial collectivities could offer the possibility of mustering sufficient power to change the conditions of political incorporation. Non-white collective action resting on the unity of the oppressed is improbable because the oppressed are not united, and such minority groups as Indians and to a lesser extent Coloureds are as vulnerable to the power of Africans as to the power of whites.

In these circumstances, it is inevitable that there should develop, in response to exclusive Afrikaner nationalism, a movement of exclusive African nationalism. This may hold some promise for a more democratic interracial accommodation, though initially sharpening the racial conflict; but Africans are so fragmented by their different life situations and their different modes of incorporation that they may not be able to mobilize effectively even by means of racial violence. In any event, in the absence of common political institutions, such as English and Afrikaners shared, and in the absence of a mediating third power, the direct confrontation of organized racial groups with a long history of conflict and oppression between them seems likely to complete the transformation of South Africa into a garrison State or to precipitate holocausts of violence and destruction.

4.

My conclusions, then, are that the collective processes of racial organization and confrontation may well be ineffective; also, they increase the probability of extreme violence, whereas I am here inquiring into the possibility of a peaceful transformation of white settler societies. Of course, this puts the problem in too stark a form. It might be approached more realistically in terms of the degree of violence or in terms of policies that might diminish the violence of political change. There are likely to be most complex relations between violence and non-violence, between revolutionary challenge and reactionary response and between parties of racial radicalism, emphasizing the collective processes, and parties of integrative moderation, concerned with the individuating processes. Democratic changes may progressively emerge from these complex interactions.

Regarding the possibly liberalizing consequences of the individuating processes, a crucial difficulty lies in the discontinuity between these ongoing social processes, promoting new interracial solidarities, and a political system under racially exclusive domination, promoting repressive, racist counteraction. Formidable barriers insulate the political institutions against liberal interracial influences. By these conclusions, I do not mean to imply that the individuating processes are without significance, even in the racially extreme Republic of South Africa, or that the racial groups are polarized. On the contrary, I tend to assume that the total polarization of groups in a society is a rare phenomenon. Groups appear to be polarized in revolutionary ideology, which sweeps aside the mediating structures and the individuating processes. They appear to be polarized, at times, in academic analysis, since we seem inclined towards dualisms and dichotomies. Probably extreme polarization is most nearly attained in the course of, and through the process of, the struggle itself. Where the struggle has finally taken the form of racial or ethnic civil war, in our preoccupation with the predominant and overriding forces we tend to overlook harmonious relations that might have been the basis for other developments. Yet these inter-ethnic and interracial relations may be appreciable, even in societies where there is extreme ethnic and racial discord. I am sure that they are also appreciable and significant in South Africa, in consequence of a long history of contact and of interaction in schools and churches and in industry and commerce.

I have examined the individuating processes in terms of the obstacles to their being politically effective, arising in particular from the constitutional structure of the society. It may be more constructive to approach these processes from a different point of view and to consider the means by which they may be rendered politically effective for change from racial domination to democratic participation. I assumed from the outset – and this assumption should certainly be qualified by reference to a relatively immediate period of time – that internal social processes would not be sufficient in and of themselves to transform the political structure of South African society. In distinguishing processes of change in colonial and white settler societies, I emphasized the role of the metropolitan power in the colonies and the absence of a mediating third party in the independent white settler societies.

Now it is inconceivable in the contemporary world that third powers should not be involved in the internal conflicts of other societies, particularly where these conflicts are between racial groups; and they are already so involved in South African society. England and the United States have large and growing investments in the country, and therefore an interest in orderly processes of change. Independent African States have declared their determination to liberate fellow Africans in South Africa and their intention to use violence for that end. The United Nations has denounced South African racism for almost two decades and explores the possibility of applying sanctions. On the one hand, there is a massive involvement of third parties opposed to racism and, on the other hand, there are internal processes stimulating interracial association, with increasing pressure under the influence of industrial growth. Perhaps under certain creative constitutional arrangements and in association with such a mediating power as the United Nations, acting in a role analogous to that of the metropolitan power in colonial society, the individuating interracial processes may provide a basis for relatively peaceful democratic change.

7

Theories of Revolution and Race Relations

1.

Most contemporary theories of revolution are derived from the analysis of conflict between social classes in racially homogeneous societies, and they may not be very illuminating when applied to situations of revolutionary struggle between racial groups. This is the problem I discuss in the present chapter, and my purpose, in general, is to raise some questions concerning the applicability of theories of class revolution to racial revolution.

The main source of many of these theories is the Marxist theory of revolution as a product of a dialectical process of polarization between classes, defined in their relationship to the means of production, and I shall deal with it in the more general terms of the role of economic stratification in racial revolutions.

I shall define revolution as a form of 'internal war'[1] in which there is a violent assumption of power and substantial change in the structure and values of the society.[2] I shall exclude from the concept of revolution used in this chapter internal wars between sections which occupy roughly the same level in the hierarchy (as for example Ibo and Hausa), and struggles for liberation from colonial rule, save where the

1 Following Eckstein's use of internal war, namely 'any resort to violence within a political order to change its constitution, rulers, or policies' (1954: 133).

2 See Bienen (1968: Section 3) for critical comments concerning the emphasis on change in conceptions of revolution.

structure of the colonial society comprised also a settled racially distinct dominant section (as for example, a stratum of white settlers or of pastoral ruling aristocracies). Thus, the cases of racial revolution (or attempted revolution) I have in mind include the revolution of Hutu against Tutsi in Rwanda (where the Belgian tutelary power supported the domination of the pastoral Tutsi over the agricultural Hutu until almost the final stage of independence), the revolution of Africans against Arabs in Zanzibar (where the British supported the Sultan and the Arab oligarchy), and the revolutionary movement of Africans and Indians against white domination in South Africa in the period 1948–64. The Algerian revolution, even if it is viewed as a revolution involving ethnically, but not racially, different groups, is also relevant, since it has provided a model for racial revolutionary struggle.

2.

If a major theme in revolutionary theory is the Marxist dialectic in the economic process, resulting in the polarization of classes, the variations on this theme appear to exhaust almost every logical possibility.[3] There are theories of a predisposing condition in the immiserization of the masses, or in economic advance,[4] or in economic growth

3 See Eckstein (1965: 136-40) for a discussion of the somewhat chaotic abundance of hypotheses about the etiology of revolutions, and his listing of different emphases on 'intellectual' factors, economic factors, social structure and social mobility, political factors, and such social processes as rapid or uneven social changes. See also the comments by Aron (1965: 250 ff.) on the different emphases in Marx and Tocqueville, both explaining political conflicts in terms of social conflicts, but Tocqueville maintaining 'the specificity, at least the relative autonomy, of the political order'.

4 Olson (1963: 543) makes the interesting point that there is nothing inconsistent in saying that both rapid economic growth and rapid economic decline would tend toward political instability, and that it is economic stability that should be regarded as conducive to social and political tranquility.

followed by recession, or in the disjunction between desire (or aspiration) and reality, or in the tension between the processes and relations of production (such as has characterized South African society for over a generation). What these situations have in common is that they involve disequilibrium, between classes as in the immiserization of the masses, or within a class, as in the disequilibrium resulting from economic progress followed by recession. The theories may then be reduced to the more basic theory that economic disequilibrium is a precondition, or precipitant, of revolutions between classes. Since classes are defined in economic terms, or largely in economic terms, the basic theory may be somewhat tautologous.

In regard to the relevance of these theories for racial revolutions, two extreme positions may be taken. The first position attaches overwhelming significance to economic relations, arguing that racial discrimination is only found in association with economic exploitation, and that racial conflict is simply a particular expression of class conflict. The causes of racial revolution are therefore the same as those of class revolution, for example, polarization of the races in their relationship to the means of production. The second extreme position emphasizes the absolute primacy of the racial structure. Racial revolutions are viewed as inherent or endemic in structures of racial domination, opportunity being the precondition or precipitant. From this perspective, economic change is somewhat marginally relevant to the preconditions or precipitants of revolution.

There is a long-standing and continuing controversy between advocates of these different perspectives. In the USA, shortly after the Second World War, Cox (1948) sought to establish the origins of racial discrimination in the growth of capitalism, and to demonstrate that black and white workers shared common class interests. In the USA today, the failure of black and white proletariat to combine, and the clashes of interest between them, lend support to the contrary view of many black revolutionaries that the conflict is essentially racial.[5] There is a similar controversy in the interpretation of African revolutions, which take the manifest form of racial conflict. Marxists find in these a class basis. Thus, with reference to Zanzibar, Bochkaryov (1964: 13-15), writing in *New Times*, charged that the British colonial administration and the imperialist press sought to interpret as racialist, a revolution which arose out of class differences and was directed against the big landowners and the Sultan. Rey, in the *New Left Review* (1964: 31), viewed the revolution in Zanzibar as a social, not an ethnic, revolution, carried out by groups representing, first and foremost, the Zanzibar City proletariat, but supported after the revolution by a general rallying of all the exploited against the Arab ruling class. In South Africa, these different perspectives of the society in terms of class or race were influential in the political division of Africans into two parties, the African National Congress being more Marxist in its ideological orientation, while the Pan-Africanist Congress emphasized the primacy of racial discrimination against Africans (Leo Kuper, 1965: Chapter 23). Fanon (1963: 32-3), examined this problem of class and race, no doubt largely in the context of the Algerian revolution, and emphasized the racial aspect, but with a complex lyricism, which gives an elusive quality to his meaning. Standing Marxism somewhat on its head (the phrase used in the translation is that Marxist analysis must be 'slightly stretched'), he argued that:

In the colonies the economic substructure is also a superstructure. The cause is the consequence; you are rich because you are white, you are white because you are rich . . . It is neither the act of owning factories, nor estates, nor a bank balance which distinguishes the governing classes. The governing race is first and foremost those who come from elsewhere, those who are unlike the original inhabitants, 'the others'.

5 See Timothy Ricks (1969: 21-6) and Cruse (1968: Chapter 10) for a discussion of some aspects of this controversy in the USA.

3.

Both aspects of Fanon's paradox, 'you are rich because you are white' and 'you are white because you are rich', are in fact inaccurate. But they do bring out a basic problem in the controversy, namely the difficulty of clearly distinguishing racial divisions from class divisions, and hence the difficulty of assessing the relative significance of class and race in racial revolutions. In the abstract the terms are quite distinct: race refers to physical differences, whether measured by 'objective' criteria or by social definitions, and class refers to socio-economic differentiation, whether defined by 'objective' measures such as the relationship to the means of production, or by social perception. In the concrete situation, however, it may be difficult to differentiate the two structures. Race and class divisions generally overlap. Race and class may be closely related genetically, since a system of stratification which is socially defined as a class system, may have originated in a system of racial stratification, the contemporary class differences coinciding appreciably with racial differences, as in many Latin-American and West Indian societies. And separation of the phenomena may be further complicated by the presence of socio-economic differentiation within each of the racial divisions. The problems raised by this merging of the phenomena can only be resolved partly. They are the empirical basis for the ideological controversy, whether racial stratification is epiphenomenal and simply a particular manifestation of class stratification, or whether racial differences provide an independent basis in the genesis and persistence of social stratification.

If racial divisions and class divisions coincided, so that, for example, the whites in a particular society were all members of the bourgeoisie, and the blacks were all members of the proletariat or peasants, some insight into the relative significance of race or class could no doubt be derived from a comparison of revolutions in such societies with revolutionary struggles between social classes in racially homogeneous societies. Where economic differentiation and racial stratification are in some measure divergent, as in the contemporary revolutions involving racial groups, interpretation becomes exceedingly complex.

The two recent revolutions, in Zanzibar and in Rwanda, may serve as an illustration of some of the complexities of the relationship between race and class, or race, class and caste.[6]

In the Protectorate of Zanzibar, comprising Zanzibar and Pemba Island, the main racial and ethnic sections were the Shirazis, Mainland Africans, Arabs and Asians; there were also small numbers of Comorians, Goans and Europeans. The total population, according to the 1958 census, was some 299,000, comprising over 165,000 on Zanzibar Island, and almost 134,000 on Pemba Island. The Shirazis were the largest section, constituting in 1948 over half the population on both islands (see Table 1, below). The Shirazis, who claimed that they had intermingled with Persians who migrated to Zanzibar in about the tenth century, most nearly correspond to indigenous African groups. The second largest section was Mainland African, comprising in 1948, almost one-fifth of the total population, that is 25.1 per cent of the population on Zanzibar Island, and 12.1 per cent on Pemba.[7] Figures are not available for 1958, but in that census, 10.9 per cent of the population on Zanzibar Island and 6.7 per cent on Pemba were shown as born on the East African mainland: most of these would be Mainland African. The

6 See Lemarchand (1968*a*) for an analysis of the problem of revolutionary change in racially or ethnically stratified societies.

7 See Zanzibar Protectorate (1953: 11-12). There are difficulties in specifying the numbers of different sections in the 1958 census, since the 'racial grouping' is Afro-Arab, Asian other than Arab, European, Somali and other. Political agitation had preceded the census, and some persons, at the instance of political parties, returned themselves as Zanzibaris (see Zanzibar Protectorate, 1960: 17). Composition of the population had probably not changed greatly since 1948.

foreign born population in general was an older population, 81.4 per cent being over twenty years of age as compared with 51.1 per cent of the local born, and had a higher sex ratio, 215.9 males per 100 females as compared with 101.7 (Zanzibar Protectorate, 1960: 32, 35). The indications therefore are of an appreciable adult male African migrant population. The Arab population, which included a variety of Arab groups, was the third largest section: in 1948, Arabs comprised 16.9 per cent of the total population, i.e. 9.3 per cent on Zanzibar and 26.7 per cent on Pemba (Zanzibar Protectorate, 1953: 2, 4). Mainland Africans, that is to say, were almost three times as numerous as Arabs on Zanzibar Island, whereas on Pemba Island they were less than one-half the number of Arabs. Finally, Asians, mostly Indians and some Goans, comprised 6.1 per cent of the total population in 1958, the great majority residing on Zanzibar Island, and indeed in Zanzibar City (Zanzibar Protectorate, 1960: 18, 21).

Zanzibar economy rested largely on the marketing of cloves, and on subsistence agriculture and fishing. There was some employment by government, some development of commerce, but little in industry, and that mainly in the processing of foods.[8] Cloves, the main export, were uncertain both as a crop and as a commodity. There was an appreciable seasonal immigration from the mainland for the picking of cloves, most of the plantations being located on Pemba Island. The dependence of the economy on cloves was such that decline in the world market for cloves created a serious economic crisis for the government, and resulted in a reduction of social services in the period immediately preceding the revolution.

It is difficult to give a clear picture of the distribution of resources and occupations among the different sections. The image of Arabs as senior bureaucrats and large plantation

8 For figures of employment in government, commerce and industry, see Zanzibar Protectorate (1963: 11-12).

182   *Race, Class and Power*

TABLE 1.
DISTRIBUTION OF POPULATION, ZANZIBAR PROTECTORATE, 1948*

Section	Zanzibar Island		Pemba Island		Total Zanzibar Protectorate	
	No.	%	No.	%	No.	%
Arab	13,977	9.3	30,583	26.7	44,560	16.9
Indian and Goan	13,705	9.2	2,187	1.8	15,892	6.1
Mainland African	37,502	25.1	13,878	12.1	51,380	19.5
Shirazi	81,150	54.2	67,330	58.8	148,480	56.2
Other	3,241	2.2	609	0.6	3,850	1.3
Total	149,575	100.0	114,587	100.0	264,162	100.0

* Source: Zanzibar Protectorate (1953: Tables 1 and 15). A small number of persons who did not state their tribal origins, I have classified with Mainland Africans.

TABLE 2.
LANDOWNERSHIP IN ZANZIBAR BY RACIAL COMMUNITY, 1948

Number of trees	Percentage of Parcels				Total Number of Owners
	Arab	Asian	Shirazi	Mainland African	
3,000 or more	68.8	31.2	—	—	240
1,000–2,999	56.1	6.1	20.2	17.7*	570
250–999	51.9	5.2	33.8	9.1	3,635
50–249	14.5	0.3	74.2	11.0	13,680
Less than 50	16.0	0.1	66.6	17.3	10,250

* This figure, which represents 100 Mainland African landowners, was recorded entirely in Pemba.

owners, of Indians as merchants, and of Africans, both Shirazi and Mainland, as fishermen, cultivators and labourers is of course quite false. Most Arabs, Shirazis and Africans were poor, and there were many poor Indians. What can be said is that senior bureaucrats and many of the large plantation owners were Arab, that merchants tended to be Indian, that most of the cultivators and fishermen were

Shirazi, and that most Mainland Africans were either employed as labourers in Zanzibar City, where many of them lived, or they were occupied as squatters or seasonally in clove-picking. There was, however, considerable overlapping of the occupations followed by members of different sections. Middleton and Campbell (1965: 39) comment on an intermingling of Arab and Shirazi plantation owners on Pemba Island, but not on Zanzibar Island. Lofchie (1969: 293–309) examines landownership (measured by number of clove trees), occupational distribution and access to education in the year 1948, when a survey was conducted; the tables he presents show appreciable overlapping. Lofchie concludes 'that Zanzibar's major communal groups were differentiated by economic and social status' and that 'Zanzibaris of different races did not share sufficient common occupational or economic interests to create politically meaningful bonds of solidarity across racial lines' (306). But it is here that difficulties begin to arise, since the figures show similarities between the different sections,[9] and there is need for a valid measure of similarities and differences in socio-economic situation (occupation, landownership and education) and for a valid methodology for drawing conclusions as to their political significance.

The population of Rwanda at the time of the revolution was some 2.5 million, predominantly Hutu (about 85 per cent), ruled by an aristocracy drawn from the Tutsi (totalling about 14 per cent) and including small numbers of Twa. The sections varied somewhat in physical characteristics, perceiving their differences in terms of racial stereotypes.[10]

9 Tables 2, 3 and 4 are here reproduced (Lofchie, 1969: 303-5).

10 I am following Maquet here, but I do not know how adequate his evidence is. Maquet (1964: 553) writes of the differences between Hutu and Tutsi that they were distinct, 'enfin par leur apparence physique: les Tutsi étaient grands, minces, au teint clair; les Hutu, de taille moyenne, trapus, de peau foncée. Tels étaient au moins les stéréotypes acceptés par tous les Rwandais même s'ils ne se vérifiaient que chez certains individus.' The Twa are pygmoid.

The country was, and continues to be, exceedingly poor and densely populated.[11] Its economy rested essentially on subsistence farming and herding. Leurquin (1960: Part 1) writes that productivity was greatly limited by geographic environmental factors, by ignorance, by poor health consequent upon malaria, intestinal parasites, tuberculosis, dysentery and malnutrition, by the rudimentary techniques of hoe cultivation and by the social and political order. With a narrow margin over bare subsistence, famine constantly threatened. Coffee was the main cash crop and export. There was little urbanization, the most important agglomeration having a population of about 20,000, and little industrialization, that being mainly in mining. Foreigners largely controlled both industry and commerce. The different sectors of industry, commerce and agriculture provided some employment for, on the one hand, the 'proletarized worker, torn from his tribal roots, living only from his work . . . and, on the other hand, the peasant labourer, the occasional plantation worker, the roadman's or foreman's often undependable day worker' (Belgian Congo and Ruanda-Urundi Information and Public Relations Office, 1960: 16). About 54,000 were so employed in 1958. In addition, there was a small professional stratum.

The nature of the distribution of resources between the sections is conveyed by the description usually applied to Rwanda, namely caste or feudal society. Maquet compares the relationship between Tutsi and Hutu to that between nobles and peasants in the *ancien régime*, or, in certain respects, to the relation between industrial capitalists and proletarian workers in Europe in the nineteenth century (1964: 552). The two sections were distinguished by their hereditary occupations of agriculture for the Hutu and pastoralism for the Tutsi. In fact, many Hutu looked after cattle and many Tutsi were not engaged in pastoral activities,

11 In *Rwanda Carrefour d'Afrique* (May-June 1967: 21), the caption to a photograph of a child beside a banana tree quotes the dictum: 'sous chaque feuille de bananier se cache un Rwandais'.

TABLE 3.

OCCUPATIONAL DISTRIBUTION IN ZANZIBAR BY RACIAL COMMUNITY, 1948

Percentage of Workers

Occupation Level	Arab	Asian	Indigenous African	Mainland African	Total Number of Workers
Upper	4.2	95.8	—	—	120
Upper middle	26.0	59.2	6.3	8.5	710
Middle (non-manual)	26.1	33.3	27.3	13.3	5,400
Middle (manual)	6.0	34.9	12.1	47.0	1,735
Lower middle	17.1	4.7	54.1	24.1	35,160
Lower	13.5	0.9	36.9	48.7	14,635

TABLE 4.

ACCESS TO HIGHER EDUCATION IN ZANZIBAR BY RACIAL COMMUNITY, 1948

Percentage of Students

Educational Level	Arab	Asian	Indigenous African	Mainland African	Total Number of Students
Standards I-VI	30.4	7.8	40.2	21.6	12,205
Standards VII-IX	29.9	41.3	12.8	16.0	1,440
Standards X-XII	31.4	46.8	3.2	18.6	620

The figures are for 1948, and though they are the best available, they relate to a period some fifteen to sixteen years before the revolution.

TABLE 5.

COMPARISON OF THE VALUE OF SUBSISTENCE PRODUCTION AND OF MONETARY REVENUE, QUANTITY OF MILK CONSUMED, AND DISTRIBUTION OF CATTLE PER FAMILY – FOR TUTSI AND HUTU IN RWANDA AND URUNDI IN THE PERIOD SEPTEMBER 1955-AUGUST 1956.

Category	Value of Subsistence Production (Francs)[1]	Value of Monetary Revenue (Francs)[2]	Production of Milk (Litres)[3]	Distribution of cattle by region[4]					
				Rwanda				Urundi	
				Vallée de l'Akanyaru	Bwana-mukare	Nduga	Kinyaga	Buyenzi	Mugamba
Tutsi	4,439	2,795	181	2.6	1.2	2.4	1.6	1.9	0.5
Hutu	4,249	2,189	66	1.7	0.7	1.2	0.5	0.3	0.2

Sources: All figures are from Leurquin (1960).
[1] Table 26, 203.
[2] Table 50, 278.
[3] 229-30.
[4] Table 45, 263.

but, nevertheless, a Hutu was always a man of the hoe, and a Tutsi a man of the cow (Maquet, 1964: 553). Economic and political relations were organized in such a way that rights over cattle provided some exemption from manual labour for the Tutsi.

Maquet, drawing on an analogy to the concept of surplus profit in Marxist class analysis, argues that the system was possible by reason of an agricultural surplus: he was obliged to add, however, that agricultural production was very little above the subsistence level, and that both surplus and malnutrition often coexisted (1964: 554). The Tutsi appropriated the agricultural 'surplus' by the effective monopoly of government, the imposition of the corvée and of heavier taxes on the Hutu, and the system of clientage through which the client, in exchange for protection and the use of cattle, undertook to render services and produce to his patron.[12]

Given the low level of economic productivity, there could not have been a great difference in standard of living between many Tutsi and Hutu. The Tutsi however constituted the privileged section. They provided the ruling class, the aristocracy of wealth, the warriors; they appropriated the control over cattle, and they enjoyed a more favoured position than the Hutu in the system of clientage, though Tutsi were also involved as clients in a hierarchical system which extended throughout the society. But the near monopoly by the Tutsi of power, privilege and wealth was an attribute of the Tutsi viewed as a collectivity. Seen as individuals or as family units, in their daily routine, there was considerable similarity between Tutsi and Hutu in material conditions of living.

Leurquin (1960), in a careful study of the standard of living of the rural populations of Ruanda-Urundi during the period from September 1955 to August 1956, provides some measure of similarity between Tutsi and Hutu in terms of

12 *Rwanda Carrefour d'Afrique* in a discussion of the animal resources of Rwanda quotes the Tutsi proverb: 'Toi, vache qui m'épargne la honte et la fatigue de la houe' (April 1965: 8).

subsistence production, daily consumption of food, distribution of cattle, monetary revenue, and expenditure. His sample of six regions included four regions in Rwanda. Traditional authorities, from whom a measure of collaboration was necessary, traders with large establishments at the beginning of the inquiry, and persons living in indigenous towns and non-traditional centres ('centres extra-coutumiers'), were excluded from the study (132-3). Thus the sample excludes chiefs and sub-chiefs, almost entirely Tutsi, and the functionaries and bureaucrats living in the urbanized zones, also predominantly Tutsi (203, 250, 277-8). These were the categories of rich Tutsi (278).

The most important economic sector for the sample population was production for subsistence which contributed two-thirds in money value, while revenue from the money economy contributed one-third (179, 274). Table 5 provides a comparison between Hutu and Tutsi in the sample population, in Rwanda-Urundi: where Leurquin gives separate comparative figures for Rwanda and Urundi, these are shown.

The figures given in the table are averages, but it is clear from the relatively small differences between Tutsi and Hutu in the annual value of subsistence production (4,439 francs as compared with 4,249 francs per family) and in the annual value of monetary revenue (2,795 francs as against 2,189 francs per family) that there must have been considerable continuity and overlapping of standards of living in the two sections. The main difference is in the annual production of milk (181 litres per family compared with 66 litres) and in the distribution of cattle (2.6, 1.2, 2.4 and 1.6 per family as compared with 1.7, 0.7, 1.2 and 0.5 in the Rwanda regions).

Leurquin (1960: 203-4), in summarizing the position, comments that the material superiority of Tutsi over Hutu is always established by reference to the holders of positions of authority, that is chiefs and sub-chiefs, and civil servants, categories virtually excluded from the sample. He points out that the cleavage: Tutsi = pastoralism = riches, Hutu = agriculture = poverty has ceased to be always true. In regions where an artisan category had developed, or where coffee plantations had multiplied, there were to be found rich Hutu, while Tutsi small-owners of cattle, deprived of their prerogatives and obliged to tend the soil, often proved to be mediocre cultivators: in a group of forty families studied at Karama, eighteen Tutsi of thirty-four possessed no cattle and in Rukoma a Tutsi died of hunger, because he had no servants and had never learnt to cultivate. Leurquin comments that the modest advantage enjoyed by Tutsi in the subsistence economy seemed to be concentrated in certain sectors, the most marked being in the production of milk. 'Pour le reste, les différences de caste ne suffisent plus aujourd'hui à expliquer les différences de revenu en milieu rural.'

4.

Among the many difficulties of interpretation which flow from the lack of correspondence between racial and economic differentiation, there is first of all the problem of the differential impact of economic change on different strata within each of the racial sections. Then, in view of this diversity within each racial section, there is the problem whether it is meaningful to define the racial sections as entities. What is the relationship between collective attributes and individual situation? In what sense were the Tutsi the dominant caste in Rwanda, or Arabs the ruling stratum in Zanzibar? Finally, there is the problem of the disjunction between the objective situation and the perception of it, facilitated precisely by the lack of coincidence between racial and economic differentiation.

First, in regard to economic change, it cannot be assumed that the consequences are the same for all members of a social class, and such general measures as economic growth and *per capita* income may be quite misleading in the analysis of class structures.[13] The assumption of a uniform impact of

13 See Oberschall (1969) and Olson (1963: 529-52).

economic change on members of a racial category may be even more misleading in the analysis of racial structures. The economic position of professionals and businessmen of the subject race may continue to improve, while that of the workers remains constant or deteriorates: or the position of the urban proletariat may improve, and that of the peasantry deteriorate. Similarly, the economic changes may have quite varied consequences for different strata in the dominant group. It is possible that the crucial stimulus which serves as a catalyst of revolution is some particular combination of these consequences for different strata within the dominant and subordinate racial sections.

The second difficulty arises from the equating of collective attributes with individual attributes. Thus, it is a very common practice among scholars, as well as laymen, to describe Indians in East Africa or South Africa as a trading class. The position varies in the different countries from situations in which most trade is (or was) in Indian hands, as in Zanzibar, to situations in which Indian trading is a negligible portion of the total trade, as in South Africa. In the case of Zanzibar, there is no published information regarding the distribution of occupations among Indians at about the time of the revolution, though there is earlier evidence, in a proposal for a survey conducted by Batson in 1946, that 'among the Indians there are a great many petty traders who are as poverty-stricken as the natives or even more so, and undernourishment exists, particularly among the Hindus' (1948: 26). Most Indians at that time were engaged as uncertified professional workers, clerical personnel, skilled and semi-skilled workers, vendors, itinerant peddlers and unskilled labourers (Lofchie, 1965: 88-9). Clearly the fact that the main traders and financiers in Zanzibar were Indian by no means constitutes Indians as a trading class. In South Africa, the great majority of Indians are working class and poor. In what sense then can they be described as a trading class? If Indians, as a category, are legally entitled to acquire the means of production in some areas of South Africa, and if in fact a few Indians have started industrial enterprises and a larger number have entered into commerce, does this constitute a class of Indian bourgeoisie? If the criterion is the theoretical possibility of mobility into the ruling stratum, or the legal right to acquire productive property, then the Marxist distinction between bourgeoisie and proletariat would be quite meaningless outside of such countries as South Africa, where the laws largely deny Africans the right to acquire productive property.

Similar problems arise with reference to the Tutsi in Rwanda and the Arab oligarchy in Zanzibar. The fact that the rulers were Tutsi or Arab, and monopolized positions of power traditionally and under colonial administration, by no means implies that these qualities of power of the dominant caste or oligarchy inhered in the rank and file of impoverished Tutsi or Arabs. Nor do the attributes of Tutsi or Arabs viewed as a collectivity necessarily affect the class situation of commoners. And yet in certain circumstances, as for example in the type of society van den Berghe characterizes as 'Herrenvolk Democracy' such as South Africa and the USA (1969: 73), the attributes of the racial section clearly affect the situation of the individual members of that race. Thus the monopoly of political power by whites in South Africa so sharply differentiates the economic position or life chances of white and black workers that they can hardly be regarded as sharing a common class situation.[14] The relationship between collective and individual attributes is clearly an

14 I have taken the position here that black and white workers in South Africa do not share a common class situation, because of the political power enjoyed by whites. Alternatively one may argue that in terms of Marxist theory of class struggle and revolutionary change, many black and white workers do in fact perform the same function in the production process, and do share a common class situation, but do not come together in an interracial working-class movement because of the racially privileged position of whites. In both types of interpretation the racial division is crucial. This is discussed in Appendix I.

empirical question, requiring systematic analysis and more refined categories than such descriptions as Tutsi dominant caste.

The perceptions of the structure of the society may be at least as significant in the revolutionary process as the 'objective reality' and they may be quite varied in their relationship to that reality.[15] Indeed, part of the revolutionary struggle consists essentially in a conflict of ideologies, and the attempt to mobilize sections of the population behind particular perceptions of the structure of the society. The very complexity of the relations of race, class and caste in a society, and the diversity of positions within the structure of that society, would encourage these varied perceptions. If Mainland Africans in Zanzibar perceived Arabs collectively as racial oppressors, or if Hutu peasants perceived Tutsi collectively as a dominant caste, what significance is to be attached to the fact that the great majority of Arabs and Tutsi did not share in the enjoyment or in the exercise of wealth and power, and had no prospects of access to wealth and power?

5.

Given the complex interrelations between racial and economic differentiation, and the consequent problems of interpretation, is it possible to test the relative significance of racial factors and of economic factors? Perhaps, the distinction used by Dumont (1966: 17-32) between the encompassing principle and that which is encompassed may be helpful. Thus, when Lofchie (1965: 10) writes that the Afro-Shirazi Party, which had attempted to unite Mainland Africans and Shirazi in Zanzibar, was motivated by a resentment of the Arab oligarchy, a resentment 'which expressed itself in virulently anti-Arab propaganda and in the publicly expressed desire of ASP leadership to transform Zanzibar into an African-ruled nation', he would seem to be describing a

15 See Chapter 2.

situation in which the encompassing principle is that of race. It can only be by virtue of this encompassing principle that an antagonism against a section of the Arabs is expressed in antagonism against all Arabs. So too, when Africans and whites in South Africa see Indians as wealthy traders, when most Indians are working class and poor, it can only be by reason of a transformation of perception in terms of a general encompassing principle of racial stratification: in an objective situation, where some Indians are traders, the subjective perception is that all Indians are traders. Similarly in Zanzibar, where most trade was in Indian hands, the categorization of Indians as traders involves the transformation of the attributes of individual Indians into the attributes of Indians as a collectivity. Again, the encompassing principle is race, and the description of Indians in Zanzibar, or East Africa generally, as traders, though seemingly a description in terms of class, is in fact a racial categorization.

There are obviously very great difficulties in attempting to determine which is the encompassing principle and which the encompassed. In the context of revolutionary change, two measures may be suggested. The first measure relates to the target group, the persons actually killed by the revolutionaries, whether persons of a particular class, or persons of a particular race and class, or members of a particular race, regardless of class. Presumably where revolutionary violence expresses itself in the indiscriminate slaughter of members of a racial group, then the encompassing principle is race. The second measure is that of the precipitating events, in terms of differences between impulses affecting racial differentiation and activating racial conflict on the one hand, and impulses affecting economic differentiation and activating class conflicts on the other. This is a more dubious measure, since subjective factors enter into the interpretation of the precipitating events by the analyst, and into the perception by the participants themselves of exacerbating events in the prelude to revolution. The measure is certainly more ambiguous than a counting and racial identification of corpses.[16]

In the Zanzibar revolution, the encompassing principle appears to have been racial. The initial revolutionary assumption of power was effected by a force made up largely of Mainland Africans on Zanzibar Island. Thereafter, Mainland Africans on Zanzibar Island came out in violent support of the revolution, with the participation of Shirazi, more particularly the Hadimu Shirazi who had been most affected by Arab occupation. Arabs were slaughtered, regardless of class.

Economic change appears to have been of little significance. Prior to the revolution, there was extreme economic stagnation as a result of a decline in Zanzibar's market for cloves, and schools had been closed and welfare programmes cut back (Lofchie, 1965: 273). But the market for cloves was always variable, and previous crises had not led to revolution. Moreover, about 85 per cent of the cloves were produced on Pemba Island (Middleton and Campbell, 1965: 35), and the revolutionary activity was on Zanzibar Island. Middleton and Campbell (1965: 40-2) refer to changing economic relationships among farmers on Zanzibar Island, expressed in competition between Africans, Shirazis and Arabs in the marketing of food crops; but this competition was between Africans and Shirazis as well as with Arabs. There was, however, a common class situation for Shirazi and African squatters in their relations with Arab landlords.

In Rwanda, the complex interweaving of race, ethnic group, caste and economic differentiation served to stimulate varied interpretations as to the dominant or encompassing principle. There was, for example, the declaration by Hutu leaders in their Manifesto of March 1957, that the question whether the conflict was a social or racial conflict was a literary question, and that it was in fact both one and the other

16 However, counts of corpses in revolutionary contexts are exceedingly unreliable. Le Tourneau (1962: 350) comments in relation to the Algerian rising in 1945, that 'les discussions statistiques autour des cadavres sont aussi vaines que dérisoires'.

(Nkundabagenzi, 1961: 22). Here the implication is that racial or economic differentiation could not be separated out as an encompassing principle. Tutsi students at Lovanium University, on the other hand, argued that the problem must be social because if it were racial, this would mean that all the Hutu were oppressed, and all the Tutsi oppressors, whereas, in fact, the great majority of Tutsi (99.9 per cent) were entirely without political, social, cultural or other privilege (Nkundabagenzi, 1961: 107). The argument perhaps carries the implication that the encompassing structural principle is a division between a small Tutsi oligarchy and a mass of oppressed Tutsi and Hutu. But the fact that many Tutsi were as underprivileged as Hutu by no means necessarily implies that racial division was not perceived as the encompassing principle or that it could not become the encompassing principle in the unfolding of the revolution. Luc de Heusch (1964), in his analysis of the revolution, in fact asserts that it did become racial, in the sense of emphasizing physical differences, during the course of the struggle. It is possible to derive from this the suggestion that the racial hierarchy was the encompassing principle, because it is otherwise difficult to understand why the struggle should ultimately have taken a racial form.

There was certainly a process of economic change in Rwanda as a result of action by the Belgian administration for the suppression of the clientage system, the development of cash crops and wage employment. Lemarchand (1966a: 602) argues that the entire political structure collapsed with the abolition of clientship, ushering in a bitter struggle for supremacy between Tutsi and Hutu. Economic change was clearly relevant for the role of the rural proletariat and intellectuals. But the conflict was not between economically differentiated groups, but between the two collectivities of Tutsi and Hutu. The actual empirical socio-economic differentiation which cut across the division between Tutsi and Hutu was encompassed within a more general principle, opposing Tutsi and Hutu as collectivities, whether by racial, ethnic and/or caste criteria. The targets of the revolutionary uprising were Tutsi, again apparently without discrimination in terms of economic position, and the precipitating events were such as to activate Hutu and Tutsi in a struggle for power, and not economically differentiated strata in Rwanda society.

In neither Zanzibar nor Rwanda, did the revolutions arise out of an economic polarization of classes, or increasing immiserization of the masses, or in economic growth followed by recession, nor are the revolutions to be explained by economic advance. The economy in Zanzibar was stagnating and there had been a decline in the world market for cloves. In Rwanda, there was some econcmic growth, the development of new economically differentiated strata, and some modification of traditional patterns of economic relationship. But the struggle was not between sections defined by economic criteria; it was a struggle between racial or ethnic sections, stimulated by democratization and the movement towards independence.

6.

However fundamental racial differences may be in particular societies, it is clearly impossible to develop a general theory of society and history based on racial differentiation, as was possible with class differentiation. Nothing could be more absurd than the proposition that the history of all living societies is the history of racial struggle. Racial difference has no intrinsic significance. Even when it is present in a society, as an objective fact, it may not be relevant in social relationships; and where it is recognized as relevant, its significance is highly variable, depending entirely on the way in which it is socially elaborated.

Under certain circumstances however, race may come to have a primary significance in the social structure. Demands for civic rights by a racial section are accompanied by labour disturbances, school and trade boycotts. An accident involving people of different race sets off racial rioting. Race is so woven into the fabric of the society that conflict between races in one situation or structure immediately ramifies to a wide range of situations and structures, whether related or unrelated; and conversely, a conflict on non-racial issues is readily transformed into a racial conflict. Racial consciousness becomes acute, and racial identity becomes the basis for political organization.

These are societies, characterized by a high degree of racial pluralism,[17] in which there has been an elaboration of racial differentiation into an encompassing principle. The structural basis of this elaboration and pluralism would seem to be 'differential incorporation', a system of racial stratification in which the racial sections are incorporated into the society on a basis of inequality (Kuper and Smith, 1969: Chapters 4 and 13). This may be *de jure*, as in South Africa where the constitution denies Africans the franchise, or largely *de facto* as in the USA. It is associated with segregation, with unequal access to power, status and material resources, and often with cultural differences, resulting in sharp discontinuities between the racial sections. Issues of conflict are superimposed on each other, lines of cleavage tend to coincide, providing the social basis for the escalation of conflict from minor incidents.

For analysis of revolutions in this type of society, it may be useful to develop hypotheses on the assumption that change in racial status is the crucial variable, in much the same way as hypotheses have been developed regarding the crucial role of economic change in revolutions between social classes. Thus the propositions in Section 2 of this chapter, dealing with theories of economic change as predisposing factors in revolution, would yield a range of propositions, one or other of which might be used to explain particular racial revolutions with some plausibility. The predisposing conditions might be found in increasing racial subordination

17 See Kuper and Smith (1969: Chapter 14).

and discrimination (corresponding to immiserization of the masses) or in the advancing status of the subordinates, or in the disjunction between aspiration and reality, or in the tension between *de facto* racial interaction and mobility, on the one hand, and *de jure* separation and rigidity on the other. No doubt, in some cases, several of these propositions might be applied with equal plausibility to the interpretation of a particular racial revolution.

But the emphasis on either race or class invites an ideological commitment. If class is seen as the major determinant, then racial differences are subordinated to the role of a dependent variable, as in the theory that they provide the bourgeoisie with the means for a more thorough-going exploitation of workers of the subordinate race, by a process of dehumanization. If the emphasis is on race, then Marxism may be declared irrelevant to the black experience, or the significance of class differences may be minimized.

The more promising perspective would be to assume that these racially plural societies are in certain respects somewhat *sui generis* and that theories of revolution derived from the analysis of revolutions in racially homogeneous societies cannot readily be applied to societies in which there is differential incorporation of racial sections. Rather, an approach should be developed which analyses the revolution-ary process in terms of the interrelations between class and race, between economic and racial differentiation.

This is an approach which is becoming well established in the analysis of ethnic conflicts in Africa. Thus Balandier (1965a: 140) sees the crises in African States since 1960 as determined by two sets of facts, namely the resurgence of old antagonisms, notably tribal and religious, and the struggle for power between members of the directing class (the *dirigeants* and the *bureaucrates*). Le Tourneau (1962) systematically analyses the role of different classes (Muslim bourgeoisie, both traditional and modern, proletariat, peasants) in the conflict between the indigenous peoples of Algeria and the French. Sklar (1967: 1-11) examines class factors in the ethnic conflict in Nigeria, arguing that the activating force was an intra-class conflict between sections of the bourgeoisie, who set the ethnic groups against each other in the interests of their own struggle for power. While Sklar is concerned to show the significance of the class factor, his argument may also be interpreted from the point of view that the social force which provided the raw power for the conflict and made it possible was the force of ethnic antagonism. The position would be similar to class conflict in Marxist theory, in which the raw power is the antithetical relationship of sections to the means of production, but in which leadership may be governed by a different principle.

If a general theory of racial revolutions is to be developed, it is not sufficient simply to demonstrate that a conflict of classes, or a process of class formation, was interwoven with the racial conflict. There is need to develop a set of propositions concerning the interrelations of economic and racial stratification in revolutionary change, as Fanon (1963) attempted in his controversial theory of the revolutionary role of peasants in the colonial situation. The two main variables would relate to economic development and stratification on the one hand, and to racial structure on the other. Presumably revolutionary potential and process will be affected by the nature of the economy, whether highly industrialized as in the USA, or rapidly industrializing as in South Africa, or largely subsistence pastoralism and agriculture as in Rwanda, or combining dependence on a major marketable crop with subsistence agriculture and a stagnating economy, as in Zanzibar. Similarly, racial structure will affect revolutionary change, with extreme racial division being represented by the systematic development of differential racial incorporation, as in South Africa. If, in addition to consummated revolutions, revolutionary movements are included, such as those in South Africa and the USA, then there is a sufficient range of cases available to cover wide variations in economic and racial structure.

7.

My initial assumption was that theories of revolution derived from the analysis of conflict between social classes in racially homogeneous societies might not be very illuminating when applied to situations of revolutionary struggle between racial groups. Indeed, I would argue more positively that the theories may be quite misleading in the context of racially structured societies. In the rapidly industrializing society of South Africa, working-class movements across the racial boundaries between whites and Africans have been negligible, and white workers have strongly supported the government in its racially oppressive apartheid policies. In the USA, under conditions of the most advanced industrialization, there are tensions between the races as white workers resist movements by black workers for equality of participation; white workers constitute a conservative stratum in race relations, and black and white workers have not come together in a significant working-class movement. As for the Zanzibar and Rwanda revolutions, I have presented discussion in this chapter to suggest that the encompassing principle was racial rather than economic, and that economic change was not the catalyst of revolution.

Of course, I do not question the very great significance of economic factors in racially structured societies. I would suppose that wherever there is racial stratification there is also economic stratification. The relations between them may be conceived as a continuum. At one extreme, racial and economic divisions tend to coincide, as in the initial stages of colonial domination. At the other extreme, perhaps purely hypothetical, there has ceased to be stratification by race, and racial differences, though present, are no longer salient in a system of stratification based on differences in economic status. Between the two extremes fall those societies in which both racial and economic stratification are present, but do not fully coincide. This is the more general case in the contemporary world, and the one with which I deal in the present chapter.

As a result of the intermingling of race and class, and of incongruities in racial and economic status, the situation is ambiguous and encourages different perspectives and ideologies. The consequences of this ambiguity may be seen in the vacillating policies of communist parties committed to a theory of revolution which is non-racialist and obliged to come to terms with racially based nationalist movements. The ambiguity is often expressed in divergent political tendencies among racially subordinate groups, a dualism in political parties, committed either to accommodation and reform, or to radical opposition and revolution. At the level of the dominant racial group, the ambiguity may be expressed in conflicting theories of economic change, as for example, the theory that the creation of a bourgeoisie among the subordinate race would be counter-revolutionary, or conversely, that it would be the catalyst of revolution. In social theory, the ambiguity may be resolved by distillation into two extreme theories, either that the causes of racial revolution are the same as those of class revolution, namely polarization of the races in their relationship to the means of production, or alternatively that the racial structure is primary and economic change somewhat marginally relevant. And it is precisely because of the ambiguity in the intermingling of class and race, that ideologies assume an added significance as directions to perceive the society, and to act, in terms of racial or class perspectives.

If the problem of the relevance of theories of revolution between social classes for the interpretation of racial revolutions is not to be left at the level of ideological preference, or in the form of a projective test into which the analyst pours his own inclinations, there is a need for comparative studies. The main variables would be different forms of economic structure and stratification, and of racial structure and stratification. This chapter stresses in various contexts the salience of subjective perceptions and it is necessary to analyse these perceptions and the ideologies in which they are conveyed. The historical dimension is also an essential aspect for analysis of the changing salience of class and race in periods preceding the revolution and during the course of the revolution itself.

In this way, it may be possible, by the comparative study of revolutionary struggles between racial groups, to test the argument in this chapter, that under certain conditions of racial pluralism, such as characterized Zanzibar and Rwanda, the racial divisions are the propelling force in the revolutions, the predisposing factors are those that affect racial status in any of its many social dimensions, and the dialectic of conflict is essentially racial.

8

Race, Class and Power: Some Comments on Revolutionary Change

1.

Such is the power of early conditioning, that it is only after many years of reflection that I have come to question the universality of the class struggle. Economic exploitation, and an intimate relationship between economic and political power, may be almost universal. But there are some societies in which the relationship to the means of production does not define the political struggle, and in which class conflict is not the source of revolutionary change.

I have in mind societies which have come to be known as plural societies.[1] This was the term applied by Furnivall to colonial tropical societies, and extended more generally by M. G. Smith to describe societies in which there are deep social and cultural cleavages. They are often characterized by racial (or ethnic) difference, and they were typically constituted by conquest and colonization, or by the introduction of slaves or indentured workers. In interpreting these societies, M. G. Smith stresses inequality in the political incorporation of the different sections as of primary significance. And it seems to me that the racial (or ethnic) structure itself, including the mode of differential political incorpor-

1 See the discussions in Leo Kuper and M. G. Smith (1969). I prefer to conceive of the relations between the different sections in terms of the extent of pluralism, as measured by a variety of indices (Kuper and Smith, 1969: 473-9). In the present context, I am using the term plural society to describe societies characterized by an extreme form of racial and/or ethnic pluralism.

ation, is the crucial variable in the analysis of revolutionary change in these societies, and that it is a source of great confusion to interpret the political conflict between the racial or ethnic sections, in terms of class struggle and the relationship to the means of production.

Some indication of the perplexing nature of racially (or ethnically) plural societies, when interpreted in terms of the class struggle, may be found in the ambiguities and ambivalences of Communist Party policy. How is the Communist Party to define its policy in a racially plural society where different sections of the working class are sharply divided by reason of the racial structure of the society? How is it to relate to white workers who perceive their interests as antagonistic to black workers, and who demand a colour bar in employment and other repressive legislation? And if the Communist Party turns away from the white proletariat and supports a black republic, or a black nationalist movement, what is the theoretical basis for this policy in class theory? If it is not a matter of expediency, but based on the assumption that the class struggle must be waged at a later stage when national or racial liberation has been achieved, then presumably class divisions are not the critical element in the initial liberatory struggle? Does this impose a need to revise the Marxist theory of revolution? Quite apart from any theoretical implications, what practical problems does the Communist Party face in its support of a movement of racial or national liberation, when many of the communist leaders or members belong to the dominant race or ethnic group?

Again, how is a Marxist to interpret many of the revolutionary struggles in racially or ethnically plural societies? Why did the conflict, and the organization for conflict, tend to take a racial or ethnic form, rather than a class form, in South Africa, the USA, Zanzibar, Rwanda and Algeria? If the Zanzibar revolution was a revolution of the oppressed masses against the Arab oligarchy, and the Rwanda revolution, a revolution of Hutu serfs against Tutsi lords, why did the revolutionaries kill poor and powerless Arabs and Tutsi, whose class situation was quite comparable to their own (see Chapter 7)? If they were driven by false consciousness, why did the false consciousness evoke racial categories? Does a revolutionary theory derived from class conflict provide an adequate basis for the analysis of revolutionary movements in racially or ethnically plural societies?

These problems of the relevance of class and plural society theories to the interpretation of revolutionary change are discussed in this chapter. The first section deals with the dilemmas which confront the Communist Party as a result (1) of the failure in class solidarity between workers of different race, (2) of the problems in relating to the national or racial liberatory movement, and (3) of the difficulties in the application of revolutionary theory derived from the class struggle. So, too, a conception of the revolutionary struggle in terms of class struggle raises difficulties for the political leaders of the subordinate race, and these difficulties are discussed in the next section. In the final section, I stress the racial or ethnic structure as the crucial factor and suggest how this emphasis may contribute to the analysis of revolutionary change. Throughout, I draw largely on case studies of South Africa, in which there is *de jure* differential incorporation of the races and the subordinate races are in the great majority, and Algeria, before the revolution, a colonial situation, with sharp cleavages between the population of *colons* and the indigenous people. The case studies are thus of societies with extreme racial (or ethnic) pluralism, and the analysis is directed more particularly to this type of society.

2.

The failure in class solidarity between workers of different race or ethnic group runs contrary to the expectations Communist Parties would derive, and did in fact derive, from classical Marxist theory. The challenge is all the more crucial if solidarity fails at the very elementary level of co-operation in demands for improved conditions of work. This was the case in South Africa, where conflict between black and white workers goes back to the very beginnings of industrial development and has continued over the entire period of industrialization, a span of about one hundred years. To be sure, there was some co-operation over the years between workers of different races, but the overwhelming majority of white workers identified with the policies of white domination and used their political power as voters to press for discrimination in employment, racial reservation of many skilled categories of work, segregation and other forms of racial oppression. Indeed, some of the early statements of apartheid political philosophy were formulated by white labour leaders (see Simons and Simons, 1969: 155, 162). I think it can be said that the hostility of white workers for blacks was among the sharpest of the racial antagonisms in South Africa, and perhaps it can be offered as a generalization that in societies with a numerically substantial dominant racial or ethnic section, it is the workers within the ruling section who express the strongest hostility against the subordinates, since they are most exposed to competition.

Faced with this challenge to Marxist theory resulting from the failure of class solidarity by reason of racial or ethnic division, there would seem to be two main categories of logical response. The first is to maintain emphasis on the relationship to the means of production as the determinant of social relations and political change, to view race conflict as an aspect of class conflict, and to seek ways of interpreting the failure in solidarity between workers of different race within the framework of class theory. The second possibility is to accept that racial or ethnic divisions, and the movements of racial or national liberation associated with these divisions, have, in some measure, an independent significance as factors of political change, and to attempt to incorporate this element in the Marxist theory of revolutionary change.

The first response then is to interpret the racial divisions as an epiphenomenon of class conflict. Social class in Marxist theory comes into existence when persons who perform the same function in the production process become aware of their common interests and unite to promote them against the opposing class (Simons and Simons, 1969: 617). One possible approach, within Marxist theory, to the failure in class solidarity, is to argue that workers of the dominant section perform a different function in the production process, or that they constitute an aristocracy of labour. This concept, which was applied to the privileged stratum of workers in the metropolitan countries who benefited from colonial exploitation (Hobsbawm, 1970; Nicolaus, 1970) could perhaps be extended to workers of the dominant section in a plural society.

Certainly, to take the South African case, the economic situation of white workers is very different from that of black workers. It is mainly black workers whose wages are at the level of subsistence or even below subsistence. The expectation that the wages of white workers would be pushed down to the same level was never realized. On the contrary, many white workers share with the white bourgeoisie the surplus profit of black labour. But this exploitative role of white workers in the economy is not due to their ownership of the means of production. They are in the same relationship to the means of production as black workers. Their privileged position derives instead from their political power, the fact that they have a franchise as whites which is completely denied to Africans and Indians and accorded only symbolically to Coloureds. Quite simply, it is due to their differential political incorporation. This is the crucial factor, this is what the white workers struggle to preserve, this is the reason that, notwithstanding spectacular economic development for more than a generation, the political oppression of blacks has become even more intense, and this is why white labour has so often identified with Afrikaner nationalists. Indeed, from this perspective, it is easy to understand the apartheid-type political philosophy expressed by some of the early labour leaders.

Even if the argument is accepted that white workers

perform different functions from black, or that the entire white labour force is a labour aristocracy, there are still difficulties in defining the revolutionary dialectic of change in a manner consistent with Marxist theory. Are white non-owners of the means of production and black non-owners antagonistic classes whose increasing polarization leads to revolution, or is the basic revolutionary conflict between black non-owners and white bourgeoisie, or between black and white?

A more plausible line of argument would be that although white and black workers do perform the same function in the process of production, and therefore have common class interests, a variety of factors, such as racial and cultural diversity, political power of the white workers, their absorption in the ruling elite, and the effects on Africans of discrimination, distort the perception of these common class interests (see Appendix 1). The task for communists then is to politicize workers of different races so that they become aware of the real nature of their interests. But this raises many difficulties. Why do white workers define their interests as antagonistic to those of black workers and why does racial identity become the basis of political organization and conflict? Perhaps it is class consciousness which is the expression of false consciousness, obscuring the reality of the racial struggle.

The second approach to the failure in class solidarity is to accord some independent significance to racial divisions, and to seek reconciliation of racial and class conflict within the framework of Marxist theory. The traditional Marxist-Leninist doctrine of the two-stage revolution, namely, that revolutions in underdeveloped areas generally pass first through a bourgeois democratic phase and then through a socialist phase, may be adapted for this purpose.[2] Thus, the

2 Klinghoffer (1969) offers a most informative analysis of Soviet perspectives on African socialism. See in particular Chapter 4, 'Socialism, the class struggle and African society: the Soviet analysis'.

first stage would be the national liberation movement or the democratic revolution, bringing about racial equality, and the second would be the socialist revolution. The theoretical supporting argument, taken for example in the context of South African society, is that racial equality constitutes a precondition for class solidarity between workers of different races. This entirely reverses the Marxist position. Instead of the elimination of classes being the precondition for the elimination of racial discrimination, it is the abolition of racial discrimination which is seen as the precondition for the classless society (Simons and Simons, 1969: 411).

This seems quite remote from class theory, since there is the implication that in the initial phase at any rate, the basic conflict is racial in character. The Marxist analyst may, however, link the racial conflict to the class struggle in a number of ways. He may analyse the national liberation movement or the movement for racial liberation in terms of its class composition or leadership. If, for example, a national bourgeoisie is leading the movement, or there is mass participation by a proletariat, or by peasantry of the subordinate race, then this is taken as evidence that class struggle provides the driving force. A large literature[3] now deals with the controversial issues arising from this approach. Is it only the proletariat which is truly revolutionary, or is the proletariat of the subordinate race in many of the racially plural societies too small or too privileged for effective engagement in revolution? And is the truly revolutionary force that of the peasantry? And can the national bourgeoisie, or a section of it, be a progressive force? The very nature of the problems, and the extent of the controversy in communist circles, testify to the difficulties in the application of class theory to the national or racial liberation movement. But I think that the difficulties are even more fundamental than indicated in these controversies. The

3 See, for example, Klinghoffer (1969); Balandier (1965*a*); Mercier (1965); and Staniland (1969).

Marxist theory of revolutionary change postulates the polarization of conflict between classes, defined in terms of their
relationship to the means of production, whereas in a
national or racial liberation movement, the antagonists are
polarized predominantly on the basis of racial or ethnic
identity, transcending class divisions.

An alternative mode of reconciling the racial liberation
movement with class struggle is to disregard the social
composition of the revolutionary forces or its leaders and to
emphasize rather the nature of the antagonist.[4] From this
perspective, the revolution is seen as directed against international imperialism, rather than against domestic capitalism,
by a four-class alliance of proletariat, peasantry, petty
bourgeoisie and national bourgeoisie. The effect is to
internationalize the conception of class struggle (Klinghoffer,
1969: 137, 173); the crucial contradiction is between
socialism and capitalism on a world scale, and not the
internal contradiction within a specific society.

3.

A second dilemma of the Communist Party concerns its

4 See comment by Ouzegane (1962: 295): 'Le critère fondamental
qui détermine le caractère d'une révolution, ce n'est pas l'origine sociale
de ses dirigeants, mais d'abord la couche sociale contre laquelle la
révolution est dirigée. C'est en partant de ce fait capital qu'un
révolutionnaire peut savoir qu'une guerre de libération nationale est
juste. Il doit la saluer, la soutenir, même si elle est dirigée par des
féodaux, socialement reactionnaires, mais nationalement progressistes
dans leur lutte contre l'oppression étrangère.' ['The fundamental
criterion which determines the character of a revolution is not the
social origins of its leaders, but first of all, the social stratum against
which the revolution is directed. It is in beginning from this principal
fact that a revolutionary can know that a war of national liberation is
just. He must hail it, uphold it, even if it is directed by feudal lords,
socially reactionary, but nationally progressive in their battle against
the foreign oppressor.'] Ouzegane had been Secretary General of the
Parti Communiste Algérien, but was expelled in 1948 for nationalist
deviations (Quandt, 1969: 82).

relationship to the racial or national liberation movement. Identifying with the movement may raise acute problems for the Communist Party. The perspectives of the Communist Party are essentially international and interracial. I think they may also be described as antipathetic to religion, and as somewhat assimilationist with respect to race and culture though profoundly anti-assimilationist with respect to class, reformism being the deadly enemy. How then are communists to relate to a movement of fervent nationalism, under bourgeois or petty bourgeois leadership, with revival of traditional culture and religious commitment, or to a racially exclusive political organization?

At the level of abstract formulation, there is no difficulty in reconciling the national liberation movement with international socialism. For example, the policy of the French Communist Party towards the liberation movement in Algeria was defined, in an article in the official journal of the Comité du Parti Communiste Français, as 'la solidarité fondée sur l'internationalisme, à la fois conforme à l'intérêt du peuple opprimé et du peuple du pays oppresseur' (Vermeersch, 1959: 164).[5] The Party's policy required that the interest of the French people be reconciled with Algerian nationalism in a context of concern for the promotion of international proletarian consciousness. The policy seems to solve the problem of the relationship between Algerian nationalism and international socialism. But at the level of practical politics, why should the leaders of a liberation movement, comprising all classes, accept the socialist commitment, or an international orientation as defined by the Communist Party? And could the interests of the French and Algerian people be readily reconciled?

The Communist Party can of course accommodate cultural diversity, not incompatible with working-class consciousness and ideology, but it is hardly at ease with cultural and

5 '. . . solidarity based on internationalism simultaneously conforming to the interest of the oppressed people and the people of the oppressing country'.

religious revivalism within a nationalist movement. It may differentiate between the reactionary and progressive elements of the religious faith (Glories, 1958: 4 ff.). Such conceptions as that 'toutes les religions contiennent dans leurs principes assez de données contradictoires pour pouvoir s'adapter suivant les nécessités aux situations sociales les plus diverses'[6] (Glories, 1958: 5), provide maximum strategic flexibility. But if these different strands are not represented by different religious bodies, and an adherent commits himself to the religious faith as a total entity, then the distinction may be simply a rationalization for expediency.

The relationship of the Communist Party to the liberation movement is further complicated in situations where the majority of the militants in the Party belong to the dominant group, as in the Parti Communiste Algérien. Mannoni (1963: 131) comments that the French society of Algeria, being a microcosm of the metropolitan society, shared its social and political quarrels, and that the Algerian Communist Party supported 'la rebellion . . . trop tard pour conquérir les Musulmans et trop fort pour ne pas perdre les Européens'.[7] The revolution posed in the most inescapable terms the dilemma of choice between ethnic political identification and support for the Algerian Revolution. Why should French workers in Algeria risk their lives or even take part in a revolutionary struggle against a colonial power which ensures them a privileged position (Glories, 1958: 39-40)?

Humbaraci writes (1966: 174), with some exaggeration, that

overnight, when the separatist movement started, all the Frenchmen living in Algeria — many of them of Spanish origin, refugees from Franco — became true *pieds noirs*. The communists were no exception, exhibiting the most violent racialist feeling, even to the extent of joining the official French forces to help put down the revolution.

---

6 'All religions contain in their principles enough contradictory basic ideas that they can be adapted to the most diverse of social situations, according to the necessities.'

7 '. . . the rebellion . . . too late to conquer the Muslims and too strongly not to lose the Europeans'.

Even where communists belonging to the dominant racial or ethnic minority identify most courageously with the liberation movement, as they did in South Africa, and in small numbers also in Algeria, they may be viewed by members of the subordinate racial section as serving their own interests, in the sense of securing their own survival and authority when the majority takes over, or indeed as serving the interests of their own racial or ethnic section in a continuing domination (see, for example, Jordaan, 1968).

4.

A third dilemma relates to the Marxist theory of revolutionary change. Basic elements in this theory are that revolution results from a dialectical process of polarization between classes, defined in terms of their relationship to the means of production: that as the social relations of production increasingly fetter the productive process, they are burst asunder in a revolutionary movement to higher productivity and to the social relations compatible with that productivity; that the economy thus tends to move towards greater productivity and rationality; and that the political structure derives from the relations of production, and changes in response to basic changes in the mode and relations of production.

There are difficulties with all these elements of theory in the analysis of revolutionary change in racially or ethnically structured societies. If class conflict is the driving force in revolutionary change, then why do struggles in these societies take on a racial or ethnic form? Why is racial identity the basis of organization, and why are the targets of revolutionary violence people of different race regardless of class situation (see Chapter 7)?

In Zanzibar the revolution was racial in form, carried out against the Arabs by Mainland Africans, with some Shirazi support. There was a small revolutionary party, Marxist in orientation and mainly Arab in membership, but it is impossible to know whether it would have launched a revolutionary struggle, and whether it could have mobilized sufficient support on a class basis. In Rwanda, the revolution was again racial in form, a struggle of Hutu against Tutsi. By a bizarre twist, the Tutsi counter-revolutionaries were attracted to communism, or at any rate to a communist alliance. In Algeria, the struggle was essentially between an Algerian nationalist Islamic movement bringing together peasants, workers and bourgeoisie in a struggle against the French colonial power and the European *colons*. In the USA, the contemporary revolutionary movements among blacks are based on race, not class, though some of the movements combine black nationalism with Marxist orientations.

The system of production may be highly irrational and restrictive, laying heavy fetters on productivity for long periods of time, without revolutionary change. This is the situation in South Africa. In all sectors of the economy, Africans, Coloureds and Indians are employed, by and large, at a level well below their productive capacities. Indeed, the colour bar in South Africa has laid social fetters on production from the very beginnings of industrialization. There has been a continuous tension between the processes and relations of production yet the society remains relatively stable. Any tendency to polarization has been based on race, or within the white section, on ethnic membership, or, briefly, on class; there has been no polarization in the society as a whole in terms of the relationship to the means of production. The economy is highly productive. For years, South Africa has maintained a very high rate of economic growth, perhaps as high a rate as it can absorb. Its white workers are among the most highly paid in the world, and the system must surely motivate them to a counter-revolutionary commitment. For a portion of the working class, then, a portion that is politically significant, the social relations of production are by no means fettered, and the revolutionary calculus must take account of the mixture of productive and fettered relations, and of motivating and alienating elements, defined by racial identity in a continuously expanding economy. The crucial point, however, is that South Africa has been in a revolutionary situation for some generations, without revolutionary change. It could be argued that there were, in fact, revolutionary movements which failed because the government adopted the coercive techniques of fascist totalitarianism; but this would mean limiting the theory of revolutionary change to situations in which the ruling class was not prepared to exercise maximum repression.

The political system, it seems, may remain relatively constant in many important respects, while the economic system is transformed. Since the establishment of the Union of South Africa in 1910, the country has changed from an agricultural society with such major primary industries as gold and diamond mines, to an advanced industrial society. Some semi-feudal relationships still persist between white employers and African labour, and there are still elements of so-called 'primitive communism' in the traditional African sector, but taken as a whole the economic system has profoundly changed. Yet, the constitution is much the same, though ensuring, to an even higher degree, the monopoly of power by whites. This is a cardinal element in the structure of the society, and it has remained a constant feature of the constitution over the years. The situation then is theoretically dissonant in two respects: the perpetuation of pre-industrial social rigidities (see Simons and Simons, 1969: 10), and the continuity of essential aspects of the political structure through a long period of economic transformation.

In any discussion of revolutionary change, there is a problem of the sense in which the term 'revolution' is used. For Marxists, revolution involves fundamental changes in the economic institutions, that is to say, in the contemporary setting, a change to ownership of the means of production by the people. But there is no reason to limit the concept of revolution in this way. In such countries as Algeria and Rwanda, or South Africa and the USA, differential incorporation is, or was, so basic a principle of social and political structure, that the abolition of that differential incorporation is a fundamental change, which cannot but bring about further transformations of the society.

Given all these difficulties in the application of class theory, perhaps one might question the concept of the universality of the class struggle, and entertain the idea that there may be an ethnocentric bias in emphasizing class conflict as a primary determinant of revolutionary change in racially or ethnically structured societies. As Memmi (1957: 51-2) observes: 'Le colonisateur de gauche se demand s'il n'a pas péché par orgueil en croyant le socialisme exportable et le marxisme universel.'[8]

5.

Also for the subordinate section in a racially or ethnically structured society, a conception of the revolutionary struggle in terms of class conflict raises difficulties. The failure in class solidarity between workers of the dominant and subordinate sections makes the theory seem not at all persuasive. The Simons (1969: 621) write from the perspective of militant Communist Party members in South Africa, that African and Coloured leaders, being unable to reconcile class theories with the white worker's behaviour, 'doubted the authenticity of the socialist vision or thought it too remote to be a sound guide to action. They preferred radical liberalism to radical socialism.' Ouzegane (1962: 82) comments of Algeria that

les petits Blancs, réfugiés de la guerre d'Espagne ou émigrants quittant les Baléares, la Corse, la Sicile, l'Italie et abandonnant l'atroce misère avec la poussière du sol natal ne peuvent qu'avoir un ressentiment naturel contre les 'ratons' au ventre creux qui menacent le colonialisme français, protecteur et bienfaiteur. Dans ces conditions, vouloir considérer l'ensemble du prolétariat algérien comme une classe ouvrière

---

8 'The leftist colonizer asks himself whether he has not committed a sin of pride in believing that socialism is exportable and that Marxism is universal.'

homogène relève de l'utopie, de l'erreur et de la cécité mentale.[9]

From this perspective, it would seem somewhat meaningless to inquire whether workers of the dominant race or ethnic group perform different functions in the process of production, or whether they perform the same functions, but have not become aware of their common class interests. The reality of everyday experience is that they enjoy a privileged position as members of the dominant racial or ethnic group, and that they may be more aggressive in the expression of their racial prejudices than the ruling bourgeoisie (Glories, 1958: 39). They do not seem to feel exploited as workers, but threatened rather in their privileged position by revolutionary change in the structure of racial or ethnic domination, and they are likely to move into the counter-revolutionary movement as the struggle becomes more intense.

It is of some interest that in both the Algerian Revolution and the South African Congress movement of the 1950s, the leaders found it necessary to establish separate trade unions. In Algeria, the Front de Libération National formed its own trade union movement, the Union Général des Travailleurs Algériens, in 1956. Later in the year, at the Soumman Conference, the Comité Révolutionnaire d'Unité et d'Action concluded, after 'un long et douloureux débat avec les

---

9 '. . . the little whites, refugees of the Spanish Civil War or emigrants leaving the Balearic Islands, Corsica, Sicily, Italy, and abandoning the atrocious poverty with the dust of their native soil, cannot but have a natural resentment towards the 'rats' with hollow stomachs who threaten French colonialism, their protector and benefactor. In these conditions, to want to conside the whole of the Algerian proletariat as a homogeneous working class savours of Utopia, of error and of mental blindness.' Ouzegane argues that only in a common struggle against the colonial bourgeoisie for the right of the Algerian people to self-determination would it be possible to raise the level of class consciousness among workers of varied national origin, language and faith.

syndicats français',[10] that political independence was the necessary preliminary requirement for all amelioration of the worker's condition in Algeria,[11] and that the new trade union fulfilled the original function of integrating workers in the national struggle by means of social struggle (Favret, 1965: 46; Humbaraci, 1966: 46-50; Lebjaoui, 1970: 35; Meynaud and Salah-Bey, 1967: 67 ff.; Glories, 1958: 37-9). In South Africa, the founding of the South African Congress of Trade Unions in 1954, and its affiliation with the Congress alliance of political movements, were a frank avowal of the political role of the workers in the liberatory struggle (Leo Kuper, 1965: 317). The Congress of Trade Unions was non-racial in membership, but the relevant point for the present argument is that it was necessary to establish a new union outside the national organizations as an affiliate of, and an instrument in, the struggle for national liberation.

To be sure, the conception of the class struggle had its devoted followers. This was particularly true in South Africa among some of the leaders and rank and file members of the African National Congress. Yet, there was a small response to communism in South Africa where conditions were particularly favourable in terms of Marxist theory: by 1957, the Liquidator charged with the liquidation of the Communist Party had placed only 608 names on his list of former members and supporters of the Communist Party (Bunting, 1964: 173). A generation earlier, in 1943, its membership was 1,500 (Simons and Simons, 1969: 538), appreciably higher, but still negligible. Indeed, the response in Africa as a whole was small, at any rate, as measured by Communist Party membership. Humbaraci (1966: 170) writes that

10 '. . . a long and painful debate with the French trade unions'.

11 An interesting defense of UGTA policy, in response to accusations that it was a political and not a trade union movement, a cover simply for the FLN, is quoted in Meynaud and Salah-Bey (1962: 122-3). See also François Weiss (1970: 42-4), for a discussion of the relations between UGTA and the French trade union movements.

on July 23 1965, the United States State Department issued a survey according to which there was a total of 12,500 card-carrying communists in Africa at the beginning of 1965. The distribution of the bigger communist groupings was: Algeria, 5,500; the Sudan, 2,500; Morocco 2,000; United Arabic Republic and Tunisia, about 1,000 each; South Africa, 800. Nigeria, the 'colossus of Africa', had only about 100.

Membership was also small in the period of decolonization.[12]

The reason would seem to be that the overriding reality for the subordinate peoples was racial or national oppression. Lebjaoui (1970: 231), one of the leaders in the Algerian revolution, justifies, as follows, his avoidance of interpretations of the revolution in terms of the social background of the revolutionaries:

Une guerre de libération nationale c'est d'abord l'affirmation de soi-même par rapport à l'occupant; c'est une soif de liberté et de dignité. Dans un contexte où l'arbitraire et la misère sont évidemment le lot quotidien de tout un peuple..Il est des conditions historiques où l'origine sociale et la situation personnelle du moment ne jouent pas un rôle primordial.[13]

And he adds that after liberation, on the contrary, the economic and social factors come to the fore. Ouzegane (1962: 176) observes that

12 Intelligence Report no. 4489 R-10 on the *World Strength of the Communist Party Organizations* (Office of Intelligence Research and Analysis, 1958) shows negligible Communist Party membership in 1957 for most of the countries of Africa, the highest membership being in Algeria (5,000-10,000) and in South Africa (1,200-2,000). For the years 1947 and 1952, that is prior to the revolution, Communist Party strength in Algeria is shown at the much higher figure of 15,000. The 1957 figures of Egypt, included in a tabulation for the Near East, are 4,000-5,000.

13 'A war of national liberation is first of all an affirmation of oneself in relation to the occupier: it is a thirst for liberty and dignity in a context where arbitrary injustice and poverty are plainly the daily lot of a whole people. There are some historical conditions where the social origin and the personal situation of the moment play no primary role.'

l'oppression nationale, politique, économique, culturelle et religieuse, qui écrasait le peuple tout entier, exaspérait le sentiment national contre la domination étrangère et lui donnait la primauté sur le sentiment de classe.[14]

Consistent with this interpretation, the Revolutionary Council's proclamation launching the revolution on 1 November 1954 offered ' la possibilité à tous les patriotes algériens de toutes les couches sociales, de tous les partis et mouvements purement algériens, de s'intégrer dans la lutte de libération sans aucune autre considération'[15] (Favrod, 1959: 170-1). So, too, the ideology of the South African Pan-Africanist Congress, which broke away from the African National Congress in 1958, was based on national or racial identity: Africans were oppressed as a nation, not as a class, and African nationalism in an all-African organization, was the liberatory outlook necessary to rouse the African masses in a struggle for genuine democracy (Leo Kuper, 1965: 373). The explanation offered in *L'Espoir* (quoted by Glories, 1958: 36) seems to be applicable to both societies:

La raison la plus profonde et d'application générale [en] est que la colonisation est l'exploitation collective d'un peuple et non l'exploitation d'individus en fonction de leur condition sociale. Aussi la situation coloniale exalte-t-elle non pas une conscience de classe qui n'existe pas, mais une conscience nationale qui se constitue très rapidement quand elle ne pré-existe pas.[16]

---

14 'National, political, economic, cultural and religious oppression, which crush an entire people, provoke national sentiment against foreign domination, giving it priority over the feeling of class.'

15 ' . . . the possibility for all the Algerian patriots of all social strata, for all the purely Algerian parties and movements, to integrate themselves in the liberation struggle without any other consideration'.

16 'The most profound reason and the one with most general application is that colonization is the collective exploitation of a people and not the exploitation of individuals as a function of their social condition. Likewise the colonial situation exalts not a class consciousness which does not exist, but a national consciousness which is formed very quickly when it does not exist originally.'

The assertion that class consciousness did not exist must certainly be qualified, but the liberation movements transcend class distinctions.

Between the national and racial liberation movements and the Communist Party are many tensions, deriving from communist perspectives based on the class struggle, from the racial or ethnic origin of Communist Party members, and from the national, community and religious affiliations of the subordinate peoples (Glories, 1958: 33). Because of the failure of class solidarity and the emphasis on race or nation in the liberatory movements, the class struggle may seem neither particularly plausible nor especially relevant in the conflict between the plural sections. Where many of the members of the Communist Party or its effective leadership, belong to the dominant racial or ethnic section, as is frequently the case, the class struggle, as the means to revolutionary change, is likely to seem even less plausible, and the motives of the communists may become highly suspect. In Algeria, there were charges of communist orientation to French national interests, or to the French Communist Party and international socialism, rather than to the Algerian movement for independence; there were allegations of subordination to Moscow, the instrumental use of Muslim Algerians, and even racism (see for example, Glories, 1958: 23-9; Lebjaoui, 1970: 30). The Front de Libération Nationale, in honouring the founding of the Union Générale des Travailleurs Algériens, attacked communist trade union leadership and complained of foreign tutelage, neo-colonialism and paternalism in the trade union movement (Favrod, 1959: 177-81). The concern expressed by communists for the fate of members of the dominant race, and their desire for interracial co-operation may be seen as conflicting with their protestations of commitment to the liberatory struggle (Jordaan, 1968: 13, 18).

Conversely, the national or racial liberation movement tends to be exclusive in its affirmation of racial or national identity, in its cultural revivalism, and sometimes, too, in its religious commitment. It emphasizes those characteristics which constitute its distinctive identity, marking it off from other sections, whatever the political affiliation of their members, and generating tension with, and suspicion of, communist secularism, internationalism, interracialism and class orientation. The reactions to Communist Party ideology may be quite varied. The Marxist theory of revolutionary change may be accepted as immediately relevant, with priority given to national liberation; or it may be conceived as relevant only at a later stage, when national liberation has been achieved, or it may be deferred for consideration until after independence; or it may be rejected as a theory derived from, and significant for, Western European industrial societies, but not specifically related to, or expressive of, the distinctive genius of the subordinate peoples. Whatever the reaction, there is an inherent tension between Marxist orientations and movements of racial or national liberation.

6.

The ambiguities in the relations between class, race and power find their counterpart in conflicting theories and predictions. Marxists assert the primacy of the class factor, and conceive of racial differences as providing a basis for the more thorough exploitation of workers. Leaders of the liberation movement, on the contrary, may see the class factor as epiphenomenal, or as mainly affecting leadership and particular manifestations of conflict, and they may find the driving force in racial differences as they come to be socially elaborated under systematic oppression. The classless society may be seen as the precondition for the abolition of racial discrimination, or conversely the elimination of racial discrimination is conceived as the precondition for the classless society. There can be no revolution in the colony until there has been a proletarian revolution in the colonizing country, or on the other hand, the colonial revolution is the necessary precursor of revolutionary change in the colonizing society.

The crucial element in revolutionary change may be seen as the class composition of the liberation movement, or this may be dismissed as immediately irrelevant, the liberation movement being conceived as embracing all classes of the subordinate race, while emphasis is placed rather on the characteristics of the ruling race, or of the system of oppression. If the class composition of the liberation movement is seen as significant, then interminable controversy surrounds the interpretation of the role of different classes. The creation of a bourgeoisie in the subordinate racial group is seen as a condition favourable to evolutionary change, or on the contrary, as predisposing to revolution. The peasantry is the truly revolutionary class, and the proletariat somewhat accommodating because of its relatively privileged position, or alternatively the peasantry is basically conservative, fragmented by regional and clan solidarities, and only the proletariat is truly revolutionary.

At a different level of analysis, economic growth is viewed as encouraging progressive change towards more equal relations between the racial sections, or as stimulating revolutionary challenge. Religion is opiate, or religion is resistance.

7.

The conflicting theories and predictions are endless. They are the product, in part, of conflicting ideologies used to influence events towards a particular outcome; in part they result from ambiguities in a situation which includes both class and racial (or ethnic) divisions. But to an appreciable extent, they flow from the assimilation of racial (and ethnic) structures to class structures.

From a political and ideological point of view, the emphasis on class is perfectly intelligible; it is part of the strategy of directing the struggle between the races towards the socialist revolution. At the level of theory, on the other hand, the concepts of race and class are so very different, that it is difficult to understand the justification for the introduction of class concepts as the crucial variable, outside of the dogma of the universality of the class struggle. Classes constitute a system of social relationships and a hierarchical order. In Marxist theory, they are defined by relationships in the economic order, the political, educational and associational inequalities being superimposed on the economic differentiation. Since classes arise out of the economic order, economic change is presumably the crucial variable. Races, on the other hand, do not constitute a hierarchical order *per se*. There is no intrinsic reason why races should constitute categories in social relationships, nor are hierarchical relations inherent in racial difference. Races only become social categories, and race relations only become hierarchical through the manner in which racial difference is elaborated as a principle of organization and association in the political and other institutions. It is these associated factors which give race an independent significance. Economic position is only one of the associated factors, and not necessarily the most crucial. Since the expression of racial domination is most diffuse, the precipitants and manifestations of racial conflict are likely to be similarly diffuse. And since racial discrimination attacks, in a fundamental way, the concept the individual has of himself, his body and his being, and the concept he has of the identity, the culture and quality of his racial group, status politics are likely to assume great importance, to the point of precipitating revolutionary change. Moreover, mobility may have very different consequences. Many mobile individuals in a class society are lost to their original class. Appreciable upward mobility is likely to tranquilize the society. In a racially structured society, the upwardly mobile are readily recovered, and appreciable upward mobility may in fact stimulate revolutionary change.

Given the difficulties of class interpretations of plural societies, it may be more productive to take, as a basis for the analysis, the racial or ethnic structure, emphasizing the mode of differential incorporation. This seems to be especially indicated where the plural society is established by conquest

as in South Africa or in Algeria. From this perspective, there
is no reason to anticipate that class divisions would have a
crucial overriding significance. Racial domination provides a
basis for interclass solidarity within the dominant racial
group, even though the interests of the various classes in the
structure of racial domination are quite diverse. There may
very well be some relations of solidarity across racial lines, òf
different extent and intensity in different classes, but these
are often overwhelmed, or rendered ineffective in crises, by
the bonds of racial solidarity. Conversely, a common oppression provides a basis for interclass solidarity in the subordinate race. Colonial oppression or racial domination is
experienced as a totality, and stimulates a racial or national
response, transcending class divisions.

Mohamed Harbi, writing in the communist journal, *Démo-
cratie Nouvelle* (June 1965: 58), about the situation in
Algeria, explains the basis for this response as follows:

De même que ceux d'autres pays colonisés, le peuple d'Algérie, toutes
classes confondues, rencontrait, une fois ses institutions détruites et son
territoire occupé, le problème de la reconstruction d'une vie nouvelle
qui prenne pour base l'état même où le choc colonial avait placé la
société. La nation constituait le type de réponse à ce problème car
c'est autant comme Algérien que comme ouvrier et paysan que
l'homme était exploité. Le colonialisme avait enfoui les frontières de
classe sous les frontières ethniques. De ce fait, la lutte se situait d'abord
sur le plan national. Dans un pays colonisé, le contraire de l'exploitation, pour les masses, c'est l'indépendance; la conscience de classe ne
peut donc pas être un phénomène de masse, car on ne peut
parler de classes que d'une manière économique, c'est à dire en se référant
à la position des hommes par rapport aux moyens de production.[17]

---

17 'Like members of other colonized countries, the people of
Algeria, all classes combined, once their institutions had been destroyed
and their territory occupied, faced the problem of reconstructing a new
life whose foundations were the precise state in which the colonial
shock had placed their society. The nation itself formed the kind of
answer to this problem, for it was equally as an Algerian and a worker
or peasant that man was being exploited. Colonialism had buried class
boundaries under ethnic boundaries. As a result, the struggle was from

If we start with an emphasis on the racial structure and mode of racial incorporation, many of the difficulties in class analysis disappear. The antagonism of workers of the dominant race for workers of the subordinate race is not a failure in class solidarity, but the anticipated response to inequality in political rights. There is a dialectical relationship between their interests, so that as workers of the subordinate race become more militant in their struggle for equality, workers of the ruling race are likely to respond with demands for protection of their privileged situation and for greater political repression. The association of increasing political repression with economic advance is thus by no means an anomaly.

As to the theory of revolutionary change, there seems to be less difficulty in interpreting the processes from the perspective of differential racial incorporation. The persistence of archaic elements, of feudal sectors in an industrial capitalist society, of extreme and continuing irrationality in the employment of labour, becomes intelligible as a product, not only of the intense exploitation of labour, but also of the exclusion of members of the subordinate race from access to sources of power. The increasing tension, over generations, between the processes and relations of production, without revolutionary change, ceases to be anomalous, if the economic transformations are interpreted in the context of the political relations between the races. It is the political relations which appreciably determine the relationship to the means of production, rather than the reverse, and the catalyst of revolutionary change is to be found in the structure of power, rather than in economic changes which exhaust the possibilities of a particular mode of production.

---

the start situated on the national level. In a colonized country, the opposite of exploitation for the masses is independence: class consciousness therefore cannot be a mass phenomenon, for one cannot speak of classes except in economic terms, i.e. by referring to the position of men in relation to the means of production.'

8.

It is facile to raise difficulties without offering constructive suggestions, and in this final section I suggest an approach to revolutionary change in racially plural societies. In taking the racial structure and the differential incorporation of the races as the basis for my argument, I do not intend to imply a political or structural determinism, nor to discount the significance of the economic relations and discrimination. The matter is rather one of offering an alternative emphasis and perspective on revolutionary change in racially and ethnically plural societies to the perspectives derived from class conflict.

(1) Whatever the origins of societies in which the races come to be differentially incorporated, these societies share certain elements in common. It is not crucial that they were established in profoundly different ways, as, for example, by capitalist imperial expansion in South Africa, or by a mixture of economic exchange and conquest, arising from the contact between Tutsi and Hutu, and leading to a central-ized system of clientage, as in Rwanda. Once established as a system of domination, with political inequality between the races, certain common consequences result (see the analysis of M. G. Smith in Kuper and Smith, 1969).

(2) There develops, over the years, an elaboration of social relations between the races on the basis of the original differential incorporation. This corresponds somewhat to the Marxist conception of the superstructure arising on the basis of the social relations of production.

A number of writers on ethnic relations in Algeria have expressed this conception of the elaboration of the original inequality. Aron (1962: 7-8) phrases the matter as follows:

La colonisation a correspondu à une phase provisoire mais nécessaire par laquelle devaient passer des régions 'sous développées' dans tous les sens de ce mot. Elle résultait d'une inégalité flagrante entre les nouveaux arrivants et les populations indigènes. Elle devait fatalement s'édifier à partir de cette disparité et la consolider dans le même temps où, plus ou moins volontairement, elle travaillait pour l'effacer.[18]

Ouzegane (1962: 215) emphasizes the consequences of the legal differentiation resulting from the application of a special code to the local people:

Bien sûr, en Algérie 'française' le code Napoléon ne recommandait pas l'apartheid yankee ou afrikander ni la ségrégation confessionelle sioniste. En fait, le code de l'indigénat, fondé sur l'inégalité politique, économique, culturelle, religieuse et technique, sous une forme brutale ou hypocrite, aboutissait au même cloisonnement racial.[19]

(3) This elaboration of the original differential incorporation is diffuse, ramifying through the institutions of the society.

(*a*) There is considerable elaboration in the economic structure of the society. Thus, in South Africa, conquest laid the basis for the expropriation of African land and for the political control of the relationship to land. This is what Marxists would expect. Clearly control over the land of a pastoral and agricultural people is a powerful weapon for political domination and economic exploitation, and it has been used in this way consistently over the years. Though Africans constitute about two-thirds of the population, only some 12 per cent of the land is

18 'Colonization has corresponded to a provisional but necessary phase through which regions, underdeveloped in every sense of this word, had to pass. It resulted from a flagrant inequality between the newly arrived and the indigenous populations. Inevitably, it had to be constructed, beginning with this disparity, and consolidated at the same time as, more or less voluntarily, it was working to erase it.'

19 'Of course, in "French" Algeria the Napoleonic Code did not recommend Yankee or Afrikaner apartheid or the Zionist religious segregation. In fact, the code of the *indigénat*, based on political economic, cultural, religious and technical inequality, under a brutal and hypocritical form, ended in the same racial enclosure.'

available for African occupation, and even their tenure
of these lands is insecure. The differential political
incorporation provides a basis for differential access to
mineral rights, industrial resources and other means of
production. It introduces a fundamental distinction in
the life chances of workers of different races, and this in
turn is a spring-board for further differentiation. The
Simons (1969: 98) in their study of labour relations in
South Africa show the antagonism of white labour to
black labour from an early period of contact, and
comment, correctly, that 'white labour policies emerged
from an all-white franchise'. By reason of their franchise,
white workers were able to exert effective pressure for
policies of racial discrimination extending to all spheres of
life.

In Algeria, the political power of the conquerors was
the basis for the expropriation of land by a variety of
procedures: land taken over from the Turks, from
religious foundations, as sanctions against rebellion, on
grounds of non-cultivation, or as communal land, or for
reasons of public utility (Launay, 1963: 113-44). At the
time of the revolution, most of the more paying crops
were in the hands of the *colons*, whose farms averaged
123.9 hectares of land, as compared with a Muslim
average of 11.6 hectares (Nouschi, 1962: 118). According to Aron (1962: 224), some 73 per cent of Muslim
exploitations were less than 10 hectares, less, that is to
say, than the minimum necessary for subsistence. To be
sure market factors entered into this unequal distribution, but the basic pattern was laid by conquest. Favrod
(1959: 32-3) observes in this connection that:

Les hectares conquis, devenus symbole et tremplin de la conquête
économique, ont dressé l'Arabe contre le Colon, contre son
pouvoir que scellait la possession de la terre, contre sa morgue
que renforçait la terre acquise, contre son ambition que justifiait
de la terre encore à prendre. Tenu à distance, chassé de son sol,

l'Arabe a vu le Colon triompher. Il a vu le vainqueur vaincre davantage, à force d'énergie, mais aussi d'aide administrative, toujours assuré de l'impunité. Il a vy, d'immigrant pouilleux et assisté, revêtir une supériorité de nature. Tandis que lui, captif de l'indigénat, devenait une sorte de negation de l'homme dans l'homme.[20]

There is, of course, continuous interaction, and reciprocal influence, between the political and economic structures and institutions.

(*b*) In the contact between Western European colonizers and people of different race, the elaboration of inequality in the educational institutions is expressed at two levels, denigration of the culture of the conquered, and meagre access to the culture of the conquerors. In Algeria, the French did not encourage the teaching of Arabic at the elementary level and at the time of the revolution, after many years of the French *mission civilatrice*, only one Muslim child out of ten went to school, 94 per cent of the men and 98 per cent of the women were illiterate (Gordon, 1966: 51). In South Africa, there was much more extensive provision of educational facilities for Africans, but it was highly discriminatory, and it withheld effective access to the skills required for control of modern technology.

20 'The conquered hectares, having become a symbol and springboard of economic conquest, have turned the Arab against the *colon*, against his power which confirmed land ownership, against his pride which reinforced the acquired land, against his ambition which justified the land still to be taken. Held at a distance, driven from his land, the Arab has seen the *colon* triumph. He has seen the victor still more victorious, by the strength of his energy, but also with administrative help, always assured of impunity. He has seen the miserable and assisted immigrant assume a natural superiority. While he, captive of the *indigénat* was becoming a sort of negation of man in man.'

(*c*) Inequality in political rights, in economic participation, in education and a variety of other elaborations
of inequality by means of segregation, discrimination in
amenities, contemptuous stereotypes, give rise to a
many-faceted generalized status of ruling race and
subject race.

(4) Given the crucial significance of the differential
political incorporation, the struggle between the races takes
the form of a struggle over the terms of incorporation. The
dominant race seeks to maintain the monopoly of political
power; it may prevent organization of the subordinates, or, at
any rate, suppress nationalist organization, reverse changes in
race relations and generally consolidate its domination. This
core of political racial domination may remain constant even
though the society changes profoundly from, say, an agricultural society with many feudal-type relationships to a predominantly industrialized society as in South Africa. Where
the system of domination derived from a Western parliamentary society, as in most of Africa, and where there were many
settlers, ingenious formulae were devised to give a more
democratic flavour to political domination.

(5) Since racial subordination constitutes a diffuse many-
faceted status, almost any element may act as a catalyst of
racial conflict and revolution. Status factors are highly
significant also in class conflict (as is clear from the
Communist Manifesto), but they appear to have greater
salience in revolutionary struggles between the races. Status
politics are a powerful instrument for mobilization to racial
revolutionary struggle, and may overshadow economic griev-
ances.

(6) Class factors enter into the racial struggle at many
different levels. They influence leadership, participation and
ideology in both the dominant and subordinate racial
sections. Since the political domination is elaborated in the

economic institutions, conceptions of the struggle as class conflict have an appeal to the subordinates. But Marxism may be simply a rhetoric in a racial movement for liberation, and imply no commitment to collective ownership of the means of production. Or it may be the commitment of a section of the liberation movement seeking to guide the struggle towards class conflict. Perhaps the hope is that class ideology and the process of struggle may create a revolutionary class in much the same way that national ideology and the struggle for national liberation may transform subordinate ethnic groups into a nation.

(7) Perhaps in the extreme case, opportunity is a sufficient occasion for revolution in racially plural societies, but presumably there are certain conditions which increase revolutionary potential. A variety of theories suggest different predisposing conditions.

(*a*) A dialectical opposition between the races, as measured (i) by a growing concentration of legal power in the hands of the dominant race, and an increasing exclusion of the subordinate race from access to power; (ii) by increasing discontinuities in other dimensions of the relations between the races, and (iii) by superimposition of issues of conflict (Kuper and Smith, 1969: 473 ff.). This is not to suggest that a movement of the members of the society into dialectically opposed camps is a necessary condition for revolution.

(*b*) Status incongruity among sections of the subordinate race, as for example, the highly educated stratum of Africans who were denied effective political participation in colonial Africa. It was from this stratum that the leaders of the revolutionary struggles against colonial domination were generally drawn.

(*c*) If some of the many theories dealing with economic

change as the predisposing condition to revolution are transformed into theories emphasizing change in racial status as the crucial variable, then the predisposing conditions might be found in increasing racial subordination and discrimination (corresponding to immiserization of the masses) or in the advancing status of the subordinates, or in an advance followed by a setback, or in the disjunction between aspiration and reality, or in the tension between *de facto* racial interaction and mobility, on the one hand, and *de jure* separation and rigidity on the other (see Chapter 7, Part 6).

(8) Conditions which might favour evolutionary change would include increasing interdependence of the racial groups, the possibility of some reconciliation in values and goals, opportunities for social mobility, and co-operative relations between individuals and strata across racial divisions (see Chapter 6 and Leo Kuper, 1970).

Many social scientists question the significance for evolutionary change of individual relationships across the racial divisions. This is the position taken by M.G. Smith who emphasizes that the races are differentially incorporated as entities. Aron (1962: 8) writes that since colonialism inevitably builds on an original flagrant inequality, 'en présence d'une telle fatalité, les efforts individuels pour s'installer définitivement dans l'impasse, ou au contraire pour en sortir, ne pouvaient donner lieu qu'à des expédients provisoires, qu'à des essais avortés'.[21] Memmi (1957: 54) writes to much the same effect that an essential feature of the colonial situation is that it is based on the relationship between one group of people and another, that colonial relations do not stem from individual goodwill or actions, but

21 '. . . in the presence of such a fate, individual efforts to establish oneself in a situation of deadlock, or on the contrary, to disengage oneself, could only result in provisional expediency, in abortive attempts'.

on the contrary determine *a priori* the place of the individual and that of the colonized and, in the final analysis, their true relationship. Certainly the change, to be effective, must be taken to the level of the differential political incorporation, which is qualitatively distinct from the sum of individual interracial relationships.

As to upward social mobility by members of the subordinate race, this does not necessarily encourage evolutionary change. The upwardly mobile are not thereby lost to their original group, in contrast to the tendency in class mobility. Race remains an extrinsic point of reference, and upwardly mobile individuals may be readily drawn back into their racial group.

Nevertheless, the cross-cutting relationships between members of different racial groups and upward social mobility by members of the subordinate race, modify the structure of race relations, and may, under conditions of interdependence, provide a basis for evolutionary processes of change. There is no inexorable predetermination, by the initial differential incorporation, of the course of race relations.

9

Political Change in Plural Societies:
Problems in Racial Pluralism

In the field of racially plural societies, with which I am here particularly concerned, the main theories relevant to political change are Marxist theories of class conflict, adaptations of Durkheim's theory of evolutionary change from mechanical to organic solidarity, and theories of the plural society or of pluralism. Each encourages different ideological uses, not necessarily implicit in the theories themselves.

Marxist theory, in emphasizing the class struggle as the major determinant of political change, conceives of racial discrimination and exploitation as an aspect of class relations. In terms of this perspective, race conflict will most probably be resolved, and racial equality established, as part of the world proletarian revolution.[1] However the application of this theory in its pure form to specific situations of racial conflict raises serious difficulties. There is not only a failure in solidarity between workers of different race,[2] but it is often workers of the dominant race who demand the most

---

1 See Cox (1948: 321-52, 583), who associates racial antagonisms with the rise of capitalism and the policies and attitudes of the leading capitalist people, the white people of Europe and North America. He argues that race relations involve a significant variation of class conflict in the tendency of the bourgeoisie to proletarianize a whole people (344) and he recognizes that ethnic (racial) antagonism may so suffuse other interests that political class differences are constantly held in abeyance (319).

2 See for South Africa, the discussion by Simons and Simons (1969: 618-19), and for the United States, Boggs (1970: 9-18).

extreme forms of racial discrimination. Moreover, members of the subordinate race, are generally economically differentiated and do not constitute a single class, with the result that racial or national liberation movements bring together different classes (peasants, workers and bourgeoisie) in revolutionary struggles against domination.

The Durkheimian models stress the cross-cutting relationship between members of the segmented sections as the basis for new forms of solidarity, transcending the old divisions.[3] The segments may be constituted by sections physically isolated from each other in their own territories or hierarchically separated by discrimination in occupation and by systematic segregation. The Durkheimian type model is essentially a model of evolutionary change, but the basic theory was developed in racially homogeneous societies in the process of industrialization, and its general applicability to racially plural societies may be somewhat doubtful. It is difficult to know what significance to attach to interpersonal relations and solidarities between individual members of different racial sections when there is an unequal political incorporation of racial sections as collectivities. Moreover, physical identifiability in a racially plural society is a more enduring identity than class membership in an industrializing homogeneous society, and mobility may have quite different consequences.

Theories of the plural society or of pluralism stress the cleavages, or discontinuities, between sections differentiated by race, ethnicity, religion or culture. These bases of differentiation are not conceived to be primordial:[4] they are socially structured in the process of interaction. Racial difference has no intrinsic social significance.[5] It comes to

3 See, for example, Gluckman (1969: 402). Despres (1967: 17-20), describes this model as a reticulated model.

4 Geertz (1963*a*: 109) emphasizes the challenge to civil politics in the new States of what he describes as 'primordial' attachments stemming from the assumed 'givens' of social existence.

5 M.G. Smith (1960: 774-5).

have social significance only as it is elaborated in systems of differential political incorporation, economic stratification and racial segregation. Since the theory of plural societies is derived from the analysis of sharp and persistent cleavage, it tends to stress the enduring nature of plural divisions and the high probability of violence in the process of political change.

At the ideological level, both Marxist and Durkheimian perspectives emphasize interracial solidarity. In the case of Marxist theory, the interracial solidarity is between persons of different race performing the same functions in the process of production; in Durkheimian theory, the interracial solidarity flows from a great variety of cross-cutting relationships. While difficulties in the application of class theory to racially plural societies lie precisely in the failure of class solidarity, and while class theory may be used to heighten racial conflict by an identification of the races with different classes, nevertheless the theory itself provides an ideology of interracialism, restraining the expression of racism and guiding action towards racial co-operation. Perspectives from Durkheimian theory similarly encourage ideologies of interracial solidarity, though, to be sure, fear of the consequences of cross-cutting relationships may stimulate a dominant group to apply a policy of systematic totalitarian racial segregation and discrimination, as in South African apartheid. Intrinsic to both Marxist and Durkheimian perspectives is a moral conception; in Marxist theory, a conception of progress towards equality by a revolutionary dialectic of change, and in Durkheimian theory, a conception of increasing contact, harmonious interrelationship and progressive withering away of racial inequality, by a process of evolutionary change. At the political level, these perspectives correspond to communist and liberal ideologies

In theories of the racially plural society, on the other hand, there is no promise of progress to interracial solidarity or to racial equality. The perspectives are somewhat sombre and the theories lend themselves readily to ideological distortion. Dominant racial groups may emphasize the

prevalence of racial and ethnic conflict as a basis for the
assertion that racial pluralism is part of the natural order, and
they may derive from this the conclusion that racial
domination is therefore justified. Subordinate racial groups
may find in the doctrine some encouragement to an unre-
strained expression of racial antagonism. Ideologists of varied
persuasion may seek to interpret the theory as postulating
innate and intractable racial or ethnic antagonism. All these
interpretations are quite foreign to the theories of plural
societies, and, in fact, totally misrepresent them. But they
arise from the preoccupation in these theories with cleavage
and conflict, and the fact that the theories do not incorporate any moral conceptions. The interest in plural societies
may indeed develop out of a strong moral commitment to
the avoidance of destructive social conflicts and to the search
for methods of peaceful change to harmony and equality.
But the moral commitment is not inherent in the theories,
which can only claim that they perhaps introduce a more
realistic approach to the study of plural societies.

1.

The concept of the plural society or of pluralism is variously
interpreted. Other terms are also used to describe the
phenomena of the plural society, such as composite societies,
feudal societies with cultural bifurcation, multiple societies,
segmental societies, segmented societies, social dualism and
sociétés multi-communautaires.[6] The very diversity of

6 See M. G. Smith (1969a: 416-17) and his reference to the work of
Radcliffe-Brown, Sjoberg, Nash, van Lier, Hoetink and Speckmann; see
also Quermonne (1961: 29-59). It should be noted that there is an
entirely different and older conception of pluralism or the pluralistic
society, 'in which the pluralism of the varied constituent groups and
interests is integrated in a balanced adjustment, which provides conditions favourable to stable democratic government' (Leo Kuper,
1969a: 7). This conception of 'democratic pluralism' has no relationship to plural society theory, but is sometimes confounded with it,
thereby encouraging charges against plural society theory which

concepts and interpretations indicates the presence of distinctive phenomena, challenging the analyst to new theoretical formulations, and the somewhat preliminary state of theory in this field.

In the evolution of the theory of the plural society, there has been a movement towards more universal and flexible formulations. As Furnivall (1948) developed the theory it applies to colonial tropical societies. Colonial domination imposes a Western superstructure of business and administration, giving relatively free rein to economic competition in a situation of cultural, social and racial diversity. No common or social will binds together the medley of peoples living by their own religion, culture or language. Instead, they are held together by pressure exerted from the outside by the colonial power and by the force of economic circumstances. The relationships between the different sections are characterized by dissensus and inherent instability, and emancipation from colonial rule raises the problem of finding some moral principle of superior validity to economic interest as a basis for consensus and integration.[7]

M. G. Smith detached Furnivall's concept of the plural society from its colonial matrix, thereby giving it a more universal significance. At the same time, Furnivall's critique of the historical phenomenon of capitalist colonialism disappears from the theory. Moreover, in the process of universalizing the concept, its moral component becomes neutralized. The emphasis on race relations also disappears from the theory. It is replaced, in M.G. Smith's earliest formulation by an emphasis on cultural pluralism, racial differences deriving significance only from cultural pluralism, and in later formulations by an equivalence, at the analytic

emanate from the abundant critiques of 'democratic pluralism' in left journals.

7 See Furnivall (1939: 464-9; 1945: 161-84; 1948: 506, 547); Rex (1959); Kuper and Smith (1969: 3, 10-11, 29, 415-30, 448-9); Layne (1970: Chapter 1); and Fortes (1970).

level, between racial and other pluralisms.[8]

Smith's first formulation of plural society theory, and the controversy it generated particularly among Caribbean scholars, are largely of historical interest.[9] In this formulation, he attaches primacy to cultural pluralism which is defined as the practice of different and incompatible forms of compulsory institutions by the sections comprising the plural society. Cultural pluralism is conceived as imposing the necessity for sectional domination by a cultural section. The plural society is typically constituted where this cultural section is a minority, a situation in which the structural implications of cultural pluralism have their most extreme expression. The societies are held together by regulation rather than by consensus, and changes in the social structure presuppose political changes and usually take a violent form.

This formulation has been criticized from a Durkheimian perspective, on the ground that it minimizes the significance of common institutions and cross-cutting relationships which develop in the contact between sections; from a Marxist point of view, or class perspective, as being insensitive to the bonds of common interest arising on the basis of similarities in class situation; and from an internal analysis of the theory itself as not providing an adequate basis for determining the presence or dimensions of cultural pluralism, and as over-emphasizing the significance of cultural differences and values. Nevertheless, the formulation retains its value as an

---

8 The equating, at an analytic level, of pluralism based on race with pluralism based on ethnic divisions is exasperating to some African analysts for whom it has the effect of reducing the moral responsibility of whites for racial oppression, and of making ethnic conflict seem more intractable, at a time when there is a great need in Africa for ethnic integration. This equating is also viewed as ahistorical, since the great majority of racially plural societies, in contrast to ethnically plural societies, result from Western colonization and imperialism.

9 See among others M. G. Smith (1960); Rubin (1960); R. T. Smith (1961); McKenzie (1966); Morris (1966, 1967, 1968); Despres (1967, 1968); Leo Kuper (1969a); and M. G. Smith (1969a).

analysis of cultural pluralism,[10] though it has been transcended in plural society theory.

Smith's later formulation of the theory is more flexible,
and emphasizes political structure rather than cultural difference. He introduces the mode of political incorporation as
a central concept. Under 'universalistic' or 'uniform' incorporation, individuals hold their citizenship directly and not
through sectional identification, and they hold their citizenship on a basis of equality, whereas under 'equivalent' (or
'complementary') incorporation, and under 'differential'
incorporation, they are linked to the polity, and their rights
and duties are defined, through their sectional membership.
In 'equivalent' (or 'complementary') incorporation, the
society 'is constituted as a consociation of complementary or
equivalent, but mutually exclusive, corporate divisions, membership in one of which is prerequisite for citizenship in the
wider unit'. In differential incorporation, 'the society is
constituted as an order of structurally unequal and exclusive
corporate sections, that is, as an explicitly plural regime'.[11]

The concept of the mode of incorporation is linked with a
distinction between three levels of pluralism; cultural, social
and structural pluralism. Cultural pluralism refers simply to
institutional differences without a corresponding collective
segregation: it may be present in societies constituted on the
basis of a uniform mode of incorporation. Social pluralism is
the condition in which institutional differentiation coincides
with the corporate division of the society into a series of
sharply demarcated and virtually closed social sections or
segments. Structural pluralism consists in the association of
cultural and social pluralism with differential incorporation.[12] The plural society, in the classic form described by

10 One is struck, for example, by the significance of ideologies of
cultural difference in many plural societies, the political conflict over
the terms of access to the culture of the dominant section, the
denigration of the culture of the subordinate section, and the revival of
cultural nationalism in revolutionary movements against domination.

11 M. G. Smith (1969a: 435).

12 ibid., 440

Furnivall, is a society characterized by structural pluralism, in which the dominant group is a numerical minority.[13]

More flexible formulations are based on the concept of pluralism conceived as a continuous variable, and not as dichotomous.[14] Among the major dimensions of pluralism, van den Berghe (1969: 69-72) specifies demographic, cultural and ideological variables, and variable patterns of social pluralism at group, institutional and individual levels.

In my own formulation (1969b: 469-79), I distinguish four dimensions of pluralism, namely: (a) particularism-universalism, which is essentially the mode of incorporation, interpreted broadly to include not only differentiation in the general political structure of the society, but also in the government of such institutional structures as industrial, educational and religious establishments; (b) segregation-assimilation, corresponding to extent of social pluralism; (c) cultural diversity-homogeneity, corresponding to extent of cultural pluralism; and (d) inequality-equality in the differential access to and distribution of power, status and material resources.

Two summarizing measures of pluralism, based on these variables, are suggested. Discontinuity-continuity is a measure of the extent of inequality in incorporation, extent of segregation, and of differences in culture and in possession of power and material resources: the discontinuities are both quantitative, as in the differential industrial wages paid to workers of different race, and qualitative, as in the distinctive roles ascribed to members of the different sections.[15]

13 ibid., 445.

14 See discussion by Haug (1967: 294-304) of the relationship between degrees of pluralism and demographic, communication, economic and political variables.

15 See for example, Furnivall's description (1948: 311) of the cleavages along racial lines in the plural society: 'The foreign elements live in the towns, the natives in rural areas; commerce and industry are in foreign hands and the natives are mainly occupied in agriculture; foreign capital employs native labour or imported coolies. The various

Superimposition-dissociation   (derived   from   Dahrendorf, 1959: 213 ff., 316-17) is a measure of the extent to which lines of cleavage coincide or diverge throughout the structures of the society. Even where the approach is based on pluralism as a continuous variable, it is useful to retain the concept of the plural society as representing an extreme form of pluralism.

What is common to these conceptions of the plural society and of pluralism is that they have come to be applied to any society that is politically unitary through being under a single, supreme political authority, or that has a unitary organization in relation to the outside world by any other structural criteria, but is internally made up of racially or ethnically or culturally diverse groups who maintain distinguishably separate ways of life.[16]

2.

Plural societies may be viewed as *sui generis*, or as characterized in more extreme form, by phenomena of cleavage or discontinuity present in all societies. From either perspective the analysis of plural societies raises questions for the more generally accepted theories of political change.

There are many problems in the application to racially plural societies of Marxist theories of the relationship between the economic and political orders, the universality of the class struggle, and the dialectic of revolutionary change. These problems result partly from the fact that while racially plural societies are characterized by both economic differentiation and racial stratification, the boundaries of race and class do not precisely coincide, thereby giving rise to

---

peoples meet only in the market as competitors or as opponents, as buyers and sellers.' See also Fanon (1963: 37-43) for a powerful description of the Manichean colonial world.

16 This is as Fortes (1970: 8) defines the current use of the concept, save that I have included racial diversity (pluralism) with which much of his article deals.

ambiguities in the social situation. In this context, plural society theory tends to emphasize the racial structure itself and the mode of differential incorporation, whether *de jure* as in South Africa or *de facto* as in the United States, and to question the primacy, though not the significance, of economic factors.

The political institutions in plural societies are by no means a superstructure built on the relations of production; on the contrary, it is the power derived from the political institutions which appreciably defines the relation to the means of production. Failure in solidarity between workers of the dominant and subordinate races, which has been a source of disillusionment among black revolutionaries (Cruse, 1968: 139-55; Simons and Simons, 1969: 621) may perhaps be reconciled with Marxist theory by an extension of the doctrine of the aristocracy of labour; but if many of the workers of the dominant race in a racially plural society do in fact constitute a labour aristocracy, they do so by virtue of their differential racial incorporation, their dominant political position, and not by virtue of a distinctive relationship to the means of production.

Commitment to the dogma of the universality of the class struggle has been somewhat weakened by criticism from leaders of national liberation movements. Cabral (1969: 77) raises the issue from one perspective when he comments that to conceive of history as beginning with the class struggle would be to consider 'that various human groups in Africa, Asia and Latin America were living without history, or outside history, at the time when they were subjected to the yoke of imperialism'.[17] Many leaders of liberation movements in plural societies, such as colonial and white settler societies, find it difficult to reconcile their own struggle with the class struggle, in a situation in which there is failure of

17 Cabral concludes that the level of productive forces, the essential determining element in the content and form of class struggle, is the true and permanent motive force of history.

solidarity between workers of different race, in which the struggle calls for the mobilization of all sections in the subordinate group, and in which the antagonists are appreciably defined by political criteria, such as colonizers and colonized, or ruling race and subject race.

In reconciling Marxist theory and reality, primacy may still be given to the class struggle in the national liberatory phase, by emphasizing the progressive or revolutionary role of particular classes within the liberatory movement, an approach which has given rise to an appreciable controversial literature.[18] Or, recourse may be had to the conception of the two-stage revolution, the national bourgeois or democratic revolution, followed by the socialist revolution, the relationship between class and race in racially plural societies being thereby reversed, so that instead of the class revolution being the precondition of racial equality, it is the social democratic revolution which is the precondition of the socialist revolution.[19] Or, finally, the class struggle may be conceived in the global terms of a struggle between the imperialist nations and the oppressed nations, or between the workers of the imperialist nations, the oppressed peoples of the world and the socialist countries on the one hand, and on the other, the international bourgeois owners of the means of production.

Each of these approaches involves the acceptance of an appreciable measure of solidarity between different classes among the oppressed peoples, at any rate in the immediate internal conflict, and this has implications for Marxist revolutionary theory of the polarization of classes in relation to the means of production. From a plural society perspective, the defining characteristic in the dialectic of conflict may be seen in political terms, as the relationship to the

18 See Staniland (1969) for a review of the controversy raised by Fanon's conception of the peasantry as the truly revolutionary element in the colonial situation.

19 See Simons and Simons (1969: 410-11), Klinghoffer (1969: 156-68) and Appendix I.

means of power, the precipitants of revolution being any factors affecting this structure of relations, and not necessarily economic process and change. The persistence of feudal-type relationships in an industrialized society, radical change in the economic institutions while the political institutions remain relatively unchanged, and a continuing revolutionary situation in Marxist terms without revolutionary change, are more consistent with plural society perspectives than with Marxist theory (see Chapter 7 and Appendix I).

Comparable difficulties arise in the application to racially plural societies of theories derived from Durkheimian perspectives. The common element in these theories is the emphasis on progressive change by the development of relationships cutting across the initial sectional divisions. The social basis for the cross-cutting intersectional relationships may be an increased sharing of a common culture, or participation in the same institutions, or varied social relationships between individuals of different race or ethnic background. Significance is attached to the cross-cutting relationships as contributing to integration or stability or change towards democracy.

Perhaps the sharing of many elements of a common culture does often contribute to integration and stability, though clearly there may be sharp divisions and revolutionary struggle in societies which are relatively homogeneous in culture, and the pursuit of the same values may, in itself, be a source of conflict (McKenzie, 1966: 59). In plural societies both cultural differences and cultural asssimilation become a focus of conflict. In colonial and white settler societies, ideologies of cultural difference are used to rationalize domination. At the same time, the opportunity to acquire the culture of the dominant section is carefully controlled, and the promise of equality of participation for the culturally assimilated proves illusory. In consequence, conflict may be expressed in part in claims and counter-claims of cultural superiority and in the revival of traditional culture, educational policy becomes a crucial political issue, and the culturally assimilated may be driven to lead their people in revolutionary struggle.

The consequences of participation in the same institutions will vary with the nature of the institution and its intersectional relationships, and its mode of articulation within the society. Colby and van den Berghe (1969: 183) comment that 'on the one hand, these common institutions are the very bases of integration of the plural society; on the other hand, the asymmetry in many of the inter-ethnic relations generates conflicts'. Characteristically, in plural societies the relationships within the economic order are markedly asymmetrical. Economic interdependence may be conducive to stability and integration under certain circumstances, but the expectation that industrial economic growth in plural societies will automatically contribute to integration and democratic change is clearly unrealistic, given the persistence of racial inequalities in the United States, and in South Africa (see Blumer, 1965: Chapter 6; Fortes, 1970). In plural societies, the response to pressure for more equal participation, generated by economic growth, may be increased political repression, as in South Africa.

The increase in networks of interpersonal relationship between individuals of different race or ethnic group may certainly be a basis for restructuring the society, but again difficulties arise in plural societies, where there is differential incorporation of the races. M. G. Smith (1969*b*: 51) argues that under these structural conditions, individual actions or alignments cannot transform the social divisions. Other analysts of colonial society have made similar observations.[20] Certainly, in such situations of extreme pluralism and violent conflict as prevailed in Algeria, the bonds of interpersonal solidarity are rendered ineffective.

Racial and ethnic division in plural societies is a very different social phenomenon from segmental division in the

20 See for example, Memmi (1957: 54) and Aron (1962: 8). See also Chapter 6 for an attempt to assess the significance of cross-cutting relationships for evolutionary change.

homogeneous societies of Durkheim's theory. In plural societies, the new relationships resulting from the progressive division of labour may be largely superimposed on the old divisions, thereby elaborating, rather than changing, the plural structure of the society. Under certain conditions, acculturation, participation in the same institutions, and cross-cutting relationships may contribute to intersectional solidarity, but they are also areas of conflict between plural sections. Models derived from Durkheim's theory of the movement from mechanical to organic solidarity can only be used with many qualifications and reservations in the analysis of political change in plural societies.

3.

Quite apart from raising critical questions in the application of Marxist and Durkheimian theories, plural society theorists offer their own distinctive perspectives. These perspectives derive from the emphasis on discontinuities, or cleavages, between the various sections, and stress the role of the political institutions, including the mode of differential incorporation.[21] They are most relevant in situations of racial or ethnic pluralism, which constitute the great majority of plural societies.

The discontinuities are not viewed as based on the assumed 'givens' of social existence, but as arising in the process of interaction within the society. In the case of the non-national State (Nash, 1958), only the dominant section is organized initially on a national scale, while the subordinate section or sections consist of many local groups. The integration of

21 Furnivall, in his conception of the plural society, emphasized the role of economic forces, exempt from the control of the social will, and acting in the context of colonial domination and racial and cultural pluralism. However, he considered that it was only at the political level that the problem of creating a common social will could be solved: 'Political reintegration is not conditional on but a condition of social and economic reintegration' (Furnivall, 1948: 506).

these local groups into a national section may result from the activities of such 'broker' institutions as ethnic associations and political parties (Despres, 1967: 22-7); or nationalism and political independence may transform ethnic categories to ethnic blocs (Freedman, 1960: 167); or the 'modernizing' process may stimulate an extension of local group loyalties to the national ethnic level.

The presence of pervasive discontinuities may raise acute problems for the maintenance of cohesion, which is based, not on shared values, but on political control exercised by the dominant section, and on economic interdependence between the different sections (Colby and van den Berghe, 1969: 10-13). Though elements of consensus are present, and they may be quite appreciable, the society is not integrated by consensus, nor may consensus be deduced from quiescence. In plural societies, potential conflict between the different sections may be a stimulus, or justification, for the one-party State or for despotic or military rule (see discussion by Fortes, 1970: 16-18, and van den Berghe, 1969: 67-81).

Notwithstanding the problems of cohesion raised by pervasive discontinuities, plural societies may be relatively stable for long periods of time. However, when political change is once in motion, the processes often tend to be violent and cataclysmic. A number of factors contribute to this tendency. Members of the same racial section are subordinate in many different institutional structures, so that conflict may move rapidly from one sector to another in a seemingly irrational and unpredictable manner. Thus minor, isolated events may have great resonance and precipitate societal intersectional conflict. So too, issues of conflict are readily superimposed, contributing to the likelihood and intensity of violence. Moreover, since there is an intimate relationship between political regulation and social process, social change and perturbation have their repercussions on the central political system.

A model of revolutionary change in societies, along the

lines of a Marxist model of polarization,[22] but substituting the racial (or ethnic) contradiction for the class contradiction, would take as its basis the differential incorporation of the sections in systems of political inequality. On the basis of this differential political incorporation, inequalities ramify throughout the institutions of the society, more particularly in the economic and educational institutions.[23] A pervasive superstructure is thus erected, giving rise to a generalized racial status. Any event which affects this racial status may precipitate conflict. Since the entire superstructure is maintained by political domination, the ruling section may respond to any pressures for change by seeking to increase the effectiveness of its political power, so as to maintain the status quo, in which case there is a dialectical relationship between the races along the dimension of political power. The primary objective of the revolutionary struggle is to change the structure of political domination. The racial or ethnic consciousness which develops is an entirely different phenomenon from class consciousness: it has different social roots, it is responsive to different appeals, and it expresses itself in different aspirations. Its goals are likely to be change in the incumbency of positions of power and wealth, rather than radical transformation of the mode of ownership of the means of production.

This model of revolutionary change is constructed on the assumption that the racial or ethnic sections confront each other as antagonistic blocs in an overall context of extreme discontinuity. But there are always both continuities and discontinuities in plural societies, as is clearly demonstrated

---

22 I am not suggesting that there is any process, comparable to the tensions between the mode and relations of production, from which polarization of the races would inevitably result. Under pressure, the ruling section may offer reforms of the system, which are acceptable to members of the subject race, thereby initiating an evolutionary process of change.

23 The model of revolutionary change is more fully developed in Chapter 8.

by the manner in which revolutionary violence turns inwards as well as outwards, as for example in Algeria (Feraoun, 1962) and in Kenya (Buitenhuijs, 1971: Chapter 12). The combination of continuities and discontinuities lends an ambiguity to the relations of the races or ethnic sections; there is no automatic polarization. Nor, on the other hand, is the conflict simply the product of the machinations of political leaders, as maintained in some of the Machiavellian theories of ethnic conflict in Africa. There are social forces conducive to racial or ethnic conflict, but also the potentiality, under certain conditions, for progressive evolutionary change, thus offering the possibility for political choice. It is for this reason that two models are suggested for political change in plural societies, corresponding to different political tendencies in the subordinate plural sections. One emphasizes accommodation and evolutionary change by progressive incorporation on a basis of equality, while the other seeks a solution by the sharpening of sectional identity in dialectical opposition and revolutionary challenge (Leo Kuper, 1969*b*).

In attempting to estimate the potentiality for evolutionary political change, it cannot be assumed that the probability of evolutionary change automatically increases with increasing continuities between the different sections in structure and culture. Some combinations of continuities and discontinuities may be particularly conducive to conflict.[24] Moreover, in racially plural societies, and to a lesser extent, in ethnically plural societies, the upwardly mobile of the subordinate section are readily recoverable. And in plural societies generally, intersectional violence is often a powerful stimulant to polarization.

The framework proposed by Beltran (1969: 93-118) may be useful for research into the potentialities for revolutionary violence or progressive evolutionary change. He distinguishes dualism between the traditional and modern sectors, primary or ethno-cultural pluralism, and secondary pluralisms, includ-

24 See, for example, the use by Galtung (1966) of the concept of status incongruity in his theory of conflict.

ing political, restratification, religious and linguistic pluralisms. And he analyses the interaction of dualism and
pluralisms, arguing that their superimposition contributes to
polarization, and suggesting that higher levels of integration
may be attained by a standardization at the base, assuring all
the members of the society a more or less equal participation.

Whatever the approach, the processes of political change in
plural societies should be seen as indeterminate. They are
affected by the political choices which the actors themselves
make within the society; and they are affected by intervention from the outside. In the contemporary period, this
intervention has stimulated conflict and heightened violence
between the plural sections, as the great powers wage their
struggles for political domination in the countries of small
nations. But, perhaps in the future, as a community of
nations develops, it may stimulate or reinforce processes of
peaceful political change to equality of participation.

CONCLUSION

10

A Personal Statement on Revolutionary Change in Race Relations

1.

There is a much abused revolutionary slogan that the history of freedom is written in blood. Under the guise of a statement of fact, it calls for the writing of even more history in even more blood. As a statement of fact, it is only partly true in the field of race relations. Societies under racial domination have changed by relatively peaceful means. But certainly under conditions of extreme racial or ethnic pluralism, political change is likely to be most violent. And in recent decades, there have been a number of very bloody racial revolutions, while others are seemingly in process.[1]

The statistics of violence are notoriously unreliable, as if ten lives, or 1,000 lives or 100,000 lives more or less were of no consequence. In the Algerian revolution, hundreds of thousands of Algerians lost their lives, perhaps as many as one million, and terrible atrocities were committed by the French army, the settler terrorist organization and the revolutionary forces. John Okello (1967: 160), who led the Zanzibar revolution, estimated that 19 of his own soldiers were killed, 1,631 civilian Africans, and almost 12,000 enemy soldiers and persons, presumably Arab. The figures

1 The chaotic nature of revolutionary phenomena is hardly conducive to definitive study. There is evidence for almost any proposition; all the variations on a theme can be documented with some plausibility (see Eckstein, 1965). The interpretation of revolutions is like a great Rorschach test, into which the analyst projects his theoretical, political and emotive predispositions.

may be greatly inflated, but there was certainly a decimation of the small Arab population on Zanzibar Island. In Rwanda some commentators described the reprisal by Hutu against the Tutsi population, in December 1963, as genocidal. If one is to be pedantic about the meaning of the word genocide, the description is greatly exaggerated, though about 10,000 to 14,000 Tutsi lost their lives (Lemarchand, 1970: 224-5) and in some areas they were simply exterminated. In the neighbouring State of Burundi, there is the reverse process of Tutsi counter-revolutionary massacres, with estimates of 50,000 to 100,000 killed.

It may be possible to derive from the study of these revolutions in Algeria, Rwanda and Zanzibar, and of the revolutionary movement in South Africa during the two decades after the Second World War, some impression of the processes of revolutionary change in racially or ethnically plural societies.[2] This would be a first step in attempting to

2 It is some indication of the ambiguity of the field that I am doubtful whether the revolutions in Algeria and Rwanda are properly described as racial revolutions or whether the term ethnic would not be more appropriate. But I am using the term race in the sense of the social definitions which prevail, and the literature abounds with reference to race, the conflict being described in these terms also in key revolutionary documents.

The 1957 Manifesto of the Hutu intellectuals, one of the precipitants of the Rwanda revolution, declared plainly that the conflict was both social and racial, the basic problem being the monopoly of political power enjoyed by one race, the Tutsi. The *Manifeste du Peuple Algérien*, drafted by Ferhat Abbas in February 1943, and signed by some fifty Algerian representatives and notables, states in a preamble: 'qu'est ce à dire sinon que le "problème algérien" — nous nous autorisons à le rappeler — est essentiellement d'ordre racial et religieux et que l'exclusive que frappe l'élément autochtone s'étend à toutes les classes de la société' (1948: 38). The Manifesto itself demands: (1) the condemnation and abolition of colonization, (2) the application to all countries of the right of self-determination, and (3) the granting of its own constitution to Algeria, guaranteeing the liberty and absolute equality of all its inhabitants, regardless of race or religion (40-1). The Proclamation of the Revolution on 1 November 1954 gave as its general objective, the achievement of national independence (1) by the

answer the question whether political change might be brought about in societies of this type by other, less violent means. In this chapter I hope to take the first step.

2.

Our thinking on revolutionary change[3] in race relations is dominated by Marxist theory, with its emphasis on the primacy of economic processes, the formation of classes on the basis of common interests, the increasing tension between the forces and relations of production, and polarization between classes leading to a forceful seizure of power and transformation of the relations of production. We are so conditioned that, quite automatically, we look for the economic causes of revolution. This accounts, no doubt, for the great variety of theories as to the role of economic factors in revolutionary change.

---

restoration of a sovereign democratic Algerian State, within the framework of Islamic principles, and (2) by respect for all fundamental liberties, without distinction as to race or religion (Courrière, 1968: 444).

Perhaps the issue of nomenclature is not very important, since the social cleavages and their expression in Rwanda and Algeria do not seem to have been essentially different from those found in unambiguously racial conflicts. Indeed I would argue that all these societies have a distinctive plural structure, and that certain common consequences for political change flow from this, whether the social cleavages are based on race or ethnicity or religious difference.

3 There is a struggle to preempt the meaning of the term revolution by insisting that it should be defined as an abrupt and violent change in the structure of power, followed by a radical transformation of the relations of production. This would exclude from the concept of revolutionary change the conquest of power by a subordinate group, but without transformation of the relations of production, as for example by the Hutu in Rwanda. I find this an unnecessary limitation on the use of the concept. Where racial or ethnic difference is a basic principle of social organization, then it seems to me reasonable to describe radical transformation of that principle as revolutionary change, whatever the economic consequences.

I would certainly not deny the significance of the economic processes in racially plural societies, which are characterized by extreme economic exploitation and inequality. It is inconceivable that one should attempt to analyse the Algerian revolution without careful study of the economic consequences of the French conquest and colonization. How can one ignore the expropriation of land, which contributed to the dichotomy between the two agrarian systems, European and indigenous, or the role of European agrarian capitalism in the resistance to reforms, in the shaping of European public opinion in Algeria, and in the exercise of political pressures in the metropole; or the decay of the traditional peasant economy, and the large movements of migrants to France and to the Algerian cities, where many remained on the margin of employment?[4]

It is equally inconceivable that one should ignore the relevance of class background or economic situation for participation in the revolutionary struggle. I interpret the Zanzibar revolution as primarily a movement of immigrant Mainland Africans against Arabs.[5] The indigenous Shirazi population, who claimed mixed African and Persian ancestry, played a rather ambivalent political role. Only one section of

4 See the excellent analysis of the political economy of Algeria by Murray and Wengraff (1963).

5 Interpretations of the Zanzibar revolution of 1964 are extraordinarily varied. In the context of the Cold War, it was inevitable that theories of external intervention or influence should be advanced, and a number of exotic possibilities presented themselves. It was Chinese-communist inspired or Russian-communist or both, or indeed backed by Cuban-trained specialists. If the revolution was seen as an essentially internal struggle, and the evidence is overwhelmingly in favour of this interpretation, then again there were varied possibilities. It might be analysed as a class struggle against the big landowners; or as a racial struggle by Africans against Arabs, with disapproval because of the racism, or with approval, as just retribution for past oppression; or race and class might be combined in a conception, somewhat at variance with the facts, that they tended to coincide. The analyst may accept the version given by John Okello, that he personally organized the revolution, and that in recruiting his revolutionary force, he largely

the Shirazi, the Hadimu Shirazi, massively supported the African nationalist movement. In explaining their distinctive participation, it seems reasonable enough to fall back, *inter alia*, on such economic factors as the greater deprivation of the Hadimu. But one must add to this, the geographic situation of the Hadimu on Zanzibar Island, and their frequent migration to Zanzibar Town, where they were described as becoming socially and politically assimilated into the Mainland African community and absorbing its racial perspectives (Lofchie, 1965: 250).

In Rwanda and Algeria, there was varied participation by different occupational strata and regional sections. Wolf (1969: 290 ff.) ascribes a distinctive and significant role to those sections of the peasantry which have some internal leverage, being either a land-owning 'middle-peasantry' or a peasantry in a peripheral area outside the domains of landlord control, or only under marginal control from the outside. In Algeria, peasants on the periphery, in remote mountain fortresses, formed the backbone of the revolution, and Wolf (1969: 230) cites evidence from one area of support by 'middle'· peasants. In the Rwanda revolution, the most violent movements were in the north, a peripheral area in which Tutsi rule had not been firmly established. The leaders of the Hutu movement were a small educated elite and they were supported by a rural proletariat (Lemarchand, 1968*b*).

But this varied participation of different occupational strata, and the highly significant role of economic factors, by

---

excluded members of the indigenous Shirazi population and relied on men who, like himself, had come from the African mainland. If the analyst has theoretical difficulty with Okello's somewhat Messianic version, he can fall back on the view that there were, in the offing, two other Zanzibar revolutions, closely related to the political conflicts of the post-war period, and that the most improper of the three revolutions, theoretically speaking, was the first off the mark. (See the following references in the bibliography: Bochkaryov, 1964; Gathani, 1966; Gross, 1966; Kyle, 1964; Nugent, 1965; Kharusi, 1967; Lieber, 1965; Lofchie, 1967).

no means convert these struggles into class struggles; nor are the processes of struggle to be interpreted in terms of a dialectic of class struggle. To be sure, if the term class is used somewhat loosely as a sort of occupational cluster, then almost everyone involved in the revolutionary struggle can be assigned to a class. But this may not be a very informative sort of statement. Some writers on the Algerian revolution, for example, were intrigued by the fact that a small core of revolutionaries in the battle of Algiers had criminal records. It is quite misleading, however, to describe them as a *lumpenproletariat*, and to introduce the terminology of class struggle, unless it is shown that there was a relatively large participation of men from the *lumpen* class, and that they were expressing, or struggling to realize, the distinctive class interests of the *lumpenproletariat* in opposition to other classes.

A somewhat plausible argument for the view that the *lumpenproletariat* does in fact constitute one of the most spontaneous and radical revolutionary forces of a colonized people is offered by Fanon (1963: 103 ff.). This is often seen as contradicting the traditional Marxist view of the *lumpenproletariat* as potentially reactionary. But Fanon uses the term *lumpenproletariat* rather broadly to include uprooted peasants, who are blocked on the outer fringes of the urban centres, and who have not yet succeeded, as he phrases it, in finding a bone to gnaw in the colonial system.[6] Moreover, in my view, he is analysing an entirely different type of struggle from the class struggle of Marx's analysis.

I think it clear that the struggles in Zanzibar, Rwanda and Algeria cannot possibly be described as class struggles. They did not bring together, in revolutionary challenge of ruling

---

6 Fanon does comment that if the *lumpenproletariat* is not drawn into the revolutionary struggle, it may support the counter-revolution. Peter Worsley (1972) offers an interesting discussion of the role of the *lumpenproletariat*, but he is surely mistaken when he writes, in his comments on the Algerian revolution (212) that the propaganda of the FLN during the struggle proclaimed impeccably socialist aims.

oligarchies, members of different race or ethnic group with similar occupations and standards of living. On the contrary, the contending parties, and the targets for attack, were predominantly defined by race or ethnicity.

It would seem from the information presently available, that Arabs in Zanzibar and Tutsi in Rwanda were slaughtered with Olympian indifference to their class background. In Algeria, the picture is greatly complicated by the fact that violence also turned inwards, as the revolutionary leaders sought to establish their claim to leadership and to eradicate support for the French. Muslim Algerians in the French administration came under special attack as did the many supplementary Muslim troops in the French army, but there were also innumerable reprisals against members of a rival nationalist movement and against peasants who supported or were suspected of supporting the French, or who did not accept the discipline imposed by the FLN. The European terrorist organization, the OAS, assassinated both French and Muslim liberals, and the French troops took disciplinary action against the *pieds noirs*, notably in the Algiers suburb of Bab-El-Oued in March 1962. But who can doubt that the conflict developed increasingly along racial or ethnic lines, as shown in the imposition of collective responsibility, the large resettlement projects, and most dramatically, in the killing of innocent people, defined simply by racial background, in the cycle of terrorism and counter-terrorism?

It might be argued that the division of labour was not greatly advanced in these three countries, and that it is under conditions of industrialization that one would expect inter-racial class formation. Certainly the fragmented patron-client relationships in peasant Rwanda would hardly encourage class organization and action. In Zanzibar, there were no large industrial organizations to bring together masses of workers of different race. Industrial development in Algeria was subordinated to the interests of metropolitan France, and the Algerian economy remained largely agricultural though with considerable development of the sector of services. But in South Africa, under conditions of relatively advanced industrialization, the failure in class solidarity between workers of different race is most marked. White labour was an important force in the development and maintenance of the apartheid structure of racial oppression. And labour relations in the most industrialized country in the world, the USA, are similarly characterized by failure in interracial working solidarity.

Let me repeat that I am not denying the significance of the economic processes and of economic differentiation for the understanding of these revolutions. What I am saying is that the revolutionary struggles in racially plural societies are not to be equated with class struggles, and that the action of classes must be set within a broader framework, which takes the racial conflict as a central phenomenon in its own right. Emphasis on the primacy of economic processes may be misleading when applied to the interpretation of these revolutionary struggles or to the planning of strategy. If the orientation is Marxist, then it seems to me necessary to develop a specifically Marxist interpretation of racially plural societies, and of the dialectic of struggle within them.

3.

Liberal theories are specially sensitive to those co-operative relations within a society which might provide a basis for radical change by evolutionary means. But the term liberal must first be defined. It is applied nowadays with equal facility to *laissez-faire* capitalists, Christians, and reactionary politicians. In a recent collection published by Oxford University Press, we learn that Western liberalism appeared to a new generation of African leaders under the guise of communism and Gandhiism.[7] A contributor to the *Socialist*

7 Fatima Meer (1971: 121-57). Strangely enough, she describes the South African Liberal Party as white (151); yet she knows perfectly well that it was interracial, that it had considerable strength among Africans in Natal, her home province, that, though the leadership was

Register 1972 (Arblaster, 1972: 83) describes Vietnam as the liberals' war, planned and mounted by liberal intellectuals inside and outside the government — at least until the war began to look like an American defeat. The term liberal has clearly lost precise meaning. In current usage, liberal is simply an object of personal anathema, and the term is more revealing of the frustrated aggressions and hatreds of the person who uses it than of the persons or views he anathematizes.

In the context of racially plural societies, I would single out the commitment to interracialism as the core of liberal ideology. Political strategy is based on interracial co-operation in the struggle for civil rights and democratic participation. At the social level, liberal perspectives stress the fostering of racial contact and interaction. There is concern for the sharing of cultures between the groups, while inclusive ideologies emphasize a common society and a common humanity. There is an emphasis, that is to say, on creating continuities of structure and culture between the racial groups, and on using these as the social basis for political change. I would add, as part of the definition of liberalism, the commitment to non-violence. This is somewhat controversial. Certainly, in South Africa a section of liberals turned to sabotage, and in Algeria, there was a conflict of views between liberals wishing to join the National Liberation Front, and those committed to nonviolent solutions. But I think it is accurate to say that, consistent with the emphasis on co-operation, and the avoidance of polarization, there is the rejection of violence, though perhaps not absolute.

There was an older, somewhat conservative form of liberalism, greatly concerned with the attitude of members of the ruling race. In the USA, it fused with empirical sociology

---

predominantly white, there were also significant African and Indian leaders, and that the party dissolved when the government legislated against interracial parties. Clearly 'liberal' must have the connotation 'white' for Mrs Meer.

to give rise to an astonishing series of experiments. These started with the measurement of attitudes; then subjects were exposed to a mind-enlarging experience, such as a series of lectures on race relations; and finally attitude change was measured at the end of the series with great technical precision. In such an intellectual ambience, it is not surprising that recognition of the institutional and structural roots of racism should have come as something of a revelation. Black Power movements were certainly influential in this change of perspective, and in emphasizing the significance of the consciousness of the oppressed. Liberals of a more radical cast, have been very conscious of the origins of most racially plural societies in conquest and exploitation, of the structures of power on which racism rests in these societies, and of the often illusory nature of the appeals to the reason and conscience of ruling strata.

The basic theory of liberalism, as I understand it, is analogous in some ways to Durkheim's theory of the progressive division of labour, though I cannot imagine that this was its source. In Durkheim's theory, the new relationships which result from increasing differentiation and interdependence, cut across the old segmentary divisions, creating a more enduring form of solidarity. So too in liberal theory, interracial solidarity is sought through new relationships which transcend the racial divisions and provide the basis for many intermediate structures. The emphasis is on relationships of relative equality, and on the sharing of common interests and values, as in religious beliefs or political goals. I shall use the term continuity to describe these shared elements of structure and culture.

These continuities were certainly a significant factor affecting the course of revolutionary struggle. In the Zanzibar revolution, Pemba Island, an area of considerable continuity in culture and structure between Arabs and Shirazi, remained relatively tranquil. In Rwanda, the most extreme violence erupted in the north, where there was great discontinuity between Tutsi and Hutu. In South Africa, a central feature of the counter-revolutionary strategy of the apartheid government was the introduction of a whole series of laws with heavy sanctions, for the control of continuities in culture and structure – marriage, sexual relations, residential contact, religious observances, political participation and other interracial association in welfare and recreation. The great number and wide range of these laws, the severity of their penalties, the suppression of political and other intermediate interracial structures under their provisions, and the establishment of separate systems of education, provide some measure of the significance of these continuities. In Algeria, the measure may be found in the almost Herculean effort required to polarize the population; the executions, reprisals, counter-reprisals; the movement from selected targets to promiscuous terrorism and counter-terrorism involving innocent civilians, identified simply by race and not by role; the ritual slaughter of Algerians suspected of supporting the French; the opposition to reforms by both revolutionaries and counter-revolutionaries; and the exemplary liquidation by the OAS of liberals, Muslim and French, who sought to mediate between the groups.

However significant these continuities may be, there is still the problem of making them effective for radical change. Powerful arguments are advanced against this possibility. Ruling strata, so the argument runs, will not give up their power and privilege because they are invited to do so by an appeal to reason or conscience or morality. They will hardly find comfort in the assurance that increases in the national wealth will permit a redistribution in favour of racial subordinates, without threat to their own possessions; the issue is in fact their domination and its attendant privileges. Many are certain to dismiss, as simply pious, the injunction that they have faith in the good intentions of the subject race; they are far more likely to believe, as in Algeria, Rhodesia and South Africa, that their whole way of life would be destroyed if they granted equal rights, or even introduced effective reforms.

Under these conditions, the argument continues, radical change can only be brought about by effective power. Is this really to be found in movements based on the association of individuals of different race in a great variety of social contexts? Can they really be politically effective, when they are so readily controlled by the power vested in the dominant race? Racial cleavage is a major force in the society, and in situations of conflict it overwhelms the interracial movements; participants in these movements tend to give their allegiance to the racial group of which they are members, or they withdraw under the strain of ambivalence, or they are liquidated or in other ways silenced.

Certainly these arguments are cogent. There are clearly many limitations on the potential use of continuities for political change. In relatively peaceful times they may be a source of stability, rather than of radical change; the networks of interracial ties act as a brake on militant action. Sharing the same values, or the same occupational interests, may be a source of conflict rather than a basis for co-operation. If there is great discontinuity in constitutional rights, as, for example, the reservation of the vote for one racial group, then it is difficult to see how common interests in employment, worship and sociability are to be transformed into political rights without direct militant confrontation.

There can be little doubt that liberals are not viable in extreme racial conflicts. They have no mass following, they have no power, they have no skill in, nor inclination for, violence. In consequence they are easily emasculated by governmental repression, or liquidated by extremists on both sides. The mediating position becomes a no-man's land.[8]

8 Camus was deeply conscious of this dilemma, when he appealed, with great personal courage, at a public meeting in Algiers, for a truce on the killing of innocent civilians: 'On peut rire sans doute à la mine que prend le prêcheur de reconciliation devant la réponse que lui fait l'histoire en lui montrant les deux peuples qu'il aimait embrassés seulement dans une même fureur mortelle' (Courrière, 1969: 257).

When combat is once engaged, and the groups begin to polarize, the appeals for conciliation, moderation and humanity become strangely insipid and meaningless. A whole series of ideological certitudes, dialectically linked, rationalize the intransigence of the parties and the commitment to violence. The revolutionary movement rejects reforms as a device for maintaining domination: corresponding to this is the conviction among sections of the dominant group that reforms once initiated lead inexorably to a reversal of power. There is the belief that since the system of domination is founded on violence, it can only be overthrown by violence; this is linked to the common belief among racially dominant groups that the subordinates only understand violence, and that there can be no concessions in response to their violent protest. Associated with these ideologies of polarization are specific strategies of polarization, such as indiscriminate terrorism and collective reprisals.

The crucial problem from a liberal perspective is how to render continuities in structure and culture, and co-operative interracial action, an effective basis for radical change in plural societies.

4.

I have argued that the racial conflicts in plural societies are not to be equated with the class struggle, that classes act within the context of the racial conflict, and tend to be subsumed under it, classes themselves being appreciably divided along racial lines.[9] And I have argued that continuities in structure and culture are likely to be rendered ineffective in times of revolutionary struggle, as those who

9 Conor Cruise O'Brien (1972: Chapter 8) analyses the somewhat analogous problem of working-class cleavages between Protestants and Catholics in Ulster. He writes (183) that 'the more articulate of the Catholic militants, as we have seen, had thought, or said they thought, in terms of class struggle, social revolution, the fight against imperialism. But what had happened was a fight between Catholics and

participate in movements of interracial co-operation are themselves divided along racial lines, comparable to the division in social classes, or are neutralized or indeed liquidated.

These arguments relate to plural societies, in which racial difference has become a basic principle of organization, either *de jure* or *de facto*. The colonial world was essentially a world of racially plural societies and this pluralism has left its stamp on the now independent States. In the contemporary world, the most extreme forms of racial pluralism are to be found in Southern and Central Africa. I would describe Northern Ireland as a plural society on the basis of the sharp differentiation and cleavages between the religious groups. Ethnic pluralisms are of course a common phenomenon. Though I am dealing with racial pluralism, I assume that many of the processes of conflict and political change are common to plural societies, whatever their constituent base. Certainly some of the manifestations of pluralism in Northern Ireland, as in the terrorism and counter-terrorism, are alarmingly reminiscent of the Algerian struggle.

The characteristic quality of plural societies is the incorporation of the groups on a basis of political inequality, such as the exclusion of Africans, Indians and Coloureds from the franchise in South Africa; or the special status of Muslims in colonial Algeria; or the virtual monopoly of political power by the Tutsi in Rwanda; or the privileged political status of Arabs in Zanzibar.

This inequality in access to the means of power (the differential incorporation[10] of the racial groups) is the core of a model I have developed of revolutionary change in

---

Protestants, at the end of which the British army – imperialists – had stepped in, to the great relief and warm welcome of the Catholics.' In conclusion, he argues that though there is class differentiation in Ulster, with Protestants having the edge over Catholics, the conflict is not a class struggle.

10 This concept is derived from M. G. Smith. See his contributions in Kuper and Smith (1969).

racially plural societies.[11] I take the plural society at the stage when it is already established, and I try to envisage the processes by which it would move to revolutionary conflict. The racial divisions are viewed as phenomena in their own right, and accorded structural significance. There is, of course, no suggestion that the racial difference gives rise to the plural society; or that it has any causal significance. Plural societies are generally established by conquest, followed by the expropriation of resources, and the exploitation of labour. No doubt ideologies of racial difference, dehumanizing the subject peoples or reducing them to the status of objects, enter into the expression of the pluralism. But peoples do not establish domination over each other because they are of different race, but in the pursuit of quite concrete interests in power and other resources.

The foundation, then, is the inequality of the racial groups in the access to the means of power. This infrastructure is the basis for a superstructure of inequality, as the original political inequality is extended to other institutions and structures. The elaboration of inequality is most marked in the economy and in education. In the economic sphere, it is the relationship to the means of power which appreciably defines the relationship to the means of production. In Algeria, the expropriations of land, which entirely disrupted the traditional economy, were the fruits of conquest. As to education, the almost general illiteracy of the Muslim population at the beginning of the revolution is as startling a commentary on the *mission civilatrice* of the French as their use of torture in the campaign against terrorism. In South Africa, there was even greater expropriation of land than in Algeria, but the educational services, though characterized by extreme discrimination, were far more extensive.

Inequalities in political rights, in economic participation, in education, ramify throughout the society. They combine with ideologies of cultural difference, contemptuous stereo-

11 See Chapter 8.

types, segregation and other discriminatory devices to give rise to a many-faceted general status of ruling race and subject race. Since inequality in political incorporation is the foundation of the general racial status, the racial struggle revolves initially around the terms of incorporation. In response to political pressure the rulers may take steps to make their power more effective, so that there is a dialectical relationship to the means of power, as in South Africa during the two decades immediately after the Second World War. Or the rulers may resist reforms, thereby heightening revolutionary potential as in Algeria. But the introduction of reforms may also heighten revolutionary potential, as seems to have been the case both in Rwanda and Zanzibar.

Perhaps a high revolutionary potential should be regarded as inherent in systems of racial domination in the contemporary world, with opportunity acting as the catalyst, or, given the diffuse many-faceted status of racial subordination, any factor affecting this general status may serve as a catalyst. The search for the economic precipitant may be quite misplaced, though to be sure there is almost certain to be some economic change in the background, failing which, one can fall back on the convenient conception of economic stagnation as the precipitant of revolutionary conflict.

5.

In this model of revolutionary change in plural societies, I have selected phenomena from the point of view of increasing antagonism between the races and of movement towards revolution. I exclude other alternatives, and ignore the continuities in structure and culture, which might provide a social basis for interracial solutions.

The lines of inequality are not rigidly drawn. Many workers of different race follow similar occupations which might provide a basis for interracial class solidarity. This was indeed an expectation of Communist Parties and the means by which they thought that racial conflict might be transcended through class struggle. It was an expectation, however, based on conceptions derived from industrializing societies, and the appreciable failure of interracial working-class solidarity in industrial plural societies naturally imposed the need to redefine the problem.

There do not seem to be many logical possibilities of redefinition. One may accept that the conflict is not a class struggle *per se*, and fall back on the conception of a two-stage revolution, the first a movement of racial liberation, and the second a socialist revolution. Strategy would then be based on the analysis of the role of different classes in the racial struggle and the forging of close ties with the potentially more revolutionary from a socialist point of view. This implies that the initial conflict is not to be interpreted as a class struggle, and that the major contradicition is not between classes but between racial groups. Would the strategy then be to encourage race conflict?[1][2]

The alternative possibility is to remain well within the framework of class analysis. One may try to exorcize the problem by the conception that race and class coincide, but this is quite misleading and merely introduces a rationalization for open race conflict. Along similar lines one may argue that workers of the dominant race perform a different function in the processes of production or constitute an aristocracy of labour, with different class interests. This by no means solves the problem, since the privileged or distinctive position of the dominant race derives from racial identity, and this

---

12 Clearly this poses a problem for Communist Parties. The South African Communist Party was highly dedicated and active in a society which has been in a revolutionary situation for perhaps two generations. Why then was the revolutionary leadership of the Communist Party not more effective? I think it can be argued, and I find this a depressing thought, that one of the factors was its principled stand on interracial solidarity and the class struggle in a social context where the lines of social cleavage were predominantly racial. Fatima Meer (1971: 121-57) offers a persuasive argument for the thesis that Communist Party policy restrained the militant expression of chauvinistic nationalism.

reintroduces the racial criterion as the basis for conflict of interest.

Indeed, I find it difficult to understand why analysis of racial conflict in societies like South Africa should give a primary emphasis to class categories and the class struggle, when the life chances of an individual are specifically defined in racial terms and appreciably determined by racial identity. Sometimes, the motive seems to be a defence of Marxism and the specific categories of traditional Marxist analysis. But surely Marxism requires no defence. It is probably the dominant social theory of our day, and it is one of the major contemporary establishment ideologies in the world.

The position of liberals and of liberal thought is quite the contrary. Liberals in the field of race and ethnic relations have become isolates. Subjected to the most articulate vituperation, they are everywhere in retreat, and this at a time of great need for the values of liberal thought, the concern for the individual and for human suffering, and the repugnance for such dehumanizing concepts as that many peoples are destined for the rubbish-bins of history, or that power grows out of the barrel of a gun.

There is certainly a need to revise traditional liberal approaches. These rested on the initiative of members of the dominant race, they were oriented to change in the perspective of dominant groups, and they emphasized the appeals to reason and morality. These approaches may still be significant in situations where racial difference is a somewhat peripheral aspect of social structure, as in England. They were not very effective in the extreme racial conflicts of plural societies, and this is one of the sources of disillusionment with liberal approaches.

The continuities in structure and culture would seem more favourable to liberal strategies of interracial action than to strategies which emphasize the revolutionary role of the working class. Where there are few large enterprises, workers of different race are not likely to come appreciably into contact and experience the need for interracial solidarity.

Where there is large scale industrialization, the situation
may be intensely competitive. This encourages workers of the
politically dominant race to entrench their privileges behind
discriminatory laws or practices and exposes workers of the
subordinate race to the experience of racism from fellow
workers in their immediate work environment.[13] The situation could hardly be more unfavourable to interracial
co-operation. By contrast, the liberal perspective encourages
the use of all continuities — between intellectuals, professionals, and workers, where there is some interest in, and
basis for, co-operation, and between people of the same
religion, or with common social and cultural interests. In an
industrialized society, a great range and variety of these
continuities are likely to be available. They are however
diffuse and amorphous, and not readily mobilized in continuing political action.

The conditions for an effective liberal movement are first, a
measure of continuity in structure and culture, so that there
are appreciable numbers whose situation and outlook might
encourage interracial co-operation. The second condition is
that of considerable interdependence, so that the dependence
of the dominant group on the subordinate becomes a source
of power for the latter. The third condition is that the social
basis of the movement rests primarily in the subordinate
group, in the sense that its members take the initiative and
participate extensively. And finally, I would suppose a
necessary condition to be support from the outside world,
through associations which transcend national boundaries
and through international involvement. This would call for a
radical change in the pattern of international intervention,
which has tended to support the ruling group, or to
encourage division and the resort to arms.

The commitment to nonviolence seems to me a necessary
continuing part of the liberal tradition. How can interracial
co-operation be fostered by violent means in a racially plural

13 See Fatima Meer (1971).

society, when the resort to violence is almost certain to canalize the conflict along racial lines? And what would be the distinctive contribution of liberalism if the search for nonviolent solutions were abandoned?

This search is, of course, anathema to many revolutionary circles. It comes under sharp attack as the ideology of a dominant group to ensure the continuity of its domination by the advocacy of futile strategies. Violence quickly politicizes, in contrast to the reasoned interracial appeals. The involvement in violence is like the mark of Cain; by contrast, the liberal can easily withdraw from the arena. Against the atrocities of civil war in massacre, torture, slitting of throats, disembowelment, impaling, rape, desolation, are placed the continuing atrocities of racial domination in the form of high infant mortality rates, low expectation of life, malnutrition, disease, poverty, and the denial of human rights and human dignity. There may be no logical connection between the proposition that systems of racial domination are based on violence and the conclusion that they can only be overthrown by violence, but the argument is persuasive all the same.

The rejection of nonviolence is no doubt motivated by the conviction that it is ineffective, and by a sense of outrage at racial oppression. But I think that it often has other roots. This is an age of passionate commitment to violence, in which vicarious killers abound, in search of a Vietnam of their own. Violence does not always offer a solution; the morality of violence is by no means self-evident. How is it possible to draw a balance sheet between the unspeakable anguish of a people, on the one hand, and the conquest of freedom and the release of creativity for the beneficiaries of the revolution on the other? How can one view the terrible sufferings in the revolutionary struggles of Algeria and Rwanda, or presently in the plural societies of Burundi or Northern Ireland, without feeling the need for other solutions?

APPENDIXES

APPENDIX I

Review of Class and Colour in South Africa –1850 -1950

Review of *Class and Colour in South Africa – 1850-1950*
by H. J. and R. E. Simons (Harmondsworth: Penguin Books,
1969)

This book raises many questions of interest in the application
of the Marxist theory of class struggle to the racially plural
society of South Africa, and analysis of the argument may
contribute to a better understanding of the relations between
race and class.

The authors were members of the Communist Party of
South Africa. As such, they devoted their lives with the
greatest courage, integrity, and selflessness to the cause of
racial and social equality, and it is a tragedy that they should
have been driven from their occupations, and so compelled to
build a new life outside the country they served so well.
Given a lifetime of involvement in the Communist Party, it is
understandable that their book should be a Communist Party
statement, with a marked component of propaganda. But it is
based on many years of scholarly research, and on a deep
knowledge of, and experience in, trade unionism and political
radicalism. Indeed, for the problem of main theoretical
interest, the relations between class and colour, the Communist Party perspective enhances the significance of the study.
It is not easy for communists to pursue a line of analysis
which may lead them to question the universality of the class
struggle, and hence one of the bases for international
communism. But this issue is confronted with integrity in the

present study, though to my mind the analysis is not pursued in sufficient depth.

South African society, among its many iniquities, which have earned it almost universal opprobium, posed three grave problems for Marxists: first, how to explain the persistence of pre-industrial relations in an industrial society; secondly, how to find a class basis for revolutionary struggle in a racially structured society; and thirdly, how to reconcile the national liberation movement with the class struggle.

The first problem relates to the Marxist theory of revolutionary change. South Africa has been industrializing for a century, and is now a relatively advanced, industrial society. Yet many pre-industrial relations persist, affecting more particularly the great mass of African workers. Relations of production, that is to say, have been in tension with the forces of production for a long time, and acutely so for more than a generation, yet there has been no revolutionary change adjusting the social relations and the forces of production in a cornucopia of productivity. The Simons phrase the matter as follows: 'South Africa uniquely demonstrates that a dominant racial minority can perpetuate social rigidities and feudalistic traits on an advanced and expanding industrial base' (p. 618). This is related to one of the propositions they offer in their introduction, namely, 'that an industrialized, capitalist society can perpetuate pre-industrial social rigidities only by adopting the coercive techniques of fascist totalitarianism' (p. 10).

I assume that this proposition is not offered as a conclusion but as a hypothesis. The authors have only analysed South African society, and they have not shown the necessity for the coercive techniques of fascist totalitarianism, but merely the coexistence of these techniques and of pre-industrial rigidities. There is, thus, no basis for generalization. Since the totalitarian methods of control are related to the structure of the society, it might have assisted the authors to probe more deeply into the sources of the movement to totalitarian control. Presumably this total coercion did not fall on the society like a plague from the outside world, but emerged from its very structure. What is the role of coercion, for example, in racially plural societies such as South Africa, in which the races are politically incorporated on a basis of inequality? What is the relationship between political power on the one hand, and the forms and relations of production on the other? To what extent are the latter dependent variables on the political structure? What are the implications of the fact that part of the relations of production, namely those affecting workers of the dominant race, are in harmony with the productive forces?

Possibly in relating their analysis and rich observation to questions in some such framework as theories of plural societies and racial pluralism, they might have been able to move to general propositions. Meanwhile, their hypothesis would seem to be in the nature of a qualification of the Marxist theory of revolutionary change, by limiting its universality to those situations in which the ruling class does not employ the coercive techniques of fascist totalitarianism.

The second problem, the search for a class basis for revolutionary struggle, was a subject of continuing controversy among South African communists. The authors discuss these controversies, adding their own comment, so that they present a great diversity of viewpoints from which I can only select a few aspects for comment.

Perhaps one may think of the revolutionary choice in a racially structured society as lying between the class war and the race war, with Marxists committed to the class war. Difficulties of orientation derive precisely from this commitment in a society where race and class do not exactly coincide, where racial sections are politically differentiated, and where workers tend to divide into antagonistic racial blocs. The authors show that the early socialists were oriented towards the white workers, who were expected to form the vanguard of revolution. Over time, however, two different political tendencies developed. One, the conservative tendency, led to participation in the white power structure, to emphasis on conflict of interest between workers of different race, and to colour consciousness. The other, the radical tendency, continued in the commitment to the concept of class solidarity between workers of different race, insisted that racial antagonisms were a variant or subspecies of class conflict, and led later to identification with the national liberation movement. I think it could be suggested, though this is not the suggestion the Simons make and it would need some qualification, that ultimately both socialist wings moved towards the race war, but aligned on different sides, and that this may be some indication of a revolutionary dialectic based on race, not class.

The problem for Marxists is how to interpret the conservative tendency leading to the abandonment of socialist principles and an involvement in white labourism, which the Simons characterize as 'a primary cause of policies that incite racial hostility, isolate colour groups and dissolve class consciousness in colour consciousness' (p. 618). How is the failure in class solidarity to be explained? One approach is to interpret the failure as resulting from the fact that white workers constitute an aristocracy of labour, or that most white workers share with the bourgeois owners of the means of production the surplus profit of African, Indian, and Coloured labour. I do not know the implications of this for Marxist theory. The Simons define social class in Marxist theory for the first time, I think, on p. 617, though I hesitate to check this since class does not appear in an index mostly of organizations and newspapers. They write: 'A social class in Marxist theory comes into existence when persons who perform the same function in the production process become aware of their common interests and unite to promote them against the opposing class.' Do white workers and African workers perform different functions in the production process, or do they perform the same function without becoming aware of their common interests? If they perform different functions, then what is the basis of the revolutionary dialectic of change? Are white non-owners of the means of production and black non-owners antagonistic classes whose increasing polarization leads to revolution, or is the basic revolutionary conflict between black non-owners and white bourgeoisie? If they perform the same functions in the production process, then why do white workers continue to define their interests as antagonistic to those of black workers?

I believe that the Simons would reply that white and black workers do perform the same function in the process of production, but that various factors obscure or inhibit or distort their perception of common interests and of the reality of the class struggle. These factors include *inter alia*, racial and cultural diversities (p. 25), racial and national cleavages (p. 56), political power of the white workers (pp. 98, 336), absorption of the white workers in the ruling elite (p. 327), effects of labour migration and discrimination on Africans (p. 616), and the reactions of African and Coloured leaders to the discriminatory policies and rabid racialism of white workers (p. 621). It is by reason of factors such as these that I think the Simons would justify their statement that 'the binary model of standard Marxist theory did not fit South Africa's multiple structure of colour, class and cultural groups' (p. 210).

In attempting some reconciliation of Marxist theory with the failure in solidarity between workers of different race, the Simons suggest that 'it is arguable on the historical facts that interracial class solidarity in the Marxist sense exists as a potential in South Africa; that the specified conditions can be realized if workers of different colour groups are allowed freedom of association. White workers actually acquired a class consciousness . . . There was also evidence of interracial co-operation' (pp. 617-18). There were indeed encouraging signs, but the great body of white workers moved into the politics of white domination, and I find it difficult to see how the specified conditions of interracial class solidarity could be realized if workers were allowed freedom of association. This seems to be a somewhat *laissez-faire* belief in the racially integrative consequences of the processes of production. But white workers, as the Simons show, used their political position to press for racial discrimination, racial segregation, protected employment, and monopoly of many skilled occupations. Freedom of association would hardly seem a sufficient condition. At the very least, political equality would be a necessary further condition, and this seems to me all the more certain, since white workers are an aristocracy of labour by reason of their privileged political position. A society, however, in which there is freedom of association between the different races and political equality is a very different type of society from such racially structured plural societies as South Africa.

A more promising line of reconciliation is one which distinguishes the revolutionary views of the authors from the theory held by their inevitable *bête blanche*, the white liberals. This latter theory is one which I was surprised to hear was held by white liberals, and which I had always thought of as one of the theories of capitalist sociology. Somewhat similar to the faith in the productive process, to which I referred in the last paragraph, this is a belief that economic expansion would prepare the way for racial integration and a multi-racial parliamentary democracy. The authors react by pointing out that, on the contrary, industrialism has not visibly eroded colour bars, and that racial discrimination is more pervasive, onerous, and humiliating today in South Africa than twenty years ago (p. 615). Their own theory (p. 610) again emphasizes the productive forces, arguing that if these were allowed free play and harmonized with social relations, skin colour would be irrelevant to status and function. This is no longer a *laissez-faire* theory, the revolutionary act entering in the harmonizing of productive forces with social relations. Now presumably this harmonizing of the free play of productive forces with social relations, would mean the elimination of racial discrimination. But in the first place, this would render tautologous the conclusion to their theory, namely, that skin colour would be irrelevant to status and function, the irrelevance of skin colour being a precondition rather than a consequence: and in the second place, it would again presuppose an entirely different type of society from South African society. I am not sure, but I think that the authors are telling us, that in South African society, race and nation and differences in culture and constitutional rights are major determinants of political affiliation and ideology, and that Marxist theory cannot be applied without qualification.

It is in their approach to the third problem, the relations between the national liberation movement and the class struggle, that the Simons believe they have found a basis in Marxist theory for the resolution of the difficulties of class analysis. Their argument may be taken at two levels, a factual level and a theoretical level.

At the factual level, the authors claim that the class struggle had merged with the struggle for national liberation (p. 609). This is presumably the basis for the general proposition they advance that where class divisions tend to coincide with antagonistic national or colour groups, the class struggle merges with the movement for national liberation (p. 10). Now the fact that members of the Communist Party were active in promoting a Congress Alliance between the African National Congress, the South African Indian Congress, and the South African Coloured People's Organization, and worked closely with this alliance, does not mean that the class struggle had merged with the national liberation movement. It means only that communists had merged with the movement, and this is an entirely different proposition.

Moreover, the term 'national liberation movement' is an over-simplification. It is a term clearly appropriate to the situation in which a nation has been conquered and subordinated, and now moves to throw off the alien yoke. But the Congress Alliance was a movement to liberate the oppressed races – African, Coloured, and Indian. Assuming for the purposes of the argument that Africans in South

Africa did constitute a nation, Coloureds and Indians were
not part of that nation. If the African nation only had been
involved, then some of the crucial questions in terms of
revolutionary struggle would concern the internal structure
of African society: whether there was a bourgeoisie, or if not
a bourgeoisie, a middle class; what its political role might be,
progressive or reactionary, and the nature of its relations with
African peasants and proletariat, and their revolutionary
potential. However, since these other races are also involved,
it becomes important to examine the relations of the African
middle class to the Indian and Coloured middle class, and the
relations between African, Coloured, and Indian workers.
This is a problem which is not sufficiently analysed, as a
result of the over-simplification in the concept of a national
liberation movement.

The general proposition the Simons advance cannot, to my
mind, be supported by evidence from the factual situation.
Moreover, it is somewhat imprecise. They write of the class
struggle merging with the movement for national liberation,.
in societies where class divisions tend to coincide with
antagonistic national or colour groups. The use of the phrase
'tend to coincide' makes it clear that there is a certain
unspecified measure of deviation from the coincidence of
class divisions and antagonistic national or colour groups. It is
precisely because of this lack of coincidence, that socialists
quarrelled so fiercely among themselves, and an intensely
fascist 'white labourism' developed within the working class
itself. Indeed, the Simons' book is essentially about the
problems which arose because race and class did not fully
coincide. But I would also question the proposition even if
there had been an exact correspondence between racial
divisions and class divisions. I can see no reason why the
liberation movement, even in those circumstances, should
take the form of class struggle, be motivated by class
ideology, or result in a radical restructuring of the relations
of production.

At the theoretical level, I have even greater difficulties.

From a strategical point of view, it is easy enough to understand the interest of the Communist Party in the association of the national liberation movement with the class struggle. It was nationalism which won a mass following among Africans, and the revolutionary fervour generated in the nationalist movement might be directed towards socialism. This could perhaps be achieved in one stage by the simultaneous pursuit of nationalist and socialist objectives. Or, it might be achieved in two successive stages, the first being African majority rule, the authors arguing that African equality was a precondition of class solidarity between African and white workers, and the second stage being the socialist revolution. That is to say, instead of the Marxist position that elimination of classes is the precondition for the elimination of racial discrimination, the order is reversed, the abolition of racial discrimination being the precondition for the classless society.

Strategically, the policy is especially plausible since most of the land in South Africa has been taken by whites, and Africans own none of its major industries. A political programme calling for the redistribution of land and the nationalization of the gold mines and other major industries should, therefore, have immediate appeal. However, even in terms of strategy, there are serious problems in the relations of colour and class. The national liberation movement and the class struggle are not necessarily mutually supportive and compatible. The introduction of the Communist Party concept of the class struggle has been a source of division within African nationalism, and a factor in its fragmentation. Perhaps the national liberation movement might have been more united, resolute, and effective with a muting of the Communist Party ideology of class struggle.

Though I understand the strategical reasons of Communist Party policy, I cannot see the basis for it in Marxist theory. The authors are not interested in justifying the policy pragmatically or as a matter of expediency. I assume that they are claiming theoretical authority for it. But what is the basis in the theory of class struggle for a national liberation movement which takes the form of a racial revolution by a subordinate race against a dominant race? And if the polarizing factor is race, what grounds are there for predicting a socialist revolution after, or concomitantly with, the racial revolution? If white workers have been a main antagonist of black workers, why should black workers come together with white workers in a movement of class solidarity? And why should the communist programme for the abolition of private property and the establishment of a socialist society appeal to Africans after the racial revolution, when it seems to have had little appeal for them in the past?

One approach to the reconciliation of the class struggle and the national liberation movement in terms of Marxist theory is to search out significant class elements within the national liberation movement. So, for example, attention is drawn to a national bourgeoisie of the subordinate group acting in the leadership of the liberation movement, and this then is assumed to give the revolutionary movement a basis in class struggle. Or, more significantly in the case of South Africa, the class basis is found in the fact that the majority of Africans are poor peasants or impoverished proletariat. But leadership by a national bourgeoisie, or participation by peasants and workers, does not render the struggle a class struggle. It is necessary to ask what social forces are engaged in the conflict, and who are the antagonists. Is the revolutionary force that of class struggle or race conflict, and are the antagonists differentiated by class or race?

I have argued that in their approach to the application of Marxist theory to a racially structured society, and in their handling of some of the major problems of interpretation, the authors have not sufficiently analysed the implications of racial pluralism. Many of the questions I raise concern the significance of racial division and conflict for the process of revolutionary change. In their introduction, the Simons argue that the issues of colour and class, with which they deal, are issues of continuing significance in the South African struggle, and that it is important to subject these issues, as they emerged in the past, to an honest appraisal from the vantage point of the present. I hope that the questions I have raised may stimulate further analysis of the relations between class and race in a racially structured society, and thereby contribute to the objectives pursued by the authors in this study.

APPENDIX II

A Matter of Surrogate Censorship

The 'surrogate censorship' refers to the exclusion of my chapter on African nationalism from the South African edition of Volume II of the *Oxford History of South Africa*. The censorship was imposed by the Clarendon Press and the editors of the *History* so as to comply with the South African Suppression of Communism Act. This is a most pernicious law, directed particularly against African nationalism, and movements for racial equality; it is one of the key apartheid laws for the suppression of freedom and political dissent. I protested at this decision of the Clarendon Press, and we entered into a correspondence which I had hoped to include in this Appendix, so that the issues could be presented through the documents. However copyright in their letters rests with the Clarendon Press, as they reminded me on several occasions, and they were clearly most reluctant to have these letters published. After almost five months of negotiation, I still did not have an agreement from them in principle, though I would possibly have received it eventually. Tired of waiting, I have finally decided on the publication of my letters, with brief summaries of those from the Clarendon Press. I do this with regret.

To the best of my knowledge, this is the first time that academic publishers and editors of works on South Africa have themselves imposed censorship on a contributing scholar. It opens a new chapter in South African censorship, and could set a dangerous precedent which would greatly extend the effectiveness of the South African government's laws for the suppression of freedom of thought. When I asked the publishers recently whether they would be interested in publishing the chapter on African nationalism and the correspondence, their representative replied that it would be difficult to persuade the Delegates of the desirability of the publication, but that the South African edition was almost exhausted, they did not plan another censored edition, and they proposed to apply to the Minister of Justice for his consent to the circulation of the full *History*. If my continued agitation about the censorship has contributed to the decision by the Press not to republish the censored edition, and if the publication of the gist of our correspondence encourages discussion of a professional ethical code in these matters, then they will have served their purpose.

Summary of letter from the Clarendon Press, 4 December 1968

[Volume II is about to go to the printer. The Press was ready to forgo the South African market rather than interfere with 'your own excellent chapter', but this would have been unfair to other contributors and to South African readers. We have therefore agreed with the editors on the publication of two editions, an International edition and a South African edition. The chapter on nationalism will be excluded from the South African edition, but there will be no attempt to conceal this fact, the chapter will be listed and there will be cross-references to it. Professor Wilson has suggested a note saying: 'Omitted from the South African edition to comply with the law in the Republic of South Africa.']

16 December 1968

Dear Sirs

I write to thank you for your letter of 4 December, though I was saddened by the thought that the Clarendon Press had decided to conform to the censorship laws and thereby submit to the repressive policies of the South African government. I feel that your readiness to forego the South African market for the second volume of the *Oxford History of South Africa* would have been more compatible with those very high standards of scholarship and of academic integrity for which the Clarendon Press is so rightly respected by scholars throughout the world.

Of course, I understand your dilemma. It was because of this understanding, and sympathy with my colleagues' desire that their work should be available in South Africa, that I at one time suggested the course you now propose. But after spending the summer of 1968 in South Africa, I concluded that this would be profoundly wrong . . .* I felt that the only honourable course in regard to the *Oxford History of South Africa*, and my own contribution, was to act with exclusive concern for scholarship and integrity, and not to waive these principles in deference to the laws of the South African government. Why should we act as agents for the repugnant repressions of the South African government, directed specifically against the democratic participation of Africans in the society; and why should we act in conformity with its policy of apartheid?

The law under which you now suggest the suppression of my paper in the South African edition is a very terrible law. It is designed to expunge people from the tablets of the living. Indeed, it goes far beyond this. It is an attempt to banish them to eternal oblivion, as if they had never existed, and this for the crime essentially of expressing those contemporary African perspectives, which it is the declared objective of your history to express . . .**

* I have omitted two sentences here which might, if published, be felt as wounding by those who have to live under apartheid and have to struggle against it.

** Some sentences have been omitted for the same reason. The question of the obligation of scholars living under apartheid is taken up in the last section of this Appendix.

I have been reflecting deeply on your letter, and would be grateful to you for a response to the questions I now raise. I assume the calculation is that if only one edition were published, it would be banned in South Africa, though circulating in the rest of the world. I think that this is almost certainly correct. The further calculation would be that if a special South African edition were published, in which my own contribution was suppressed, it would not be banned by the South African government. This is a disturbing reflection, given the objectives of your *History*, and the nature of the South African government. It is disturbing because it would mean that you have published a history, dealing with contemporary events in South Africa, in a way which is not altogether unacceptable to the South African government. But I think the calculation is probably correct that Volume II will not be banned. However, your expectation may be wrong, and Volume II of the history may in fact still be banned: the government's discretion is quite arbitrary. You would then have compromised on principle, without gaining the objectives you sought to achieve. I could give you so many instances of this in South Africa, including the assurance by the University of Natal that its segregatory policies complied with the principles of apartheid. The assurance failed to realize the objective of permitting the university to retain its African and Indian students, but it succeeded in deeply wounding many members of the faculty and undermining morale.

Presumably the intention in the International edition is that there should be absolutely no compromise with apartheid, and absolutely no censorship. But has this in fact been realized? If the only difference between the International edition and the South African edition is the suppression of my contribution, then I do not doubt that some of the other contributions have already been written in conformity with the censorship laws. When I saw Professor Monica Wilson in Zambia in June of this year, she told me that four South African contributors, including herself, had agreed to omit reference to proscribed sources, but that she would add an appendix, explaining that reference would have been made to the works of the appended list of writers, but for the laws of the Republic of South Africa. However, following legal advice, which seemed to me as a lawyer probably wrong, there would be no reference to the names of the books by these authors, simply a bare obituary, which is certainly to be preferred to the practice of no obituary at all. There is surely no reason why any of these restrictions should be imposed on the International edition, and presumably this will appear in as scholarly a form as we can attain.

I appreciated the decision that the South African edition would carry references to my contribution, even though the contribution itself did not appear, but I was puzzled by Professor Monica Wilson's suggestion that the omitted paper should be preceded by the phrase, 'Omitted from the South African edition to comply with the law in the Republic of South Africa'. There is clearly no need for so telegraphic a form of communication, conveying so little, and cryptic, information, and suggesting as it were something happening of itself. The decision to suppress my paper has been taken by the publishers and the editors, for reasons which they consider valid, and would presumably be ready to defend. These reasons include particular apartheid laws of the Republic of South Africa, and a very real dilemma of choice. Moreover, it is surely a significant aspect of South African history, that the repression of thought, action and African political expression has reached such extremes, that it becomes impossible to publish a scholarly account of African nationalism in South Africa. I believe that all this should be stated, both in the South African edition and in the International edition, and I have attached a suggested form of statement. I would feel deeply humiliated that readers might suppose that the exclusion of my paper was at my own request and for my protection. But, apart from this aspect, I feel that the issue is important and should be clearly stated.

I have one final question. I have advanced arguments in an

attempt to persuade you that the preferable course is to publish one International edition, and to leave it to the South African government to ban local circulation, rather than that you should comply with their laws in anticipation of their action. If, however, you should abide by the decision you have taken, then I will accept that, but I ask the following in return. I was not invited to contribute a chapter which would comply with South African censorship laws, and I would have rejected any such invitation utterly and contemptuously. Instead I have worked for two years on this chapter, on the basis of the invitation to me. I have responded as sensitively as I could to the assignment, trying to write as a historian, complying with many suggestions from Professors Leonard Thompson and Monica Wilson. Only months after I had submitted the final revised version of my paper did I learn that Professor Monica Wilson wished me to conform with the censorship laws. I am saying that I have fulfilled the obligations I was asked to undertake, and did undertake.

You have now made a decision to exclude my paper from the South African edition. I have completed my work to the satisfaction of all parties, save on the question of censorship. Both you and Leonard Thompson have expressed your appreciation of the paper, as did Professor Monica Wilson of the first draft, now greatly improved. The exclusion of my paper is something less than I had the right to expect. But, as I have already said, I understand your dilemma, and I would accept your decision if you allow me the right to use my chapter in the following way. I would deal in a preface with the problem of censorship, analysing some of the effects of the laws on scholarship. I would amplify my chapter, and add a new chapter dealing with the sociological aspects of African nationalism, which I did not develop in deference to Leonard Thompson's wish, naturally, that I should write so far as possible as a historian; and I would seek publication of this small volume – perhaps the Clarendon Press would be interested – and offer it also for circulation in South Africa.

Leo Kuper

Suggested draft

The basis of the laws for the suppression of political opposition to apartheid is the Suppression of Communism Act, no. 44 of 1950. This defines communism to include not only communism, but any doctrine or scheme which aims at bringing about any political, industrial, social or economic change by the promotion of disturbance or disorder, or by unlawful acts or omissions, or threats of such acts or omissions. Refusal by Africans to carry the 'pass' documents as a protest against the curfew laws, or a strike by Africans to improve labour conditions, constitutes the statutory crime of communism.

Under this law, persons may be proscribed and organisations liquidated at the arbitrary discretion of the Minister of Justice. By virtue of section *11 (g) bis*, it is made a criminal offence save with the consent of the Minister of Justice or for proceedings in court, to record, reproduce, publish or disseminate any speech, utterance, writing, statement or extract from any speech, utterance, writing or statement by proscribed or liquidated persons. The main African political organizations have been liquidated under this law, and many African leaders have been proscribed, as well as some of the historians and political analysts of African nationalism.

Legal opinion on the chapter by Leo Kuper, entitled 'African Nationalism in South Africa 1910-1964', was to the effect that it infringed South African law in many respects, mainly by references to books and articles dealing with African nationalism, policy statements of the African National Congress, and statements by African leaders. The legal opinion listed over fifty contraventions, advised that the chapter could not lawfully be published in South Africa as it stood, without the consent of the Minister of Justice, and concluded as follows: 'I do not think that it would be possible to conceive an honest and scholarly account of "African Nationalism in South Africa 1910-1964" which would be publishable in this country without the consent of the Minister of Justice.'

This posed a difficult dilemma for the publisher and editors. If Volume II of the *History* was published or disseminated in South Africa with the inclusion of the chapter by Leo Kuper, the South African editor would be liable to prosecution: but the probability, perhaps certainty, is that it would not be allowed to circulate in South Africa. In consequence, South African scholars would be denied access not only to the chapter on African nationalism, but to all the contributions in Volume II, and the editors and contributors would be denied South African readers and recognition. In the circumstances, the publishers and editors decided that the better course was to exclude Leo Kuper's chapter from the South African edition. It is with great regret that the decision has been taken to exclude this scholarly contribution; but it is available, in precisely the form in which it was written, in the International edition of the *History*.

Summary of letter from the Clarendon Press, 31 December 1968

[The letter of December 16 seems most just and reasonable. The Press is sad to have been driven, or appear to have been driven, into this wretched compromise. 'If it had been purely a political issue there would have been no problem, but it became also a personal one.' The writer does not know whether the Press could get away with the publication of the proposed statement. Indeed it is not clear to him how the Press are to explain why they did not seek the consent of the Minister of Justice in the first place, or how they are to disarm those who ask the question. They are somewhat consoled by the thought that the omission of the chapter would be conspicuous, serving as something of an indictment. The writer cannot say anything for the moment about the suggestion that other chapters were written in compliance with the censorship laws. The Delegates of the Press would be prepared to consider the possibility of publishing an ampli-fied version of the chapter on nationalism separately in a different context. The substance of the chapter would in any event be available in the International edition, which was quantitatively more important, and copies of which would certainly find their way into the country.]

Summary of letter from the Clarendon Press, 11 February 1969

[We are reconsidering matters in the light of the letter of 16 December. The editors have recommended that there should be two editions, the South African edition omitting the chapter on African nationalism. The Delegates of the Press, after considering the case for and against, have accepted this recommendation. The Press would be willing to consider the proposed manuscript on censorship and African nationalism for publication preferably after the appearance of the International edition of Volume II. They would however have to weigh the possible consequences for their Cape Town branch. If the International edition is certain to be banned, the writer does not see how they can hope to sell the suggested book, though 'some improbable and "subversive" books do manage to escape the censors'.

The Press have difficulty about the proposed statement of explanation. They doubt whether they could legitimately quote from Counsel's confidential opinion, and the writer supposes that the statement was something of a manifesto, belonging more appropriately in the other book.]

26 February 1969

Dear Sirs,

Thank you for your letter of 11 February. I am sorry to hear of the decision taken by the Delegates, but I do appreciate your response to the other suggestions I made.

In regard to your willingness to consider a manuscript from me on the operation and effects of censorship in South

Africa, which would include my chapter on nationalism, I can well understand that this could be embarrassing for your Cape Town branch and perhaps it would be better to have it published by a publisher who does not have a South African branch. I am not sure when I would find the time to write this analysis, but I would certainly not seek any publication until after the appearance of the International edition of Volume II of the *History*.

With reference to the statement which is to be published, I do not think there would be any difficulty in quoting from Counsel's opinion if you wish to do so; his permission could readily be sought and I am fairly sure that he would agree. I was a little puzzled by your suggestion that my own draft was something of a manifesto. Perhaps, I am reacting oversensitively, but it seemed to me that my draft was a rather straightforward statement of the factual position and that there were no other important relevant facts which should have been included. In any event, I will be hearing from you later in regard to the wording of the statement.

Leo Kuper

Summary of letter from the Clarendon Press, 20 May 1969

[We enclose a copy of the Note the Press propose to include in the South African edition. After discussion with the two editors, the Press feel that this note says all this is necessary.]

Note

Legal opinion on the chapter by Leo Kuper entitled 'African Nationalism in South Africa 1910-1964' was to the effect that it infringed South African law in many respects, mainly by references to books and articles dealing with African nationalism, policy statements of the African National Congress, and statements by African leaders. In the circumstances, the publishers and editors decided that the better course was to exclude Professor Kuper's chapter from the

South African edition. It is with great regret that the decision has been taken to exclude this scholarly contribution; but it is available, in precisely the form in which it was written, in the International edition of this *History*.

18 July 1969

Dear Sirs,

May I refer you to your letter of 20 May. In replying, I forgot to ask whether the International edition will contain reference to the fact that my chapter will be excluded from the South African edition, and the reasons for it. I would like this to be done and hope you will agree. I think it is highly relevant to the *History* that conditions, and repressive censorship laws, in South Africa were such as to oblige you to exclude my chapter from the South African edition, and I think it is relevant too for readers to know that you judged that the remaining chapters complied with these censorship laws.

Leo Kuper

Summary of letter from the Clarendon Press, 28 July 1969

[The Press are not proposing to include the Note in the International edition. They will consult with the editors. Neither the Press nor the editors 'would wish to imply that the other chapters in the book had been written in order to comply with the South African censorship laws'.]

7 August 1969

Dear Sirs

Thank you for your letter of 28 July. The issue seems to me to be a very simple one. I am sure that the Clarendon Press would not knowingly publish a history of South Africa, which had been censored in the preparation, without informing its readers of the fact. To do otherwise would certainly be to depart from those standards of scholarship for which the Clarendon Press is so greatly respected.

On the question whether the *History* has in fact been censored (or self-censored) so as to exclude reference to banned persons and sources, I can only say the following:

(1) That Professor Monica Wilson told me in Lusaka last year, that she and other South African contributors had decided not to refer to censored sources, but that they would give a list of the authors thereby excluded with the comment that they would have cited these authors but for the censorship laws.

(2) It is surely inconceivable that a contemporary history of South Africa should not refer to any banned sources, save by deliberate design.

If there has been compliance with the censorship laws – and I have no doubt that this is the case, if the same text is being used in the South African and International edition – then surely readers must be informed of the fact. The publishers cannot shelter behind the wishes of the editors. They have an independent responsibility to their readers, and to scholarship.

Leo Kuper

Summary of letter from the Clarendon Press, 13 August 1969

[The Press are not sheltering behind the wishes of the editors: in any event, they have complete confidence in their integrity. It is indeed inconceivable that a contemporary history of South Africa should not refer to any banned sources. Since the Press are publishing the chapter on African nationalism which infringes South African law in some 87 instances, according to information given to the writer, they can hardly be accused of publishing a volume which does not refer to banned sources, or is in compliance with South African apartheid laws.]

25 August 1969

Dear Sirs

Thank you for your letter of 13 August, though I am sorry you responded to some phrases in my letter, and not to its intent or the broad issues. The Clarendon Press, in excluding my chapter from the South African edition, has, of course, most fully complied with the censorship laws of the Republic of South Africa. Indeed, compliance by the Clarendon Press goes beyond the strict requirements of the laws. The South African government does not, and could not, attempt to control publication and distribution outside the area of its jurisdiction. Readers of the South African edition are to be informed of the exclusion of my chapter from the South African edition, and I have asked that readers of the International edition should also be informed of the exclusion of this chapter from the South African edition, and the reasons for it.

On the remaining issues, I have suggested that there may be compliance with these censorship laws in other chapters of Volume II. The relevant questions seem to me to be the following:

(1) Do the chapters in Volume II, apart from my chapter, refer to banned sources, or to the decisions or proceedings of banned organizations, and in this way infringe the censorship laws?

(2) If these chapters do not infringe the censorship laws, is this because the works of banned authors and the proceedings of banned organizations are of little or no significance for students of contemporary South African history outside of the field analysed in my chapter? Or has there been a deliberate policy of compliance by some of the contributors, dealing with the more contemporary phases?

(3) If there has been compliance with the censorship laws in some chapters, is not the Clarendon Press under a duty to inform its readers of the fact, and to mention the names of authors excluded, as suggested by Professor Monica Wilson in the discussion I mentioned to you?

The decision is, of course, one for the Clarendon Press. I can only raise the issues which seem to me important for scholars and protest if I feel there has been a compromise with standards of scholarship. I think it very sad that the Clarendon Press should have made any concessions whatever to the South African censorship laws.

Leo Kuper

Summary of letter from the Clarendon Press, 28 August 1969

[The typescript is with the printer, and there are some points which the writer cannot answer precisely. 'The main point seems to be, however, that Professor Wilson and the other South African contributors have taken cognizance of every relevant source: their chapters and their conclusions are free from any constraints created by the laws of South Africa. They may have refrained from quoting and from making express reference to certain sources, when to do so would make them liable to prosecution, but in essence there has been no self-imposed censorship.']

10 September 1969

Dear Sirs

Thank you for your letter of 28 August. If the documentation is incomplete to comply with the censorship laws, then surely readers should be so informed. This is particularly necessary in the International edition which is not subject to the censorship laws. Readers of the South African edition might realize that reference to banned sources would have been omitted: readers of the International edition would never suspect this and they would be gravely misled.

I have still not heard from you whether you will include the statement I asked for in the International edition informing readers that my chapter was excluded from the South African edition, and giving the reasons for the exclusion. I am puzzled by your hesitation in making the facts known.

Leo Kuper

Summary of letter from the Clarendon Press, 19 September 1969

[The writer is not convinced that there is a need for a general statement in the International edition. Readers can draw conclusions from the fact that the International edition will be marked as not being for sale in the Republic of South Africa. The Press would not wish to imply that the documentation* is incomplete. The author of the earlier chapters states several times that it is not possible to quote certain sources. This is followed by quotations from Hansard or from Court Records. To an anthropologist like Professor Wilson direct observation is the preferred source. There are many direct observations in the earlier chapters. The writer thinks that all the authors have made all the points they believe to be true and relevant.]

1 October 1969

Dear Sirs

Thank you for your letter of 19 September. I think this brings us to the end of our correspondence, and to a conclusion I am sorry about. I have tried my best to persuade you to take the course which seemed to me the honest course

---

* The writer recently told me that 'documentation' should read 'authentication'.

for a press which publishes scholarly works. I am sure that neither of us knows what conclusion readers will draw from the fact that the book is not for sale in the Republic of South Africa. You say that.you do not wish to imply that the documentation is incomplete. But both this letter and your last letter show that you know the documentation to be incomplete: and there is no need for you to rely on implication, when you can simply ask‛ the editors for the facts. There is a large volume of banned literature, including scholarly analyses, for which there is no possibility of substituting Hansard Reports or Court Records. When contributors write that they could not refer to certain authors, the statement would be true in the South African edition but, to the best of my knowledge, false in the International edition, even in the case of South African contributors. And I think it would be a strange history in which the historians said that their readers need not concern themselves too much about the sources, but could be sure that the authors had taken all relevant views into account, and had made all the points that they believed to be true and relevant.

I assume I may go ahead, as we agreed, with the separate publication of my paper, as it is only to appear in the International edition. I am wanting to raise, at the same time, the broad issues of the duties of scholars and publishers in the field of South African studies, and to comment on the problems arising from a concealed censorship.

Leo Kuper

P.S. You cannot seriously mean that Professor Wilson prefers a sort of observational history (not requiring documentation) when her contributions cover early African migrations and nineteenth-century wars, with meticulous and extensive references . . .*

* Three words are omitted here which, on reflection, seem to me unfair.

Summary of letter from the Clarendon Press, 20 November 1969

[The editors have agreed that the same note should appear in the International edition, as in the South African edition. 'This may not say all that you could have wished, but it will make matters a little more explicit.']

1 December 1969

Dear Sirs

Thank you for your letter of 20 November, and for letting me know the decision of the editors. It is sad that it took so much correspondence to arrive at this minimal level of information to your readers. I am assuming that I may proceed to publish my paper after the second volume of the Oxford *History* has been published.

Leo Kuper

Summary of letter from the Clarendon Press, 27 May 1970

[There has been a last minute intervention by the South Africa Foundation who have approached the Minister of Justice. He was very sympathetic, and expressed the view that there was nothing to worry about. However he felt unable to give an unequivocal authorization, or to assume full responsibility himself.]

Note: It appears from an article by Stanley Uys, published in the South African *Sunday Times*, 6 June 1971, that the Foundation wished to avoid the effect that the publication of an expurgated edition, with '53 blank pages', would have on the South African image abroad. The Minister said he could not give formal permission or refusal because he had not been approached formally. Nor did he know what the views of the Publications Control Board would be. 'The publishers and editors did not want to approach him formally and submit Professor Kuper's chapter, because they felt he might then ask to see all the other chapters, and possibly take exception to one or more of them.'

On 20 June 1971 the London *Sunday Times* printed the following story:

HISTORY BOOK CENSORED
by Tony Geraghty

Oxford University Press is publishing two versions of its new and authoritative history of South Africa: one for the free world and a second version for the South African market censored to meet that country's Suppression of Communism Act.

The book – the *Oxford History of South Africa*, Volume II, 1870-1966 – is now being sold in South Africa with 53 blank pages in place of a chapter on African nationalism. The only reference to the subject is a chapter-heading in the book's contents table.

The decision to excise 'the offending chapter' was taken by senior members of the university, headed by the Vice-Chancellor, who sit as delegates to the University Press. The chapter was removed despite protests from its author, Professor Leo Kuper, a South African who now lives in Los Angeles.

A spokesman for the publisher, Clarendon Press – the most prestigious division of OUP – explains that the main reason for OUP's action was to protect one of its two editors, the social anthropologist Professor Monica Wilson, who lives in South Africa.

The spokesman says: 'When we received Professor Kuper's contribution it was clear that it contravened the Suppression of Communism Act by quoting the works of banned persons including Chief Albert Luthuli [a Nobel peace prize winner]. We consulted lawyers in Johannesburg who said it would be quite impossible to publish an honest account of African nationalism in South Africa.'

The University Press delegates discussed the problem in January, 1969 and considered whether to produce a separate edition for South Africa or 'publish and be damned'. Professor Wilson's welfare and the possibility that the entire book would be denied students in South Africa were considered.

The committee had before it the advice of Professor Wilson, who agreed the chapter should be deleted, and Professor Kuper who argued for its retention.

Eventually the committee decided unanimously to drop the chapter from the South African edition if necessary. The publishers then submitted the complete work, in galley proof form, to the South African Minister of Justice, Mr Pieter Pelser, for an opinion.

At the end of 1970 the publisher was told that the Minister would not commit himself. In any case, he said, he could not accept galley proofs in place of the completed book. The OUP spokesman adds: 'As we got no final assurance we decided to carry on as planned. The committee did not consider the matter further.'

The publisher decided, at this stage, to save binding costs of £200 by including blank pages in the South African edition, thus making it the same size as copies printed for Europe and America. It was in this form that the work was submitted to the South African Publications Control Board, which has passed it as acceptable. The board made no comment about blank pages.

On 6 July I wrote the following letter to the editor of the London *Sunday Times*. It was not printed.

Sir

May I be permitted to comment on the report you published on 20 June 1971, dealing with the censorship of my chapter on African nationalism from the South African edition of the *Oxford History of South Africa*. I am afraid the report is very misleading in an important respect. Your correspondent writes that the committee of the Clarendon Press decided to drop the chapter from the South African edition 'if necessary' and then submitted the complete work in galley proof form to the South African Minister of Justice. On the contrary, the Clarendon Press informed me on 4 December 1968 that they had decided to publish two editions, an International edition with my chapter and a South African edition excluding it. On 31 December, the Clarendon Press wrote to me that they did not know 'how we are to explain why we did not seek the consent of the Minister of Justice in the first place, or how we are to disarm those who may ask the question'. It was only seventeen months later, on 27 May 1970, that the Clarendon Press informed me that there had been a last minute intervention by the South Africa Foundation who approached the Minister of Justice, who was very sympathetic, and expressed the view that there was nothing to worry about, but felt unable to assume full responsibility himself or to give an unequivocal authorization.

I understand very well the concern of the Clarendon Press for the welfare of one of the editors, Professor Monica Wilson, who lives in South Africa. I know well the terrorizing effects of censorship, since I was teaching at the University of Natal, when my own book, *Passive Resistance in South Africa*, was banned, and the laws have become even more terrorizing. But the difficulties of the South African editor arose from her retention of the position of editor of the second volume, and not from her contributions, which comply fully with the censorship laws. Moreover the implications of the action taken by the Clarendon Press is that the Press accepts an obligation, where there is a South African editor, to ensure that the publication does not offend against the censorship laws. In the present case, it is not only my contribution which has been excluded to satisfy these laws, but other contributions have been self-censored so as to produce a censored *Oxford History of South Africa*. I believe that the Oxford Press may have already published censored books, but quite unwittingly, and hence without informing readers. The present case however is one of deliberate censorship.

There is however a much more fundamental issue. The censorship laws provide the means for denying freedom of expression, and many books, including works of outstanding scholarship, have been suppressed. The laws are particularly directed against African freedom and opposition to apartheid. There is in these censorship laws something reminiscent of the burning of books by the Nazis, or the proscription lists by which individuals were totally expunged from all records. And the question I ask is a simple one, namely whether it is appropriate that scholars, or a leading firm of publishers of scholarly works, should be the agents for implementing laws which so gravely restrict the free and responsible expression of scholarship? Or should they say that the laws are so repugnant to us, that we will have no part in them?

As I see it, censorship in South Africa has moved through three stages. The first is the imposition by the government of censorship, with government agencies to enforce the laws. Since there is an arbitrary element in the whole process, fears tend to be magnified beyond the requirements of the law. In the second stage, there is a self-censorship to comply with the laws – inevitably, because of the severity of the penalties. But to the best of my knowledge, readers are for the most part not told this, so that there is a concealed censorship. The controversy over my chapter has served to bring this issue into the open. The third stage is the enforcement of the censorship laws against writers, by persons acting on their own initiative and not charged with that function by the government. It is a surrogate censorship which enormously increases the effectiveness of repression. It is this step which the Clarendon Press and the editors have now taken.

There was in fact a very simple alternative available to the Clarendon Press. It appears from your report that the publishers submitted the South African edition, that is the

edition without my chapter, to the South African Publications Control Board for approval, and that this Board
passed it as acceptable. Why then could not the International
edition, published in England, have been submitted to the
appropriate board and minister? If it were approved, and I
think the government might have hesitated to reject an
Oxford History of South Africa, there would have been no
problem. If it were rejected, the editors could then have
decided whether to go ahead with a special South African
edition. The banning would have been the responsibility of
the South African government. Now I reflect with bewilder-
ment that two distinguished scholars and a distinguished
press have acted, on their own initiative, as agents for the
South African government by suppressing my chapter in
order to comply with a repugnant law, which severely curtails
freedom of scholarly expression.

Leo Kuper

SOME COMMENTS ON SOUTH AFRICAN CENSORSHIP

(1) South African scholars, who oppose apartheid policy,
and work on subjects relevant to race relations, have a
hazardous task, threatened as they are by a most oppressive
regime. Some write as if to challenge or stretch the censorship
laws, or as if indifferent to them. Others seek to convey their
meaning, as precisely and accurately as possible, within the
constraints of these laws. It is for them to choose their course
of action, and we can only accept their decision. It is wrong
to be judgmental, as I have been in my correspondence with
the Clarendon Press. But I do think that where there is
compliance with the censorship laws, this should be clearly
stated, and the implications shared with the reader.

(2) South African scholars working in these censored fields
of race relations and political freedom, certainly have an
important contribution to make as editors. If they decide

that the volume they edit should comply with the censorship laws, this is their prerogative in a matter affecting their own safety. But a number of very difficult problems are raised, calling for careful consideration.

(i) The effect may be to impose censorship on South African contributors, who accept self-censorship out of consideration for the editor, when they might reject it for themselves.

(ii) It may impose censorship on an outside contributor, as in the present case, where I had the choice, *after* my chapter was completed, of voluntarily self-censoring my contribution or having it forcibly censored by the editors and publishers. I think that where it is intended to produce a censored volume, the invitation to the contributors, and the contract, should be absolutely specific on this point. The invitation should read more or less to the effect that: 'You are invited to contribute a chapter on ———, which must comply with the Suppression of Communism Act' and the various other acts which restrict freedom of expression. The interpretations the editors give to these acts in terms of their implications for the contribution should also be explicitly stated. In the present case, it did not cross my mind that I might be expected to comply with these laws. I think one must ask whether it is justifiable to impose such a condition *after* fulfilment of the contract.

(iii) The publishers may feel that the participation of a South African editor imposes on them the need for censorship of contributions. There was a phrase in a letter from the Clarendon Press, dated 31 December 1968, which always puzzled me. 'If it had been purely a political issue, there would have been no problem, but it became also a personal one.' Recently I asked in what sense it had become a personal issue, and I understand that the reference was to the personal consequences for the South African editor if my chapter had been included. But the vulnerability only arose because of the retention of the editorship of the second volume. And I think one must ask: is the censorship of this volume really of consequence in the context of a distinguished career with original contributions extending over some forty years? Could the costs of retention be high?

(3) The desirability of making available the other chapters of the *History* to South African readers and students has been advanced as the justification for the compulsory censorship. I am sure it is desirable that these chapters should be readily available. But the argument of the greater good is the almost invariable justification for repression. It is surely the justification the South African government would advance for the Suppression of Communism Act. If this principle can be invoked by distinguished scholars, it must certainly set an authoritative precedent.

I think a number of questions should be asked.

   (i) Are the means irrelevant? Does the service rendered in making the *History* available, outweigh the disservice in exercising political censorship?

  (ii) Are the expectations realistic? In my own letters, I had assumed that if my chapter were included, Volume II would almost certainly be banned. No doubt I was influenced by my own experience, my main works on South Africa, *Passive Resistance in South Africa* and *An African Bourgeoisie* having been banned by the South African government. But there are many scholarly works circulating in South Africa which refer to proscribed sources. The expectations may have been quite unrealistic.

(iii) Were the fears of the South African editor realistic? The editors did not wish permission to be sought from the Minister of Justice for the publication of references to, and quotations from, proscribed sources in my chapter, in case he asked to see other chapters, and objected to one or other of them. Was this a realistic fear? Repressive regimes act by creating fears and anxieties, which greatly extend the effectiveness of the repressive laws. Have the editors in this censorship, imposed in anticipation of the government's action, gone far beyond anything the government would have done.

(4) The decision by the publishers to ban my chapter seems to me to have involved them in a whole series of further consequences — an unwillingness to publish a forceful statement on South African censorship, to include adequate information on the censorship in the International edition, and to make available to the general public our exchange of correspondence. In thinking of the role of a leading academic publisher, working from Oxford and I suppose associated with the University, I do not seem to be able to go beyond the following somewhat blunt statement. In excluding my chapter, the Clarendon Press, whatever the motives of its representatives, has committed an act of political repression. And I cannot see how political repression, particularly in the self-appointed role of surrogate censor for compliance with the Suppression of Communism Act, can be consistent with the high ideals of scholarly publication.

(5) My own role in all this leaves much to be desired. I moved between a sense of outrage and an appreciation of the dilemmas and contributions of South African scholars working under the incessant barrage of political oppression. But I hope that these concluding comments may contribute to a better understanding of the issues raised by the South African censorship laws for scholars and publishers.

Postscript

It appears from correspondence with the Clarendon Press early in 1973, and from a report in the *Sunday Times* dated 9 September 1973, that the South African Minister of Justice has granted an application by the Press for the publication and distribution in South Africa of the complete, unexpurgated edition of Volume II of the *Oxford History of South Africa*. Thus I can only conclude that, in effect, the suppression of my chapter by the editors and publisher has turned out to be a purely gratuitous act of political repression.

The gratuitous nature of the censorship is all the more clear from the fact that Peter Walshe's detailed and carefully documented history of the African National Congress from 1912-52,* published in the same year as Volume II of the *Oxford History of South Africa* circulates freely in the country.

* *The Rise of African Nationalism in South Africa: The African National Congress 1912-1952*, University of California Press, Berkeley and Los Angeles, 1971.

Bibliography

Adam, H. (ed.)	1971	*South Africa – Sociological Perspectives.* London: Oxford University Press.
Adotevi, S.	1969	'Discours sur la mélanisme', paper presented to the First Pan-African Cultural Festival, Algiers.
	1969*a*	'Négritude is dead: the burial', *Journal of the New African Literature and the Arts* (Spring and Fall), 70-81.
Allen, S.W.	1962	'Négritude: agreement and disagreement', in American Society of African Culture (1962).
American Society of African Culture (eds.)	1962	*Pan-Africanism Reconsidered*, Berkeley and Los Angeles: University of California Press.
Apter, D.E. and Joll, J.	1972	*Anarchism Today*, New York: Doubleday.
Arblaster, A.	1972	'Liberal values and socialist values', in Miliband and Savile (1972).
Aron, R.	1965	*Main Currents in Sociological Thought*, New York and London: Basic Books and Weidenfeld.
Aron, R., *et al.*	1962	*Les Origines de la guerre d'Algérie: textes et documents contemporains*, Paris: Fayard.
Balandier, G.	1955	*Sociologie actuelle de l'Afrique Noire*, Paris: Presses Universitaires de France.
	1962	'Les Mythes politiques de colonisation et de décolonisation en Afri-

que', *Cahiers internationaux de sociologie*, 33, 85-96.

1965 'The colonial situation', in van den Berghe (1965).

1965a 'Problematique des classes sociales en Afrique Noire', *Cahiers internationaux de sociologie*, 38, 131-42.

Banton, M. 1967 *Race Relations*, New York: Basic Books.

Barbour, N. (ed.) 1959 *A Survey of North West Africa (The Maghrib)*, London: Oxford University Press.

Bastide, R. 1972 'Millenarianism as a strategy in the search for a new identity and dignity', paper delivered at the Conference on Race, Identity and Dignity, UNESCO, Paris.

Batson, E. 1948 *Report on Proposals for a Social Survey of Zanzibar, 1946*, Zanzibar: Government Printer.

Belgian Congo and Rwanda-Urundi Information and Public Relations Office 1960 *Rwanda-Urundi Economy 1*, Brussels.

Beltran, L. 1969 'Dualisme de pluralisme en Afrique tropicale indépendante', *Cahiers internationaux de sociologie*, 47, 93-118.

Berque, J. 1961 'Recent research on racial relations: North Africa', *International Social Science Journal*, 13, 2 (1961), 177-96.

Bienen, H. 1968 *Violence and Social Change: A Review of Current Literature*, Chicago and London: University of Chicago Press.

Biko, B.S. 1971 'White racism and black consciousness', paper delivered at the First Inter-University Research Workshop on Students and Youth in South Africa, at the Abe Bailey Institute of Interracial Studies, University of Cape Town.

Birdsell, J.B.	1963	'A review of the origin of races', *Quarterly Review of Biology*, 38 (June), 178-85.
Blumer, H.	1965	'Industrialization and race relations', in Hunter (1965).
Bochkaryov, Y.	1964	'Background to Zanzibar', *New Times*, 5 (5 February), 13-15.
Boggs, J.	1970	*Racism and the Class Struggle*, New York: Monthly Review Press.
Bourdieu, P.	1962	*The Algerians*, trans. A.C.M. Ross, Boston: Beacon Press.
Buitenhuijs, R.	1971	*Le Mouvement 'mau mau'*, The Hague: Mouton.
Bunting, B.	1964	*The Rise of the South African Reich*, Harmondsworth and Baltimore: Penguin Books.
Cabral, A.	1969	*Revolution in Guinea*, New York: Monthly Review Press.
	1970	*National Liberation and Culture*, Syracuse University, Programme of East African Studies, Occasional Paper no. 57.
	1972	'Le Rôle de la culture dans la lutte pour l'indépendance', paper delivered at UNESCO Conference on Race, Identity and Dignity, Paris.
Carter, G.M. (ed.)	1963	*Five African States*, Ithaca: Cornell University Press.
Cleaver, E.	1969	*Post-Prison Writings and Speeches*, New York: Random House.
Cohen, J.	1955	'Colonialisme et racisme en Algérie', *Les Temps modernes*, 2, 580-90.
Cohn, N.	1967	'The myth of the demonic conspiracy of Jews in medieval and modern Europe', in de Reuck and Knight (1967).
Colby, B.J. and van den Berghe, P.L.	1969	*Ixil Country*, Berkeley and Los Angeles: University of California Press.
Coleman, J.S. and Rosberg, C.G., Jr. (eds.)	1964	*Political Parties and National Integration in Tropical Africa*, Berkeley and Los Angeles: University of California Press.

Cooper, D. (ed.)	1968	*The Dialectics of Liberation*, Harmondsworth: Penguin Books.
Corfield, F.D.	1960	*Historical Survey of the Origins and Growth of Mau Mau*, London: HMSO.
Courrière, Y.	1968	*Les Fils de la Toussaint*, Paris: Fayard.
	1969	*Le Temps des léopards*, Paris: Fayard.
Cox, O.C.	1948	*Caste, Class and Race*, New York: Doubleday.
Cruse, H.	1968	*Rebellion or Revolution?*, New York: Morrow.
Dahrendorf, R.	1959	*Class and Conflict in Industrial Society*, Stanford and London: Stanford University Press and Routledge.
Davidson, B.	1964	*Which Way Africa?*, Harmondsworth and Baltimore: Penguin Books.
	1969	'Pluralism in colonial African societies: Northern Rhodesia/Zambia', in Kuper and Smith (1969).
De Heusch, L.	1964	'Massacres collectifs au Rwanda?', *Synthèses*, 221 (October), 416-26.
	1964a	'Mythe et société féodale', *Archives de sociologie des religions*, 9, 18, 133-46;
	1964b	'Nationalisme et lutte des classes au Rwanda', in Frölich (1964).
De Kiewiet, C.W.	1942	*A History of South Africa, Social and Economic*, London: Oxford University Press.
Depestre, René	1969	'Les Fondements socio-culturels de notre identité', paper presented to the First Pan-African Cultural Festival, Algiers.
	1970	'Les Métamorphoses de la négritude en Amérique', *Présence africaine*, 75, 3, 19-33.
De Reuck, A. and Knight, J. (eds.)	1967	*Caste and Race: Comparative Approaches*, Boston: Little Brown.
Desai, N.	1969	*Contribution to Liberation and Revolution: Gandhi's Challenge*,

		Thirteenth Triennial Conference on Gandhi's Centennial Year of the War Resisters' International, Haverford, 60-2.
Despres, L.A.	1967	*Cultural Pluralism and Nationalist Politics in British Guiana*, Chicago: Rand McNally.
	1968	'Anthropological theory, cultural pluralism and the study of complex societies', *Current Anthropology*, 9, 3-26.
D'Hertefelt, M.	1960	'Myth and political acculturation in Rwanda', in Dubb (1960).
	1960*a*	'Les Élections communales et le consensus politique au Rwanda', *Zaïre*, 14, 5-6, 403-38.
	1960*b*	'Stratification sociale et structure politique', *La Revue nouvelle*, 31, 5, 449-62.
	1964	'Mythes et idéologies dans le Rwanda ancien et contemporain', in Vansina *et al.* (1964).
Dickson, K.A. and Ellingworth, P. (eds.)	1969	*Biblical Revelation and African Beliefs*, Maryknoll: Orbis Books.
Dubb, A. (ed.)	1960	*Myth in Modern Africa*, Lusaka: Rhodes-Livingstone Institute.
Duffy, J.	1963	*Portugal in Africa*, Harmondsworth and Baltimore: Penguin Books.
Dumont, L.	1966	'A fundamental problem in the sociology of caste', *Contributions to Indian Sociology*, 9 (December), 17-32.
Dunn, J.	1972	*Modern Revolutions: An Introduction to the Analysis of a Political Phenomenon*, London: Cambridge University Press.
Eckstein, H.	1965	'On the etiology of internal wars', *History and Theory*, 4, 2, 133-63.
Emerson, R.	1960	*From Empire to Nation*, Boston: Beacon Press.
Epstein, A.L.	1958	*Politics in an Urban African Community*, Manchester: Manchester University Press.

Fanon, F.	1963	*The Wretched of the Earth*, trans. C. Farrington, New York: Grove Press.
	1963*a*	'Concerning violence', in Fanon (1963).
	1964	*Pour la révolution africaine*, Paris: Maspero.
	1965	*A Dying Colonialism*, New York: Grove Press.
	1965*a*	'Algeria's European minority', in Fanon (1965).
	1967	*Towards the African Revolution*, New York: Grove Press.
Favret, J.	1965	'Le Syndicat, les travailleurs et le pouvoir en Algérie', *Annuaire de l'Afrique du Nord, 1964*, Paris: Éditions du Centre National de la Recherche Scientifique, 44-62.
Favrod, C.H.	1959	*La Révolution algérienne*, Paris: Librairie Plon.
Feraoun, M.	1962	*Journal, 1955-1962*, Paris: Éditions du Seuil.
Fortes, M.	1970	*The Plural Society in Africa*, Johannesburg: South African Institute of Race Relations.
Fraenkel, M.	1964	*Tribe and Class in Monrovia*, London: Oxford University Press.
Freedman, M.	1960	'The growth of a plural society in Malaya', *Pacific Affairs*, 33, 158-68.
Frölich, W. (ed.)	1964	*In Afrika im Wandel seiner Gesellschaftsformen*, Leiden: E.J. Brill.
Furnivall, J.S.	1939	*Netherlands India: A study of Plural Economy*, London: Cambridge University Press.
	1945	'Some problems of tropical economy', in Hinden (1945).
	1948	*Colonial Policy and Practice: A Comparative Study of Burma and Netherlands India*, London: Cambridge University Press.
Galtung, J.	1964	'A structural theory of aggression', *Journal of Peace Research*, 1, 95-119.

	1966	'International relations and international conflicts: a sociological approach', *Transactions of the Sixth World Congress of Sociology*, 1.
	1969	'Feudal systems, structural violence and the structural theory of revolutions', *Philosophy of Peace Research*, 1, 110-88, Oslo: International Peace Research Institute.
Gann, L.H. and Duignan, P.	1962	*White Settlers in Tropical Africa*, Harmondsworth: Penguin Books.
Gathani, B.	1966	'Ghostly Zanzibar', *Atlas*, 12, 2 (August).
Geertz, C.	1963	*Old Societies and New States*, New York: Free Press of Glencoe.
	1963a	'Integrative revolution: primordial sentiments and civil politics in the new States', in Geertz (1963).
Germani, G.	1966	'Social and political consequences of mobility', in Smelser and Lipset (1966).
Gerth, H.H. and Wright Mills, C. (eds.)	1946	*From Max Weber: Essays in Sociology*, New York: Oxford University Press.
Glories, J.	1958	'Quelques observations sur la révolution algérienne', *L'Afrique et l'Asie*, 11, 12, 3 23.
Gluckman, M.	1963	*Custom and Conflict in Africa*, Oxford: Blackwell.
	1965	*Politics, Law and Ritual in Tribal Society*, Chicago.
	1969	'The tribal area in South and Central Africa', in Kuper and Smith (1969).
Goldman, L.	1971	*La Création culturelle dans la société moderne*, Paris: Éditions Gonthier.
Gordon, D.C.	1966	*The Passing of French Algeria*, London: Oxford University Press.
	1971	*Self-Determination and History in the Third World*, Princeton: Princeton University Press.
Görög, V.	1968	'L'Origine de l'inégalité des races—

étude de trente-sept contes afri-
cains', *Cahiers d'études africaines*, 8,
2, 290-309.

Gross, F.   1966   *World Politics and Tension Areas*,
New York: New York University
Press.

Guillaume, P. and   1969   'La Critique de la "négritude" au
Lagroye, J.   festival culturel d'Alger de juillet
1969', *Année africaine*, 251-63.

Gumplowicz, L.   1963   *Outlines of Sociology* (2nd English
edition), New York: Paine-Whitman.

Harbi, M.   1965   'Les Paysans dans la révolution',
Democratie nouvelle (June),
56-62.

Hartz, L. (ed.)   1964   *The Founding of New Societies*,
New York: Harcourt Brace.

Haug, M.R.   1967   'Social and cultural pluralism as a
concept in social system analysis',
American Journal of Sociology, 73,
294-304.

Herskovits, M.J.   1941   *The Myth of the Negro Past*, New
York: Harper.

Himmelstrand, U.   1966   'Conflict, conflict resolution and
nation-building in the transition
from tribal "mechanical" solidarities to the "organic" solidarity of
modern (or future) multi-tribal
societies', paper presented at the
Sixth World Congress of Sociology,
Évian.

Hinden, R. (ed.)   1945   *Fabian Colonial Essays*, London:
Allen and Unwin.

Hobsbawm, E.   1970   'Lenin and the aristocracy of
labour', *Monthly Review* (April),
47-56.

Hoetink, H.   1967   *The Two Variants in Caribbean
Race Relations: A Contribution to
the Sociology of Segmented
Societies*, London: Oxford University Press.

Humbaraci, A.   1966   *Algeria: A Revolution That Failed*,
New York: Praeger.

Hunter, G. (ed.)   1965   *Industrialization and Race Rela-*

tions, London: Oxford University Press.

Idowu, E.B.	1969	Introduction to Dickson and Ellingworth (1969).
Isaacs,H.R.	1965	*The Ex-Untouchables*, New York: John Day.
Jones, L.	1969	*Four Black Revolutionary Plays*, Indianapolis and New York: Bobbs-Merrill.
Jordaan, K.A.	1968	'The Communist Party of South Africa – its counter-revolutionary role', *World Revolution*, 1, 2, 12-20.
Kealey, P.	1963	*The Politics of Partnership*, Harmondsworth and Baltimore: Penguin Books.
Kharusi, A.S.	1967	*Zanzibar – Africa's First Cuba*, Richmond: Foreign Affairs Publishing.
Ki-Zerbo, J.	1962	'African personality and the new African society', in American Society of African Culture (1962).
Klinghoffer, A.J.	1969	*Soviet Perspectives in African Socialism*, New Jersey: Associated University Presses.
Kornhauser, W.	1960	*The Politics of Mass Society*, London: Routledge.
Kunene, D.P.	1968	'Deculturation – the African writer's response', *Africa Today*, 15, 4, 19-24.
Kuper, H.	1964	'The colonial situation in Southern Africa', *Journal of Modern African Studies*, 2 (July), 149-50.
	1969	'Strangers in plural societies: Asians in South Africa and Uganda', in Kuper and Smith (1969).
	1970	'Colour categories and colonialism: the Swazi case', in Turner (1970).
Kuper, L.	1956	*Passive Resistance in South Africa*, London and New Haven, Jonathan Cape and Yale University Press.
	1965	*An African Bourgeoisie: Race, Class*

		and Politics in South Africa, New Haven: Yale University Press.
	1965*a*	'Sociology: some aspects of urban plural societies', in Lystad (1965).
	1965*b*	'The heightening of racial tension', in van den Berghe (1965).
	1967	'Structural discontinuities in African .towns: some aspects of racial pluralism', in Miner (1967).
	1969*a*	'Plural societies: perspectives and problems', in Kuper and Smith (1969).
	1969*b*	'Ethnic and racial pluralism: some aspects of polarization and depluralization', in Kuper and Smith (1969).
	1970	'Nonviolence revisited', in Mazrui and Rotberg (1970).
Kuper, L. and Smith, M.G.	1969	*Pluralism in Africa*, Berkeley and Los Angeles: University of California Press.
Kuper, L., Watts, H. and Davies, R.	1958	*Durban: A Study in Racial Ecology*, New York: Columbia University Press.
Kyle, K.	1964	'Gideon's voices', *The Spectator* (7 February), 175.
Laing, R.D.	1968	'The obvious', in Cooper (1968).
Launay, M.	1963	*Paysans algériens*, Paris: Éditions du Seuil.
Layne, N.	1970	*The Plural Society in Guyana*, Ph.D. Dissertation, Department of Sociology, University of California, and Los Angeles.
Leach, E.	1964	'Anthropological aspects of language: animal categories and verbal abuse', in Lenneberg (1964).
Lebjaoui, M.	1970	*Vérités sur la révolution algérienne*, Paris: Gallimard.
Lemarchand, R.	1962	'L'Influence des systèmes traditionnels sur l'évolution politique du Rwanda et du Burundi', *Revue de l'institut de sociologie*, 2, 2, 333-57.
	1966	'Political instability in Africa: the

		case of Rwanda and Burundi', *Civilisations*, 16, 3, 307-37.
	1966*a*	'Power and stratification in Rwanda: a reconsideration', *Cahiers d'études africaines*, 21, 6–4, 592-610.
	1968	'Les relations de clientèle comme agent ˙de contestation: le cas du Rwanda', *Civilisations*, 18, 4, 553-78.
	1968*a*	'Revolutionary phenomena in stratified societies: Rwanda and Zanzibar', *Civilisations*, 18, 1, 16-51.
	1970	*Rwanda and Burundi*, New York: Praeger.
Lenneberg (ed.)	1964	*New Directions in the Study of Language*, Cambridge, Mass.: MIT Press.
Le Tourneau, R.	1957	*Les Villes musulmanes de l'Afrique du Nord*, Alger.
	1962	*Afrique Nord musulmane*, Paris: Librairie Armand Colin.
Leurquin, P.	1960	*Le Niveau de vie des populations rurales du Rwanda-Urundi*, Louvain: Éditions Nauwelaerts.
Liebenow, J.G.	1964	'Liberia', in Coleman and Rosberg (1964).
Lieber, J.	1965	'Memories of Zanzibar', *Ramparts*, 4, 4, 55-8.
Lipset, S.M.	1960	*Political Man*, Garden City: Doubleday.
Lofchie, M.F.	1965	*Zanzibar: Background to Revolution*, Princeton: Princeton University Press.
	1967	'Was Okello's revolution a conspiracy?', *Transition*, 7, 33 (October-November), 36-42.
	1969	'The plural society in Zanzibar', in Kuper and Smith (1969).
Lystad, R.A. (ed.)	1965	*The African World*, New York: Praeger.
McKenzie, H.I.	1966	'The plural society debate: some

comments on a recent contribution', *Social and Economic Studies*, 15, 53-60.

M., A.   1963   'Regards sur l'enseignement des musulmans en Algérie', *Confluent*, 2 (June-July), 596-645.

Mandela, N.   1965   *No Easy Walk to Freedom*, London: Heinemann.

Manifeste Algérien,   1948   *Le Manifeste algérien parle aux* Union *français*, Algiers.
Démocratique du

Mannoni, E.   1963   Algérie: le présent – le passé – l'avenir', *Confluent*, 27 (February), 131-6.

Mannoni, O.   1956   *Prospero and Caliban*, London: Methuen.

Maquet, J.J.   1961   *The Premise of Inequality in Rwanda*, London: Oxford University Press.

                         1964   'La Participation de la classe paysanne au mouvement d'indépendance du Rwanda', *Cahiers d'études africaines*, 16, 4-4, 553-68.

                         1969   'En son devenir, l'africanité', paper presented to the first Pan-African Cultural Festival, Algiers.

Marcuse, H.   1970   *Five Lectures: Psychoanalysis, Politics and Utopia*, London: Allen Lane.

Marx, G.T.   1967   *Protest and Prejudice*, New York: Harper.

Marx, K.   1970   'Contribution to the critique of Hegel's philosophy of law', in O'Malley (1970).

Maunier, R.   1949   *The Sociology of Colonies*, trans. E.O. Lorimer, London: Routledge.

Mazrui, A. and   1970   *Protest and Power in Black Africa*, Rotberg, R. (eds.)   New York: Oxford University Press.

Mbiti, J.S.   1969   'Eschatology', in Dickson and Ellingworth (1969).

Meer, F.   1971   'African nationalism – some inhibiting factors', in Adam (1971).

Memmi, A.   1957   *Portrait du colonisé précédé du*

		portrait du colonisateur, Paris: Buchet/Chastel.
	1964	'Essai de définition', *La Nef*, 19-20 (December), 41-7.
	1967	*The Colonizer and the Colonized*, Boston: Beacon Press.
Mercier, P.	1965	'Les Classes sociales et les changements politiques récents en Afrique Noire', *Cahiers internationaux de sociologie*, 38, 143-54.
	1965*a*	'The European community of Dakar', in van den Berghe (1965).
	1965*b*	'Evolution of Senegalese elites', in van den Berghe (1965).
Meynaud, J. and Salah-Bey, A.	1962	*Fondements idéologiques du mouvement syndicat africain*, Paris: Fondation Nationale des Sciences Politiques.
	1967	*Trade Unionism in Africa*, London: Methuen. .
Michels, R.	1962	*Political Parties*, New York: Collier Books.
Middleton, J. and Campbell, J.	1965	*Zanzibar: Its Society and Politics*, London and New York: Oxford University Press.
Miliband, R. and Savile, J. (eds.)	1972	*The Socialist Register 1972*, London: Merlin Press.
Miner, H. (ed.)	1967	*The City in Modern Africa*, New York: Praeger.
Mitchell, J.C.	1960	*Tribalism and the Plural Society*, London: Oxford University Press.
Mitchell, P.	1954	*African Afterthoughts*, London: Hutchinson.
Morris, H.S.	1966	Review of M.G. Smith, *The Plural Society in the British West Indies*, in *Man*, 1, 270-1.
	1967	'Some aspects of the concept of plural society', *Man*, 2, 169-84.
	1968	*Indians in Uganda*, London: Weidenfeld.
Mulago, V.	1969	'Vital participation', in Dickson and Ellingworth (1969).
Murray, R. and Wengraff, T.	1963	'The Algerian revolution', *New Left Review*, 22 (December), 14-65.

Nash, M.	1957	'The multiple society in economic development: Mexico and Guatemala', *American Anthropologist*, 59, 825-38.
	1958	'Political relations in Guatemala', *Social and Economic Studies*, 7, 65-75.
Nehru, J.	1962	*Autobiography*, New Delhi.
Newton, H.	1968	'Huey Newton talks to the movement about the Black Panther Party, cultural nationalism, SNCC, liberals and white revolutionaries', *The Movement* (August), 8-12.
Nicolaus, M.	1970	'The theory of the labour aristocracy', *Monthly Review* (April), 91-101.
Niebuhr, R.	1932	*Moral Man and Immoral Society*, New York: Scribner.
Nkundabagenzi, F. (ed.)	1961	*Rwanda Politique*, Brussels: Centre de Recherche et d'Information Socio-Politiques.
Nouschi, A.	1962	*La Naissance du nationalisme algérien*, Paris: Éditions de Minuit.
Ntwasa, S.	1971	Report on the National Seminar on Black Theology, Roodepoort, South Africa, March 1971.
Nugent, J.P.	1965	*Call Africa 999*, New York: Coward-Melann.
Oberschall, A.	1969	'Group violence: some hypotheses and empirical uniformities', paper presented at the meeting of the American Sociological Association, San Francisco.
O'Brien, C.C.	1972	*States of Ireland*, London: Hutchinson.
O'Malley, J. (ed.)	1970	*Critique of Hegel's Philosophy of Law*, London: Cambridge University Press.
Office of Intelligence Research and Analysis, United States Department of State	1958	*The World Strength of the Communist Party Organizations*, Intelligent Report no. 4489 R-10.
Okello, J.	1967	*Revolution in Zanzibar*, Nairobi: East African Publishing House.

Oliver, R. and Fage, J.D.	1962	*A Short History of Africa*, Harmondsworth and Baltimore: Penguin Books.
Olson, M.	1963	'Rapid growth as a destabilizing force', *Journal of Economic History*, 23, 4, 529-52.
Ossowski, S.	1963	*Class Structure in the Social Consciousness*, trans. Sheila Patterson, New York: Free Press.
Ouzegane, A.	1962	*Le Meilleur combat*, Paris: Juillard.
Quandt, W.B.	1969	*Revolution and Political Leadership*: *Algeria, 1954-8*, Cambridge, Mass.: MIT Press.
Quermonne, J.L.	1961	'Le Problème de la cohabitation dans les sociétés multi-communautaires', *Revue française de science politique*, 2 (March), 29-59.
Radcliffe-Brown, A.R.	1952	*Structure and Function in Primitive Society*, London: Cohen and West.
	1952*a*	'On social structure' in Radcliffe-Brown (1952).
Reich, C.A.	1970	*The Greening of America*, New York: Bantam Books.
Rex, J.	1959	'The plural society in sociological theory', *British Journal of Sociology*, 10 (June), 114-24.
Rey, L.	1964	'The revolution in Zanzibar', *New Left Review*, 25 (May-June), 29-32.
Rhav. P.	1971	'Kid stuff: the myth of consciousness III', *Modern Occasions*, 1, 3 (Spring), 307-13.
Ricks, T.	1969	'Black revolution: a matter of definition', *American Behavioural Scientist*, 12, 4 (March-April), 21-6.
Roux, J.P.	1969	'Les Troubles du Rwanda et du Burundi', *Revue française d'études politiques africaines*, 39 (March), 48-62.
Roy, J.	1960	*La Guerre d'Algérie*, Paris: René Juillard.
Rubin, V. (ed.)	1960	'Social and cultural pluralism in the Caribbean', *Annals of the New York Academy of Sciences*, 83, 761-916.

Rwanda Carrefour	1965	April issue.
d'Afrique	1967	'L'Économie rwandaise', 66-7 (May-June), 1-27.
Sawyerr, H.	1969	'Sacrifice', in Dickson and Ellingworth (1969).
Senghor, L.S.	1967	*Les Fondements de l'africanité ou négritude et arabité*, Paris: Présence africaine.
	1971	'Problematique de la négritude', *Le Soleil*, 305 (8 May), 5-10.
		tude', *Le Soleil*, 305 (8 May), 5-10.
Simmel, G.	1950	'Subordination under a principle', in Wolff (1950).
	1950a	'On the significance of numbers for social life', in Wolff (1950).
Simons, H.J. and Simons, R.E.	1969	*Class and Colour in South Africa, 1850-1950*, Harmondsworth: Penguin Books.
Sjoberg, G.	1952	'Folk and feudal societies', *American Journal of Sociology,* 58, 231-9.
Sklar, R.	1967	'Political science and national integration — a radical approach', *Journal of Modern African Studies,* 5, 1, 1-11.
Smelser, N. and Lipset, S.M. (eds.)	1966	*Social Structure and Mobility in Economic Development*, Chicago: Aldine.
Smith, A.L.	1969	*Rhetoric of Black Revolution*, Boston: Allyn and Bacon.
Smith, M.G.	1960	'Social and cultural pluralism', *Annals of the New York Academy of Sciences*, 83, 763-85.
	1965	*The Plural Society in the British West Indies*, Berkeley and Los Angeles: University of California Press.
	1965a	*Stratification in Grenada*, Berkeley and Los Angeles: University of California Press.
	1969	Contributions in Kuper and Smith (1969).
	1969a	'Some developments in the analytic

framework of pluralism', in Kuper and Smith (1969).

1969*b* 'Institutional and political conditions of pluralism', in Kuper and Smith (1969).

1969*c* 'Pluralism in pre-colonial African societies', in Kuper and Smith (1969).

Smith, R.T.   1961   Review of 'Social and cultural pluralism in the Caribbean', *American Anthropologist*, 63, 155-7.

Soustelle, J.   1956   *Aimée et souffrante Algérie*, Paris: Librairie Plon.

Spiro, H.J.   1963   'The Rhodesias and Nyasaland', in Carter (1963).

Staniland, M.   1969   'Frantz Fanon and the African political class', *African Affairs*, 68, 4-25.

1969*a* 'Frantz Fanon et les classes politiques africaines', *Études congolaises*, 12, 1, 37-68.

Sundkler, B.G.M.   1961   *Bantu Prophets in South Africa*, London: Oxford University Press.

Talmon, Y.   1966   'Millenarian movements', *Archives européennes de sociologie*, 7, 2 (1966), 159-200.

Thomas, L.V.   1965   'Senghor and négritude', *Présence africaine*, 26, 54, 102-33.

Thompson, L.M.   1964   'The South African dilemma', in Hartz (1964).

1966   *The Republic of South Africa*, Boston: Little Brown.

Turner, R.H. and Surace, S.J.   1956   'Zoot-suiters and Mexicans: symbols in crowd behaviour', *American Journal of Sociology*, 62, 14-20.

Turner, V.W. (ed.)   1970   *Colonialism in Africa: 1876-1960*, vol.3, *Profiles of Change: African Society and Colonial Rule*, London: Cambridge University Press.

Valentine, C.A.   1968   *Culture and Poverty*, Chicago:

University of Chicago Press.

Van den Berghe, P.L.   1964   'Toward a sociology of Africa', *Social Forces*, 48 (October), 11-18.

1965a   *South Africa: A Study in Conflict*, Middletown: Wesleyan University Press.

1965b   'Toward a sociology of Africa', in van den Berghe (1965).

1965c   'The economic system and its disfunctions', in van den Berghe (1965a).

1967   *Race and Racism*, New York: John Wiley.

1969   'Pluralism and the polity: a theoretical explanation', in Kuper and Smith (1969).

Van den Berghe, P.L. (ed.)   1965   *Africa: Social Problems of Change and Conflict*, San Francisco: Chandler Publishing.

Van Lier, R.A.J.   1950   *The Development and Nature of Society in the West Indies*, Amsterdam: Royal Institute for the Indies.

Vansina, J., Mauny, R. and Thomas, L.V. (eds.)   1964   *The Historian in Tropical Africa*, London: Oxford University Press.

Vermeersch, J.   1959   'Le Problème algérien et l'intérêt national', *Cahiers du communisme*, 35, 155-67.

Warner, W.L.   1949   *Social Class in America*, Chicago: Science Research Associates.

Washington, J.R., Jr.   1969   *The Politics of God*, Boston: Beacon Press.

Weiss, F.   1970   *Doctrine et action syndicales en Algérie*, Paris: Éditions Cujas.

Wittfogel, K.A.   1957   *Oriental Despotism*, New Haven: Yale University Press.

Wolf, E.R.   1969   *Peasant Wars of the Twentieth Century*, London: Faber.

Wolff, K.H. (ed.)   1950   *The Sociology of George Simmel*, Glencoe: Free Press.

Worsley, P.   1972   'Frantz Fanon and the lumpenproletariat', in Miliband and Savile (1972).

Zanzibar Protectorate 1953   *Notes on the Census of the Zanzibar Protectorate, 1948*, Zanzibar: Government Printer.

1960   *Report on the Census of the Population of Zanzibar Protectorate, 1958*, Zanzibar: Government Printer.

1963   *Labour Report for the Years 1960 and 1961*, Zanzibar: Government Printer.

1964   Presidential Decrees, nos. 5 and 6, *The Zanzibar Gazette* (25 February).

Zolberg, A. and V. 1967   'The Americanization of Frantz Fanon', *Public Interest* (Fall), 49-63.

Index